SUBURBAN SWEATSHOPS

SUBURBAN SWEATSHOPS

The Fight for Immigrant Rights

JENNIFER GORDON

THE BELKNAP PRESS OF
HARVARD UNIVERSITY PRESS
Cambridge, Massachusetts, and London, England

2005

Copyright © 2005 by Jennifer Gordon

ALL RIGHTS RESERVED

Printed in the United States of America

Library of Congress Cataloging-in-Publication Data

Gordon, Jennifer (Jennifer Lynn)
Suburban sweatshops : the fight for immigrant rights / Jennifer Gordon.
p. cm.
Includes bibliographical references and index.
ISBN 0-674-01524-X (alk. paper)
1. Alien labor—United States. 2. Employee rights—United States.
3. Workplace Project (Organization) I. Title.
HD8081.A5G67 2004
331.6′2′0973—dc22   2004052241

For Linda, Sophie, and James

CONTENTS

Absurdo suponer que el paraíso
es sólo la igualdad, las buenas leyes—
el sueño se hace a mano, sin permiso . . .

Absurd to think that paradise
is only equality and good laws—
we make our dream by hand, without permission . . .

—Silvio Rodriguez, lyrics from
   "Llover sobre mojado," *Tríptico (Volumen Dos)*,
   Musicrama, 1999

No tengo sueños imposibles.

I do not have impossible dreams.

—Zoila Rodriguez, Workplace Project member

INTRODUCTION

Nine million undocumented immigrants call the United States home. Most of them—over 80 percent—are from Latin America.[1] As immigrants long have, the vast majority come to this country to work. But where most earlier immigrants found their first jobs in cities, the scraps of paper these newcomers carry over rivers and deserts are quite likely to bear suburban addresses. While this country's manufacturing base has withered, calls have increased for lawns to be mowed, bedrooms to be cleaned, pools and homes to be built, and office park floors to be swabbed. Once the place where the second and third generation moved to escape the immigrant taint of city life, the suburbs are now the immigrant destination of choice. Long Island, New York, mother of all suburbs, typifies the trend. Today it is home to over 300,000 Latino immigrants. Whole villages from Ecuador and Honduras, El Salvador and Mexico, now send their strongest and their brightest to Hempstead and Farmingdale, to Freeport and Huntington.

Low-wage immigrant work in the suburbs is no kinder than immigrant work in cities. It is often scattered among small businesses and spread out along suburban sprawl, harder to locate than the clustered buildings of an urban garment district that have come to signal "sweatshop." But in its long hours, illegally low wages, and staggering rates of injury, it is sweatshop labor all the same. What few statistics we have sketch an outline of the problem. In the year 2000, 74 of 111 people who died on the job in New York City were immigrant workers.[2] In the mid-1990s, immigrant dishwashers in Long Island earned an average of $2.50 an hour for 75 hours or more of work in a week.

The personal stories of immigrant workers tell the tale better. Jorge Bonilla was hospitalized with pneumonia after sleeping all winter on tablecloths mounded on the floor of the Long Island restaurant where he worked, the heat capped at 50°. He had been evicted from the room where he had been living because his wage of 30¢ an hour was so low that he could not pay his rent, even working 80 hours a week.

As a live-in domestic worker, Yanira Juarez cared for two children and cleaned house in Suffolk County. Duped by her employer's claim that her wages were being paid "into a savings account," she worked for 6 months with no pay, and then was fired without seeing a penny.

A day laborer, who did not want me to use his name, stumbled dazed and bleeding out of his employer's truck and through a Long Island hospital emergency room door one summer afternoon, his right hand cradled in his left, one finger hanging by a flap of skin and gristle. A new boss had picked him up that morning and taken him to his jobs. After he cut twenty lawns, grass clogged the lawnmower. In a hurry, the employer had ordered the worker to clear the blockage without cutting the motor. The powerful blades, spinning free, had sliced his finger through the bone. As the worker told the doctor what had happened, his employer fled in his truck, confident that the worker had no information about him and no way to track him down.

This book has its roots in grim sweatshop stories like these. But it also has an unexpected tale to tell. In Long Island, in the 1990s, hundreds of the most vulnerable and desperate immigrant workers—including Jorge Bonilla and Yanira Juarez—shook off their fear, came together, and took on suburban sweatshop employers. Through the Workplace Project, which I founded and directed from 1992 to 1998, these workers demanded better wages, safer work, and respect from their employers.

These recent immigrants were unlikely leaders. And they faced daunting obstacles. At work they felt the press of global competition, at times in the form of their employers' threats to move operations overseas, more often through a sea of new immigrants vying for a limited number of jobs. Many were undocumented. They changed jobs and industries frequently, moving among small and highly mobile businesses. Subcontracting and short-term work put much of their labor outside the realm of workplace laws. Few unions were interested in them as members, given the tremendous challenges and unlikely rewards of organizing workers in such settings. In 2003 an all-time low of 8.2 percent of workers in the private sector were represented by unions, but that is a tidal wave of organization compared to the situation of the lowest-wage workers, only .6 percent of whom claim union membership.[3]

The Workplace Project refuses to accept that the newest and worst-off immigrants are unorganizable. Through a resourceful combination of collective action and legal advocacy, the Workplace Project has won noteworthy victories, including the most far-reaching state wage-enforcement legislation in the country. It has also created and maintained a stable membership organization run in large part by immigrants. In the process, its members have transformed themselves from outcasts in exile to active and effective political participants.

The story of the Workplace Project is not, in the end, a traditional tale of triumph. It is messier and more complex than that; it is about guts and the willingness to experiment in the face of tremendous odds. I remember in particular one pre-dawn spring morning in 1997, when I was speeding down the unusually empty Long Island Expressway to a picket line at a factory whose managers had fired twenty-five immigrant workers for objecting when their supervisors called them "stupid" and "dogs." As light filtered into the dark gray sky, I wanted nothing more than to pull off at some anonymous exit, douse the headlights, and disappear until I could figure out some answers to the questions constantly on my mind. In this case, the workers' solidarity under pressure during the previous months had been remarkable, but I was having familiar doubts about the ultimate outcome. How could the most vulnerable workers organize when even those with stable jobs were struggling to form unions? What alternate organizational forms and strategies could take those workers where the mainstream methods seemed unable to go? In some respects, the Workplace Project and other immigrant organizing centers, often called worker centers, were leading the way. But in others, the path was far from clear.

Alongside the organizing dilemmas loomed another perpetual question, the debate about the role of law. A graduate of Harvard Law School, I had been challenged at the Workplace Project to use law in ways my legal education never anticipated in order to create change in a lawless setting. The Project had filed legal cases on behalf of these factory workers, but the prospects that they would get their jobs back through a legal challenge were slim. Their best hope for change lay in collective action. In some ways, legal strategies were doing a good job of supporting the organizing effort—and in others they were undermining it. For many immigrant workers, learning about their rights had given them a sense of strength and hope. But the faith rights had engendered was fast coming into conflict with the real-life workings of courts and administrative agencies. Slow and cumbersome as they were, these workers' legal claims had helped keep the group together after its members were fired, and had drawn publicity to their cause. But would winning the cases now become the focus of their organizing work rather than their broader goal of winning a union on the job? These and other debates about what role law could fruitfully play in supporting an effort that was primarily about organizing rang in my ears as the highway blurred by.

Not surprisingly, the organization found much it could not do. Sweatshops flourish where workers have little power; where workers have little power, organizing is hard. Long Island is no exception. The Workplace Project has yet to figure out how to exert sustained rather than sporadic pressure on employers or government officials, how to raise the wages and improve the working conditions of substantial numbers of workers beyond the level set by the inadequate laws on the books, or how to grow beyond its current small size of about five hundred members. In the end, the Project has created no miracles. And yet, to track its growth is to witness an unexpected realm of possibility emerging from what at first appears to be impossible terrain.

In the chapters that follow I examine the strategies that the Project brought to bear on the obstacles to organizing new immigrants in the lowest-wage work, where they succeeded and where they floundered.

Organizing is not only about the external battles a group chooses (or that choose it). It is also about the internal process of building an organization, a process that takes on particular importance when the group is—as the Workplace Project is—dedicated to creating a participatory, member-run center. I focus on how the Project built its "path to participation," on how immigrant workers were first attracted to the organization, how they became involved, why they chose to commit in the long term, and through what structures and practices the organization maximized immigrants' participation in decision-making. I argue that while this emphasis on democracy was not itself sufficient to make change in the outside world, it proved a philosophically and strategically important component of the group's organizing strategy.

The Workplace Project path to participation had many elements, but one of the most prominent was the *creative* use of law. The Project used law to support its organizing in various ways: through outreach about rights; through a legal clinic designed to draw immigrants to the organization and introduce them to organizing as a complement to litigation; and through its Workers Course as a bridge between talking about rights and collective action. All of these are unconventional in that their goal was to build a strong organizing effort, as well as or more than to win legal victories.

I provide three perspectives on the Workplace Project's use of law. The first is about rights education and broader discussions about rights ("rights talk") as a path to collective action. Many immigrant workers—particularly those who are undocumented—believe that laws about minimum wages, safe working conditions, and the like protect others but not them. Working without papers, living under the government's radar screen, they fear that the only possible response to a pay envelope amounting to $2.00 an hour, a workday of 14 hours, a demand that they operate machines without safety guards, is to submit or to lose their jobs. The culture of the underground economy, flourishing with its back to the law, reinforces that assumption. Under such circumstances, learning about rights can be a powerful component of organizing. It can galvanize people to see themselves as legitimate actors, those with a right to claim rights.[4] It can support the creation of a group identity that carries within it the seed of forward motion, toward new demands for change. Rights talk does have some disadvantages from an organizing perspective. It can individualize problems. It can channel the group's energy away from collective action and toward litigation and the courts. It can blind participants to visions of the possible that are outside the realm of existing rights. Yet despite the inherent tensions, an approach to teaching and talking about rights that is critical in outlook and collective in orientation can be a powerful source of support for organizing.

Moving from rights talk to rights enforcement, I offer a close examination of the Workplace Project's unusual effort to develop a legal clinic that worked in tandem with the group's collective goals. If rights talk hinted at ways that organizing and lawyering can seem contradictory in goal and approach, the legal clinic put them in bold relief. In a series of experiments, the Project tried to make its clinic a draw to the organization and a bridge to organizing. These experiments were a source of controversy at the organization (as well as outside it, albeit for very different reasons). Some of the tensions related to the particular expectations the Workplace Project had for its clinic, but others seem inevitable no matter what structure was chosen. Good organizing moves people from resignation or private pain and an-

ger to an awareness of the shared, public nature of their suffering—and from there to a commitment to fight for change so that
suffering will no longer be the norm. Good lawyering can do
many things, but lawyers tend to be more focused on solving clients' problems than on generating a collective vision for change.
Although offering legal services is a way to encourage those still
numb or inward-looking to take the first step toward redress,
considerable tensions arise when the individualistic outlook and
remedies of the law are required to act as a pivot-point for a collective focus.

Imperfect as it is as a bridge, under the right circumstances a
legal clinic still can bring valuable benefits to an organizing effort. Some are very concrete. The Workplace Project clinic drew
new members and resources to the organization, prevailed in
hundreds of workers' claims against their employers, and collected previously unavailable data about the conditions of immigrant work. Other benefits are less tangible, but equally
important. Precisely because it highlights tensions in the organization's work, a clinic can force a group to pay attention to questions it might otherwise rather avoid. What is the relationship
between helping individuals resolve immediate problems and organizing? When is it legitimate to make the interests of an individual secondary to the group's larger organizing agenda? Who
decides what those interests are, and how they would best be
served? Because of the light it trains on issues that all too often
get ignored once a group commits to one approach or another, a
legal clinic can make a group more honest about law, about organizing, and about change.

Rights talk and rights enforcement merged in the campaign
for the Unpaid Wages Prohibition Act. This was an unconventional legislative effort, carried out by members of the Work-

place Project and of two other worker centers, despite their inability to vote. In the process, people with an initial sense of themselves as "afraid," "invisible," and "nobody," became effective political actors. The campaign raises a series of questions about power, political participation, and citizenship. Admirable as immigrant workers' leadership in that campaign is, it is inadequate—indeed, counter-intuitive—as an explanation for the success of the campaign. How did people with little to offer in the political currency of money or votes build the power necessary to succeed in participating politically, and what does that process suggest about how we should rethink citizenship education and citizenship itself?

In the end, I reflect on what the experiences of worker centers such as the Workplace Project suggest more broadly about participatory organizing, about the roles of law and lawyers in supporting collective action, and about barriers and opportunities for the labor movement as a whole. These issues begin with immigrants in the new suburban sweatshops, but they do not end there. In a world of ever-increasing global connections, the question of how to guarantee human beings fair wages, safe working conditions, and the opportunity to live with dignity as full participants in society is everywhere urgent, and demands answers that reach across cities, countries, and continents.

1

THE NEW SWEATSHOPS

Carmen Lelys Maldonado sits in an apartment rank with the smell of damp carpeting, the walls bare, the furnishings minimal except for two beds and an extra mattress propped up against a closet. His lanky body is perched on one of the beds, head bent to a tablet of paper, hand poised to write but seemingly unable to move downward into action. Maldonado thinks of his wife, who will receive this letter he is about to write, of his six children gathered around her on the farm in Honduras he once ran and his father ran before him. He thinks of their hope on opening the envelope, expectations of money for new shoes and books for school and a radio, and thinking of their hope reminds him of his, the hope with which he set off two years earlier for the grueling eight-week voyage to Long Island, New York, hope born of what has now been revealed as a miserable miscalculation.

As a boy and a young man, a leader in his small village, Maldonado saw immigrant after immigrant return with piles of cash, telling tales of weekly salaries that surpassed the unthinkable sum of $200 a week—a third of the annual income of the average Honduran at the time, himself included. His mistake, he now thinks, lay in not wanting to read between the lines, not asking the obvious questions: How many hours a day does it take to make that kind of money? How often do you actually get paid what you are promised? And, most of all, how much does it cost to *live* in the United States? He had spent his whole life growing the food he ate and sleeping in a place his family had built. No landlady charging $600 to rent a single room for a month. No supermarkets, with their cruel fluorescent lights illuminating row upon row of unthinkably expensive produce. No taxi fare, no electric bill. Who would not make the same mistake?

Maldonado lowers hand to paper. He forces himself to put a salutation on the page by reviewing the string of misfortunes that brought him to this point. A job as a dishwasher at a pizzeria that demanded 6 14-hour days a week for $250 in pay, and the pay was sporadic. A fruitless attempt to stretch that money to cover Long Island prices for housing, food, transportation. The night he was fired from the restaurant, only to arrive home and learn that his father had died. And still, he cannot bring himself to write the sentences he hears in his head, simple sentences that depict a travesty of the immigrant experience he had hoped to have. "Dear Nicomedes," he would begin. "I am very sorry. Things are bad. I need *you* to send money to *me*." Maldonado drops the pen and turns his head slowly toward the room's one warped window. He wonders, not for the first time, whether its view points toward home.

Not far away, night has fallen in the kitchen of a middle-class Long Island family. Lilliam Araujo, who lives with the family, cleans their home, and cares for their daughter, sits in the dark at the breakfast table, the phone line wound tightly around her shoulders like an umbilical cord. Her voice, hushed to avoid waking up the sleeping people on the second floor, is warm but firm: "Did you do your homework, *papi?* Is your brother home? No, you can't wait up for him to come from work. It's late already. Ten more minutes of Nintendo and then I want you in bed. I love you. Sleep well. I'll call in the morning." She hangs up. Even in the dim light, the strain of raising her two boys by phone is evident in her face. Seven years old and seventeen, they live alone in a small apartment she rents two towns away.

She left El Salvador for them: to keep the older one from being recruited by the military or the guerrillas in their increasingly conflict-ridden town, to save the younger one from being caught in the ever more frequent crossfires of the Salvadoran civil war. But the best work she could find on arrival was a live-in domestic job at the rate of $160 a week for 65 hours of work, less than $2.50 an hour. A single mother, she took the job and got the nearest apartment she could afford for her sons. Bathing and dressing and hugging a child not her own, she is plagued by the question of whether she is doing better by her boys here, or worse. As for herself . . . as she moves out of the kitchen and toward the stairs, her mind drifts toward her days in El Salvador, the coffee-growers' cooperative where she served as secretary, the degrees she had been earning at night and on weekends in psychology, social work, and teaching, the courses she taught at the local business college, the house she owned. It feels like another life.

These are individual moments in individual lives. But as they struggle, Carmen Lelys Maldonado and Lilliam Araujo also offer a window onto a more universal picture: the immigrant experience at a time when the United States is undergoing a disturbing renaissance of sweatshop work.[1] For a while in the middle of the twentieth century, sweatshops were more present in our national

consciousness as examples of what our grandparents had overcome than as a modern reality. No longer. In a country where reformers, unions, and workers once declared victory over sweated
labor, we live in an era of the sweatshop reborn.

Many sweatshops can be found today in the same places
where they proliferated in the earlier part of the last century. The
garment industry in the United States is a prime example, running once again on the back of sweated labor after at least a
partial hiatus of some fifty years.[2] The hellish conditions of
turn-of-the-century Chicago immigrant meatpacking workers
that Upton Sinclair famously revealed in *The Jungle,* relegated to
history for decades in the mid-twentieth century after the plants
were unionized, play out again—and worse—as a new century
turns, in the enormous meat-processing plants that dot the
Midwest and West.[3] Farm work is a perennial sweatshop, it
seems. The sweatshops in the fields revealed to the American
public by Edward R. Murrow's 1960 documentary *Harvest of
Shame* still exist. They grow in Florida's hypnotically repeating
rows of tomatoes and groves of citrus fruit. They thrive in the
thousands of acres of cucumbers stretching southward from
Ohio, destined for the jars of the Mt. Olive pickle empire, and
flourish in the vast commercial strawberry farms of California
and Washington state. So too with domestic work. Lilliam and
many of her fellow woman immigrants have come to discover
what African-American women in this country have long known,
that private homes can also harbor sweatshops, with domestic
workers laboring for 70 or more hours a week for $2.00 an hour
or less.

New kinds of sweatshops are emerging these days too. No barrier keeps sweatshop conditions—long hours, low wages, high
rates of injury—in traditional sweatshop industries. Jobs in the

United States in general have shifted from manufacturing to service; sweatshops have followed suit. We have sweatshops in restaurants such as the one that hired Carmen Lelys, with dishwashers earning far less than the minimum wage as they bend over sinkfuls of crusted pans for 14-hour shifts. We have sweatshops in carwashes and construction, sweatshops in home renovation and auto repair, sweatshops in landscaping. Sweatshops may look different in some places today than their predecessors of an earlier era, but in their effect on workers they are often devastatingly the same.

Ask the average person to imagine "sweatshop in the United States" and she may recall some of the particularly horrific situations that garnered public attention in the 1990s. In the summer of 1995, for example, 72 Thai workers in El Monte, California, were found held in bondage in a barbed-wire–enclosed apartment building, where they stitched garments for up to 18 hours a day. Some had been enslaved for as long as seventeen years. In 1997, more than 60 deaf Mexican workers—including 10 children—were discovered living together in crowded and dirty conditions in Queens, New York, after two of them reported their situation to the police. They had been recruited from schools and homes for the deaf in Mexico by smugglers on the promise that they would find "prosperous jobs and life styles" in the United States, but since their arrival had been forced to sell trinkets on the streets of New York for a dollar a piece. When they tried to escape, their captors turned electric stun guns on them. Farm workers and domestic workers, too, have in recent times been made to work under conditions akin to slavery. And slavery is not the worst of it. The story of Eduardo Gutierrez, who immigrated from Mexico, found work for a construction boss notorious for his use of undocumented immigrants in unsafe conditions, and died shortly thereafter when he fell three stories into wet cement, is but one of a litany of the tales of immigrants who have paid for their dreams with their lives.[4]

Such situations of super-exploitation are certainly a part of the world of sweatshop work. The vast majority of sweatshops, though, attract little notice. Shocked by stories of slave and child labor, of death on the job, we become numb to the grimness and dangers of low-wage immigrant work, and indeed low-wage work in general.[5] Most immigrants are not forced to work for nothing, but like Lilliam Araujo many will at some point in their work life make less than the minimum wage or be cheated of their wages entirely. Most immigrants do not work in conditions of slavery, but like Carmen Maldonado, many labor 12, 14, even 16 hours a day to make ends meet. The "everyday sweatshops" that hire them pay $4.00 an hour when the minimum wage requires $5.15. They offer no time-and-a-half for overtime, either flagrantly ignoring the law or creating ruses to avoid it. Others avoid the whole issue by keeping no records and paying only in cash.

As appalling as the illegally low wages and extended hours are the injuries immigrants suffer on the job. Most sweatshops are unsafe. The question is not whether any workers will be hurt, but how often, how many, and how badly. All too many immigrants lose fingers to machines operated without safety guards, suffer debilitating back injuries from lifting huge loads, and struggle with headaches and blurry vision from working with dangerous chemicals without appropriate protection or training. Other serious injuries are also common. Within one two-year period as an advocate for immigrant workers, I paid a hospital visit to a Salvadoran mechanic whose ribs and legs were mangled when he was pinned by a backward-rolling car in an underground auto repair shop; met a Honduran who had inhaled so much toxic paint while sanding yachts for his employer that within months he went from dizziness and nausea to violent headaches and then death; sat with a Salvadoran woman whose hands were covered with puffy blisters from being forced to operate the searingly hot press in a commercial laundry with only thin cotton gloves to protect her; talked with a Guatemalan restaurant worker whose boss intentionally burned him with hot pans of oil when he did not chop ingredients and wash dishes fast enough; and took to the emergency room a Salvadoran day laborer whose arm was crushed by falling scaffolding.[6] In the not infrequent worst case, death is the result. A 2001 *Newsday* investigation concluded that "Hispanic immigrants are particularly at risk for getting killed in the workplace," a conclusion graphically corroborated two years later by the National Academy of Sciences' estimate that Latino immigrants die on the job at a rate nearly 250 percent higher than the average workers in the United States. Death rates for Latino workers have risen over the past decade even as workplace fatality rates for non-Latinos have fallen.[7]

A broad brush can paint only so clear a picture. To really understand the challenges of taking on the modern sweatshop, we need to turn to a specific context: particular immigrants and particular jobs set in a particular local economy. Long Island, New York, may not be the first place that comes to mind as a prototype of an immigrant community. But a confluence of factors have turned it into a setting that aptly illustrates the resurgence of sweatshops.

Zoila Rodriguez laughs as she remembers the morning in 1990 when she arrived in Long Island. In El Salvador she had lived the relatively comfortable life of an office worker in the country's capital, moving from secretarial work with an oil company into the growing field of international development aid. But she was a single mother, and she urgently wanted to get her daughter, Mónica, out of war-torn San Salvador. From television, other immigrants' stories, and movies, she thought she knew what she was choosing when she decided to move to New York: skyscrapers, apartment buildings, metropolitan bustle. She was a city dweller, and bustle was exactly what she wanted. She made plans to stay with a friend in New York until she got settled. The friend came to meet Zoila at the airport. It was only as the car pulled out of the airport parking lot and onto the Belt Parkway that Zoila realized that they were driving away from New York City's skyline, not toward it. "That was a shock," Rodriguez says now, shaking her head. "According to me, 'New York' *was* Manhattan's buildings!"[8] After what felt like an interminable drive, they pulled up on a street of neat ranch homes. She asked for a map to understand where she was. The answer: Brentwood, Long Island. Brentwood was an hour and a quarter from Manhattan with no traffic, but there was always traffic. In any case, she didn't own a car. It would be months before Zoila so much as visited the city she had once believed would be her new home.

By the early 1990s, a river of immigrants was pouring from Latin America into Long Island. They were from over a dozen countries, from rural villages and urban high-rises, from all political perspectives, those with university degrees and those who struggled to write their name, those who had had maids and those who had been maids. In 1970, Long Island was 95 percent white. By the 2000 Census almost one in four of the Island's residents would be people of color, the majority of them foreign born.[9] Whatever its slightly stunned longtime residents may tell you now, Long Island is no stranger to immigration. Irish, German, Italian, and Jewish newcomers have lived and worked in

Long Island's two counties, Nassau and Suffolk, since the late 1800s.[10] But the recent arrivals are different in number and in race. Where the older generations came in relatively small numbers and were largely white skinned (although often not seen as "white" by the Northern Europeans who preceded them), the newest arrivals have come in large waves, and are predominately people of color.

Today, Long Island is home to one of the largest communities of people from El Salvador in the United States: 100,000 by one recent estimate, 150,000 or more by another. Those numbers would put Long Island on the list of the five largest cities in El Salvador. The motivation for these immigrants' flight was political upheaval, intertwined with growing economic need. A violent civil war, prolonged and harshened by the intervention of the United States on the side of the Salvadoran government, released a flood of refugees in the 1980s and 1990s—a sixth of the country's population by some estimates. Some had no direct involvement in the conflict, but were unable to make a living or, like Rodriguez, raise their children as the army and the guerrillas battled in their fields and neighborhoods. Some were direct participants in the war. Close on the Salvadorans' heels came thousands of other Latino immigrants, from Mexico and Honduras, Colombia and Ecuador. Official data from the 2000 Census show 283,000 Latinos living in Long Island, a 280 percent increase over 1980; experts estimate that accurate numbers may be as much as 50 percent higher. And they have company. During the same time period, South and East Asian, Caribbean and other immigrants have come to live and work in Long Island in large numbers.[11]

Long Island has grappled with its new identity. For the most part, communities have adapted over the two decades since the new wave of immigration began, albeit slowly, with some public resistance and not a little private grumbling. Public schools began to offer bilingual education; hospitals added translators; adult education programs saw ESL enrollments swell. Churches started Spanish masses. At times and in places, though, there has been open backlash. In 1994, the Suffolk County legislature was refused permission by the state to deny health care and welfare benefits to noncitizens.[12] The 1990s also repeatedly saw English-only bills proposed in Suffolk County. Things worsened dramatically in 1998, when a group of Suffolk County residents founded the Sachem Quality of Life committee, an organization with an explicit mission to rid the area of undocumented immigrants, whose quest for work at day labor sites they believe "adds to the degradation of our quality of life." The Sachem group persistently tried to get the Suffolk County legislature to pass a series of anti-immigrant bills, from an English-only measure to a resolution to sue the Immigration and Naturalization Service (INS) for failing to do its job to a law that would forbid day laborers to seek work on public property. Their methods were not subtle. In 1999, as a day laborer tried to give testimony at a public hearing, dozens of members of the group stood, put their hands on their hearts, and began to shout the Pledge of Allegiance to drown him out.[13]

Violence against immigrants increased. In one terrible incident in the fall of 2000, two young members of a neo-Nazi group picked up two Latino day laborers in Farmingville on the pretense of offering work. They brought them to an abandoned basement and attacked them with a knife and post-hole digger, intending to kill them. Xenophobia flared again in the "immigrants go home" aftermath of September 11, 2001. Even as the intensity of that period faded, a Farmingville immigrant home was firebombed in the summer of 2003.[14]

Long Island is not the only unlikely place to have become an immigrant mecca over the past decade. Its shift in demographics is reflected around the country. Immigrants are now settling in large numbers in places such as rural Tennessee and Georgia, where Latino and Asian faces fall outside the black and white social categories that have held sway for hundreds of years. They are coming by the hundreds and thousands to small midwestern towns where the last wave of immigrants arrived more than a century and a half ago from Germany and Scandinavia. They are making homes in suburbs—in Alexandria, Virginia, and Silver Spring, Maryland, in the residential sprawls outside Chicago and Dallas and Los Angeles.[15]

Above all, it was work that led this demographic change. Work, and in particular, the shift from manufacturing jobs to service.

Long Island is often stereotyped as a "bedroom community," home to families whose breadwinners pile on the trains to New York City every morning and pile off again at night. Since World War II, Long Island has developed a rich economy of its own. The bulk of the area's jobs were once in defense manufacturing. Then major defense contractors such as Grumman and Lockheed shed over 40,000 jobs on Long Island in the period from 1985 to 1994. More than 10,000 additional manufacturing jobs vanished during the recession of the late 1980s and early 1990s. This pattern reflected a shift from manufacturing to service within the United States economy as a whole. In 1970 the U.S. economy counted 25 percent of its jobs in the manufacturing sector. The number of manufacturing jobs in the United States has fallen by 20 percent since 1970, while the number of private service-providing jobs has grown by 140 percent, many of them at the low-wage end.[16]

When Long Island's economy picked up a few years later, it

was far more diverse on the high end: biotechnology, high-tech, and financial industries drew new well-paid families to the suburbs, where they both lived and worked. Their demand for workers to clean their homes, clip their lawns, build their pools, care for their children, and cook their restaurant meals created a ballooning market for low-wage service jobs. Between the new firms hiring high-end employees and those employees in turn hiring landscapers and domestic workers, service industries drove Long Island's economic recovery. Service work—childcare, housecleaning, janitorial duties, restaurant work, landscaping, and construction jobs, among others—now accounts for 86 percent of Long Island's nonfarm employment. The manufacturing work that remains in Long Island is largely low-wage and low-skilled. At the lowest end, many of these service and manufacturing jobs are run as sweatshops. Wages are low, hours are long, injury rates run high. Few of them are unionized. And by and large, these jobs are filled by Latino immigrants.[17]

The problems that go with this work vary from job to job and industry to industry. Restaurant dishwashing and busboy work is notorious for its long hours—often upward of 70 a week—and its low wages, often below the legal minimum. Live-in domestic work has even longer hours and even lower wages; live-out domestic work can provide a higher income once a worker builds up a set of clients, but requires more English and more contacts to succeed. Landscaping *offers* more than the minimum wage, but employers frequently fail to pay for work done. In addition, it operates only for half the year (and only on days when the weather is good), and has a strikingly high injury rate from razor-sharp mower blades, chainsaws, and work high in trees without training or safety gear. Similar things could be said for construction, with the added dynamic that unlike the landscaping industry, where unionization is rare, in the building trades unions were once a strong presence in Long Island.[18] Today, immigrant workers have made significant inroads into jobs that once were unionized, yet by and large the Long Island building trades unions have not brought immigrant workers into their fold. Subcontracting is rampant in many immigrant occupations. Finally, immigrant workers on Long Island have little industry identification, and change jobs frequently. A Latino immigrant man in Long Island may work as a landscaper during the summer and in a restaurant in the winter; if he loses his restaurant job he may spend some time doing day labor and end up working for a roofer. A woman may begin as a live-in domestic worker and move on to a patchwork of factory work, live-out housecleaning, and part-time janitorial jobs.

If immigrant workers could have figured out a way to get more stable, safer, and higher-paying jobs, most would have. As Lilliam Araujo says, "As human beings, I have always believed that we must work to support each other and fix the problems we face." Even during her first seven years in the country, years spent working for that one family without a single raise, high among her goals was "to be able to work to achieve a better socioeconomic state for other people"—and herself too. But how? Between being undocumented, living in someone else's home, working at all hours, and attending to the needs of her boys, she couldn't figure out what shape that work might take. Carmen Maldonado was frustrated too. He had asked his family and his coworkers at the restaurant about his legal rights on the job, but no one seemed to know anything. "At times I cried for the unjust way the bosses would treat us. I didn't know what else to do. Such low wages, 14 or 15 hour workdays, abuse, racism, all of that." He was angry. A leader in his home community, cofounder of an agricultural cooperative, he felt there had to be a way to fight the mistreatment he and others faced. And yet, he remembers, without a clear alternative, "I felt I had to stand for it."

Workers are not the only ones who struggle with the question of how to take on the modern sweatshop. Across the country, advocates grapple with it, and so do government inspectors, and union and community organizers. We used to think we knew what to do about sweatshops. *Legislate. Enforce the law. Unionize.* But the solutions that are most familiar were crafted for another time, for the rules and rhythms of industrial mass production. It is worth asking whether they can simply be lifted from Detroit's shop floors, Chicago's slaughtering pens, New York's hulking garment factories and dropped a hundred years later on the modern versions of those prototypes, much less on the day labor street corners, the janitorial subcontractors, the busboys and domestic workers and home health aides of the new sweatshop economy.

A closer look suggests that, by and large, they cannot. Sweatshop work today is different in significant ways from what it was a century ago. Sweatshops in the United States today are entangled in a context of globalized production, undocumented immigration and underground work, and restructured workplaces that has complicated every response to the abuses of sweated labor.

In today's sweatshops, enforcement of workplace laws is far more difficult than it once was. The problem, by and large, is not a lack of regulation. If the abuses of immigrant and other low-wage workers a century ago could once be laid at the door of a failure to create protective laws, they no longer can. Thanks to decades of work by unions and reformers, most immigrant workers, even the undocumented, have the right—on paper, at least—to a minimum wage, to overtime wages, to protection from discrimination, and to safe and healthy working conditions.[19] Enforcing existing laws is thus a major thrust of the current fight against sweatshops. Yet sweatshops are founded on—are literally defined by—their refusal to comply with these basic laws governing the workplace. The underground economy is structured to avoid detection. Sweatshops are notoriously small and mobile, paying in cash and maintaining low capital investments in order to operate below the radar screen. For much low-wage service work, it is often difficult even to locate a physical place to inspect, since construction contractors, landscapers, domestic workers, and others move hourly, daily, or weekly from site to site. Once an enterprise is found, investigating it before it disappears is a challenge. And where government inspectors are able to complete an investigation, enforcement of a finding or judgment against a company before it dissolves and reopens under another name can be next to impossible.

Compounding this is the fact that government agencies responsible for enforcing protective labor laws are sorely underfunded. Where in 1977 there was one federal wage inspector for every 43,000 employees covered by the Fair Labor Standards Act (FLSA), by 1996 that number had plummeted to one inspector per 91,000 covered workers. The Occupational Safety and Health Administration (OSHA) today has an even lower ratio, one inspector for every 99,000 workers covered. The federal Department of Labor's efforts to address sweatshop conditions by concentrating inspections in industries with high percentages of violators and by enforcing FLSA's "Hot Goods" provisions, which permit the seizure of goods made under conditions that violate the law, have had limited impact due to low staffing and legal loopholes.[20]

Long Island provides a graphic example of the resulting problems. As Long Island's sweatshops grew through the eighties and early nineties, government agencies there turned a blind eye to the largest labor problem in their midst. Suburban branches of state and federal labor department agencies were never set up to handle serious problems in any case. Given the staffing of the OSHA office in Long Island in 1994, if each inspector had visited a different site every workday—a highly optimistic scenario—it would have taken eighteen years for the agency to complete a single round of inspections. Moreover, fines were minimal and could often be "abated" if the offense was remedied before a certain date. Thus employers had no incentive to maintain health and safety standards in the absence of an OSHA order to do so. Paying OSHA fines and penalties once caught was often cheaper for an employer than complying with the law before an inspection. And OSHA was not the agency in the worst shape. The New York State Department of Labor's Division of Labor Standards was so understaffed that it would have required more than twenty-seven years for its inspectors to finish a one-time inspection of each of the state's private businesses.[21]

Over and above these staffing problems, immigrant workers in low-wage industries hit brick walls when they tried to file claims with Long Island labor enforcement offices. The critically important state Division of Labor Standards, charged with enforcing the minimum wage and overtime laws, was a particularly closed system. For a time, immigrants who wanted to file claims were told in English that they could return to the office every other Friday morning, when a Spanish speaker might be available to help them—although in fact she was often called away. Those who penetrated the translation system were met with insult and outright rejection: inspectors told immigrants, "I don't like to take claims for domestic workers and restaurant workers," lectured them about not paying taxes, complained to them that "illegal aliens" rob the taxpayer of money, and dissuaded them from filing cases with warnings that they would owe more in taxes than they received in back wages if they pursued their claims.[22] The office of the U.S. Department of Labor had its own problems. It was drastically underfunded, and until 1998 was further hampered by regulations that meant reports about nonpayment of wages could trigger a raid in addition to a wage inspection at a particular workplace, resulting in the deportation of the workers who stood up for their rights.[23] This made the Labor Department a risky partner in the effort to combat abusive working conditions for immigrant laborers.

Where the government fails to enforce its own laws, legal advocacy groups have an important role to play. But Long Island in the early 1990s was not a target of the few advocacy organizations in New York City that focused on conditions of low-wage work. Federally funded legal services, another institution that might have pressed government to respond by bringing individual claims, offered equally little to the Island's immigrant workers. Banned by Congress like all such offices from serving undocumented immigrants or engaging in organizing, the legal services offices on Long Island were not in a position to offer help.[24] This was compounded by the legal services tradition of offering assistance with housing problems, benefits issues, and family law—but not work-related issues.[25] One other resource might have been the network of churches, home-country associations, and social service agencies that had either developed in the 1980s or been reconfigured during that period to serve the needs of new immigrants. But beyond the actions of an intrepid minister here or there, in the early 1990s on Long Island these institutions rarely ventured into the world of work.

Even if legal representation had been more widely available, individual legal victories in the sweatshop world are both hard to enforce and fleeting in their impact. Once caught, many employers continue to pay sub-minimum wages to other workers not involved in the lawsuit. Another approach might be to seek a more effective body of law through impact litigation. But in a setting where every law on the books is flouted, the incentive to add one more rule to the list of those already ignored is minimal. Lobbying for changes in the law faces the same problem. Both litigation and stronger legislation can be important tools in the arsenal of the fight against sweatshops, but without effective government enforcement or organizations of workers that have the power to see that legal rulings and new laws are enforced, they are unlikely to have much of an impact.

What, then, of union organizing? After all, it was unions that lifted generations of immigrants out of sweatshop poverty and into decent jobs with decent pay. Any reader who has a passing familiarity with labor history can list unions known for their immigrant traditions that are still active today: the International Ladies Garment Workers Union (ILGWU, now UNITE HERE!), the Steel Workers Organizing Committee (now the United Steelworkers of America), and the United Auto Workers, to name just a few. And yet thinking about organizing modern sweatshop workers along the model that has come to typify union organizing in the United States highlights how much today's conventional organizing strategy is shaped by assumptions that no longer hold in many workplaces.

A realistic assessment of why unions struggle to organize low-wage immigrants today involves untangling several strands of an argument too often presented as an undifferentiated whole. One element is the shameful history of xenophobia in the U.S. labor movement. Yet while racism and anti-immigrant sentiment have unquestionably been a recurrent theme in union organizing in this country, they are insufficient to explain the obstacles to effective organizing of the lowest-wage immigrants. As other observers have suggested, immigrants may have their own doubts about joining a union. I also examine those concerns. Although important, they too provide an inadequate account of the reasons that unionizing has been stymied in the new sweatshops. To fully comprehend the challenges faced by such an effort requires an exploration of the structural barriers to organizing low-wage newcomers.

The American Federation of Labor and the Congress of Industrial Organizations (AFL-CIO) and its predecessors have a long and messy history of nativism. After Chinese immigrants laid the rails over some of the most difficult terrain connecting the eastern United States to the West, labor organizations played leading roles in barring new Chinese immigrants from entering the United States and keeping those already inside the country from becoming citizens through the Chinese Exclusion Act, passed in 1882. In 1891, the American Federation of Labor passed a resolution calling for a halt to all immigration.[26] In 1954 unions backed Operation Wetback, during which the INS hunted down and deported over a million Mexican immigrants, many of them the relatives and home-country neighbors of *braceros* who had been invited into the country to harvest U.S. crops.[27]

Labor movement history is not by any means a single story. At the same time as the mainstream national labor movement fought for anti-immigrant public policies, other unions—sometimes including the locals of national unions that supported anti-immigrant policies—courted immigrants and saw some of their greatest victories won by them. The participation and leadership of Jewish immigrants in the International Ladies Garment Workers' organizing of New York's garment industry in the early 1900s, of Irish, Italian, Lithuanian, and other immigrants in the Industrial Workers of the World Lawrence textile mill strike of 1912, of the Greek and Italian immigrants who died in the 1914 Ludlow Massacre in Colorado fighting for membership in the United Mine Workers: these are the stuff of labor movement legend. So, too, is the CIO's wall-to-wall organizing approach to mass production, beginning in the 1930s, that often included both African American and immigrant workers.[28] In the last twenty years many unions have actively sought to organize immigrants.

It is not always easy to draw the line between unions with anti-immigrant positions and those that actively seek to organize newcomers. The United Farm Workers in the 1970s is a prime example. In many ways, the UFW was the most pro-immigrant of unions. It had a decidedly immigrant "feel": Spanish was the language of daily work, and the culture and religion of its largely Mexican and Mexican- and Filipino-American members played important roles in its organizing model. The union's membership included recent immigrants from Mexico and elsewhere, both documented and not. When undocumented immigrants were working on a ranch where the UFW was organizing, the union sought to include them, offering help with immigration issues and treating them like any other member.

But undocumented workers were also often brought in by growers as strikebreakers, and when that happened the UFW fought to exclude them by every means at its disposal. Union staff frequently asked the INS to intervene and deport immigrant workers who had crossed picket lines or whose willingness to take jobs threatened a strike. At various times, UFW organizers pressed the INS to arrest and deport five hundred undocumented workers, submitted to the INS individual names of undocumented immigrants who were working in struck fields, and met with the INS commissioner to demand that the INS extend its raids to labor camps where undocumented strikebreakers were living. Despite organizers' and members' ambivalence about the INS due to many of their families' bad experiences with the agency, and despite the fact that the resulting raids occasionally netted undocumented UFW members from the picket lines as well, the union felt this was a necessary step given the labor situation. The union's general counsel, Jerry Cohen, recalls that "Cesar [Chavez]'s posture at that point was, 'We want to get contracts, come hell or high water; if somebody's busting our picket line the hell with them.'" The UFW's policy and tactics were particularly controversial among Chicano activists, who felt the UFW's strategy reinforced the false concept of a border and sharpened divisions among Latinos.[29]

These examples illustrate the conflicts that arise as unions seek to protect their members from wage competition. Some new immigrants become members. Those who don't, the newer newcomers, become a threat to the organizing that has been achieved. Today, the UFW recognizes that it must continually seek to organize undocumented immigrants, not deport them. But the pressures its former policy reflects remain a real concern for many unions in the labor movement whose members face intensive competition for jobs from undocumented immigrants.

Long Island is no stranger to these tensions. By the time Latino immigrants were a significant presence in Long Island, the Island's labor movement—once a vibrant and even militant extension of New York City's unions—had slowed to a crawl. Union-heavy manufacturing sectors were disappearing, taking union memberships with them. Globalization was taking its toll: the ILGWU, for example, lost more than half of its Long Island membership during the 1980s.[30] Little new organizing was taking place in the service and light manufacturing industries that came to replace the jobs that left. This trend had a profound impact on Long Island's newest workers.

Consonant with the anti-immigrant union tradition, some Long Island unions in industries where newcomers worked in the 1990s either ignored immigrants or actively sought to exclude them. In heavily subcontracted industries on Long Island, immigrant firms operating in the underground economy were often in direct competition with union firms for jobs. Several of Long Island's unions were both angry about this situation and stymied by it. In 1998, I met with a prominent local labor leader. He was acutely aware of what was happening in the industry—as he bluntly characterized it, "'Francisco' is taking our members' jobs." But he was unable to imagine an alternative to the unions' continuing to represent almost exclusively native-born workers. When I suggested that his union might seek to incorporate immigrants, including the undocumented, he told me he believed that was not legally possible. He promised to consider my argument to the contrary, and eventually paid a visit to the Workplace Project to invite its members to join the union's apprenticeship program. When the union failed to provide support for Spanish-speaking apprentices, though, the connection fizzled, and within a few years this leader and his union were publicly voicing their opposition to the establishment of organized day labor sites in Suffolk County.[31]

Other Long Island unions, including the Communication Workers of America and the United Food & Commercial Workers, did try to reach out to immigrants, although they were often defeated by the myriad challenges of organizing workers who spoke different languages and came from countries with different organizing traditions and disparate images of unions. Others, such as the Service Employees International Union (SEIU) and Teamster locals in Long Island, took in new immigrant members as the hiring patterns of the factories, janitorial services, warehouses, and other businesses they had organized years ago changed, but did little to incorporate them into the union's culture. Few unions translated contracts into Spanish, or even gave workers copies in English. Even shop stewards—workers elected or appointed to represent coworkers—rarely spoke languages other than English. Because of this lack of linguistic and cultural fluency, among other reasons, unions were also ill equipped to confront undocumented immigrants' fear that they would be reported to the INS and deported in retaliation for organizing, or to build on the strengths that immigrant workers brought and to understand their needs and concerns.

At the same time, immigrants wondered if what the unions offered was something worth fighting for. Immigrant workers on Long Island—like all workers, but with even greater obstacles and fears—struggled over the question of whether to invest the time and take the risks necessary to raise their wages and improve their working conditions.

In part their doubts grew from their immediate experience of unions in New York. Some Workplace Project members had concluded that they were more likely to earn decent wages with union representation than without it, and they appreciated the benefits that union membership provided, although they had

critiques of the way unions had failed to engage them person-
ally. But most were disillusioned, saying things such as "I have a
union and it never does anything" (Wilma Chavez); "the union
. . . works more for the employers than the employees" (Rony
Martinez); "the unions I belonged to were not interested in their
members" (Rene Arguello); "a friend of mine [at work] . . . was
fired unjustly. The union did not defend her . . . They don't listen
to what we say" (Angela Sarmiento).[32] Juan Carlos Molina offered his personal assessment of the officers of the Teamsters local that had represented him as "bad guys, totally bad guys. They
would negotiate the contract in advance and then come out to
the workers to say 'Look, we're going to ask for so much.' People
would agree. But they already had it in hand . . . I always used to
say to them, 'You call this democracy?'"[33] Maria Aparicio, an Ecuadorian woman, recalls that after eight years as a unionized
warehouse worker "I had no idea we had a union contract. They
had never read it to us. Sure there was one—but it had been filed
away who knows where."[34] These same workers might have been
positive about the *idea* of unions, but their experience had left
them disenchanted.

It is often argued that the real problem is not that unions
such as these have served immigrants poorly, but that immigrants have little interest in organizing. Immigrant workers are
often portrayed as grateful for any work in the United States,
glad to earn a few dollars an hour instead of the same amount in
a day or even a week. Why would a person in that situation, if
immigrants are indeed in that situation, want to organize?

Carmen Lelys Maldonado's story typifies the mindset of many
immigrants who depart for the United States imagining that the
wages they will be paid here will amount to riches compared
with the wages they could earn back home. The word on the

street in Latin America is: Go to the United States and in two years you'll return with enough cash to settle back home for good. As it has been on many continents and for at least a century, of course, the word on the street is wrong. Nonetheless, it is so commonly believed that Latino immigrants refer to it with a rueful smile as "those famous two years," or "the two-year myth." Zoila Rodriguez remembers friends promising her that if she went to work as a housekeeper in the United States, her residency would come through in two years, allowing her to travel back home. That was in 1990. In fact, it was 2002 before she was able to arrange for permanent legal papers, and then not through her job but through a new law that benefited Salvadorans. Maldonado recalls, "According to my calculations, in two years I would have enough to go back home."[35] In advance, he savored the triumphant return: his children's education paid for, his farm grown fat on his savings. It was not to be. Lilliam Araujo had also heard that two years would be enough time to make some money, let the political situation calm down, and return to El Salvador. That was over a decade ago, and she has yet to return for so much as a week's visit.

The two-year myth began to unravel when immigrants discovered the impossibility of earning enough money to both live and save while working in one of Long Island's suburban sweatshops. As the Salvadoran immigrant Carlos Canales ruefully recalls, it took a only little while before he "began to analyze why it is that in this country you need two jobs just to survive."[36] At the root of the two-year myth and the sense of betrayal among immigrants is a basic miscalculation. For those with access to television in their home countries, the media portrays life in the United States as exclusively middle class. Print articles and advertising send the same message. Earlier migrants exaggerate their success, sending home pictures of themselves standing next to fancy cars they do not own in fancy neighborhoods they do not live in, and returning home to visit laden with expensive gifts. All this is compounded by what might be called pre-immigration math, in which immigrants calculate the wages they imagine they will earn in dollars and compare them to the much lower wages in their home countries. The large nest egg they imagine accumulating within a year or two fails to take into account the cost of living in Long Island, which eats up those dollars as fast as they can earn them.[37]

A simple calculation shows the dimensions of the problem. A parent with two children working full time *at* (not below) the current federal minimum wage—$5.15 an hour—earns a gross annual salary of $10,712 a year. If she puts every penny of that toward rent, paying not a dollar in taxes, eating literally nothing, going nowhere, buying her children not a single item of clothing or a school notebook, never visiting a doctor or taking an aspirin, she will still fall $4,048 short of the amount she would need to pay fair market rent on a two-bedroom apartment in Long Island for a year.[38] (She will also be $3,400 below the poverty line for a family of three.) Disturbing as they are, even these figures assume that the worker is paid a minimum wage for a steady job. For many immigrant workers, stuck in sweatshops, that assumption does not hold.

So although new immigrants might have been grateful for whatever they could earn, those with more than a month under their belts soon realized that the price of basic living was far higher in Long Island than they had ever imagined. Furthermore, a few chances to observe native-born workers led many to the conclusion that the dirtiest, hardest, and most dangerous jobs were reserved for immigrants. That things were rough, then, most immigrants had no doubt. *We work like oxen,* they would say, *and they treat us like dogs.* But what to do about it? For undocumented workers fear of detection was obviously a strong deterrent to taking action to improve working conditions. More surprising, for documented and undocumented immigrants alike, was the inhibiting role of the two-year myth.

Sociologists call immigrants who plan to return home (and those who travel back and forth) sojourners. Migrant workers are classic examples. They contrast them to settlers, immigrants who put down roots and intend to remain. But what is complicated about the two-year myth is that it creates immigrants who are settlers in fact but sojourners in attitude. Although many Latino immigrants in Long Island dreamed of returning home for good or for extended visits, very few actually did so. Flights were too expensive, land travel took too long, and, for the undocumented, the risks of the clandestine border crossing on the return trip grew greater year by year. For the immigrant who had fled persecution, return was not possible, at least in the short term. But the fantasy died hard—especially when for an immigrant to see himself as a settler required admitting that he had failed in his original goals of saving substantial sums in a short time. So like Araujo, Rodriguez, and Maldonado, many settled here while remaining sojourners in their hearts, ever imagining that they would soon be able to travel back.

The sojourner attitude makes labor organizing hard. As the Salvadoran worker and organizer Samuel Chavez notes, "one of the reasons it's so difficult to organize new Latino immigrants . . . is that they come with that mentality, 'two years and I'll go home.'"[39] The sociologist Roger Waldinger, a long-time student of immigrant labor patterns, and his colleague Claudia Der-Martirosian, have explored the behavior of settlers and sojourners in labor organizing campaigns. Not surprisingly, they found that settlers, whose frame of reference is more firmly rooted in this country, may be more likely to look to a union if they feel their wages are insufficient and their working conditions dangerous. But sojourners, or those who at least imagine returning home shortly or who travel regularly back and forth, continue to measure their earnings to some extent by home-country standards. This "dual frame of reference," they conclude, "blunts the impact of those frustrations encountered in the United States."[40] Such immigrants may decide that their current wages and working conditions are good enough in the short term, which is the only term in which they imagine themselves living here.[41]

Chavez encountered this attitude head on when he led an organizing drive among his largely Latino coworkers in a Long Island paper goods factory, against owners and supervisors who, according to the workers' complaint filed with the Equal Employment Opportunity Commission, called Latino workers "Spanish animals" and "fucking Salvadorans" and said "your children are like dogs."[42] This was the group of workers whose picket I mentioned driving to join in the Introduction. Chavez reflects on this experience: "I remember that when we were talking with coworkers we would say to them, 'Look, we can make changes here, we can make these people treat us differently.' And we would explain to them what we'd have to do, that we had to bring in a union and all of that. But often some of them would say, 'Why should I put myself at risk? I'm earning money, I work 40 hours a week, I get normal wages, they pay me overtime, which plenty of places don't—and I'm only going to be in this country for two years.'"

Whether they are sojourners or settlers is not the only factor that influences how immigrants see unions. Experience with labor activism before immigrating is another important influence. It plays out both ways. On the one hand, it stands to reason that immigrants who were organized or fought to organize in their home countries would have a great deal to offer to a union drive here. And often they do. Many of the Latino immigrants in Long Island are from El Salvador, a country with a vibrant (and violent) history of union organizing. As Chavez notes, "Sometimes people come who are new in the fight for rights *here,* but perhaps they have been involved in another country, in their country of origin . . . that person already had the seed inside him, so probably he'll stay [to organize]." Immigrants who witnessed severe repression of labor activists in their home countries may also see the negative consequences of organizing in the United States as minimal. As one SEIU organizer from the Los Angeles Justice for Janitors campaign noted of workers from El Salvador, "there, you were in a union, they killed you. Here, you [were in a union] and you lost a job at $4.25."[43] Similarly, Salvadoran Workplace Project member Rodolfo Sorto remembers that he was heartened when he first began organizing a union in this country. "I could see that here in the United States you could raise your voice. You can make demands, you can yell. You may receive many kinds of abuse. But perhaps not a bullet like you would have gotten [in El Salvador]."[44]

Yet coming from a country with a violent labor history turns out to be no guarantee that workers will want to become involved in a union here. Sometimes, Salvadoran workers were *more* afraid to become involved than others, because they assumed that repression would follow. Some activists had promised their families they would leave unions and politics behind when they immigrated; their loved ones were so traumatized they wanted to hear nothing about organizing. And those who had been active with other social movements often struggled to figure out how to make their organizing experience at home relevant in such a foreign context. Juan Carlos Molina, who as a university student fought as a part of the Salvadoran revolutionary forces, found that the United States is different. "The organizing approach is different." And still others were so relieved to be out of an atmosphere of life-threatening terror that they were willing to tolerate just about anything. Samuel Chavez again: "people have lived in terribly abusive situations, so in some sense when people come here they feel freed. Why would you care that your boss calls you 'stupid'? That's nothing compared with them coming to take you from your house at midnight."

Immigrants, then, feel the pull in both directions. A number of them bring experience with social movements and, indeed, union organizing of a breadth and depth few workers in the United States have experienced. At the same time, many are doubtful that they will settle here. They are often wary of activism, and experience has led not a few to be dubious about union organizing in the United States.

The uneasy relation between immigrants and unions is only the beginning of the story. Even a labor organizing effort that was entirely welcoming to immigrants, even a group of immigrants deeply desirous of organizing, would face serious obstacles that grow out of the structure of sweatshop work today. Three such challenges are global competition, undocumented immigration and the underground economy, and restructured work.

It is common to refer to the globalized economy as if it were a new phenomenon, and yet the old economy was not exactly domestic. Even in the seventeenth century, colonial powers were mining countries around the world for raw materials and seeking to open new markets for their finished products. By the early twentieth century, international trade and multinational production were a fact of life for many large companies in the United States and other parts of the "developed" world. But the international economy in the 1920s was structured very differently than it is today. Global trade then was limited in scope, taking place among perhaps a few hundred transnational firms. Global trade now is pervasive, involving over 60,000 transnational corporations.[45] And what was traded was different, too. Most of what companies in the United States imported in the first half of the century were raw materials required for domestic production. By comparison, multinational companies now shift the making of clothes, electronics, and other products to factories in whatever country sells its labor for the least money, importing the resulting products to sell here and abroad.

Global competition is not limited to manufacturing. Service work, too, is fast relocating overseas. Only a faint hiss on the line and the gentle accents of the women who answer the phone hint that a health insurance provider has shifted its claims processing operations to India, where companies run workshops in American slang for Indian employees and require them to choose an Americanized name to make callers feel more comfortable. Airline and hotel reservations, as well as the record-processing, customer service, and technical support functions of other U.S.-based companies, now often are handled through "call centers" located in foreign countries. Word processing and telemarketing similarly have moved offshore.[46]

It is trite to say that globalization has made us all neighbors. But it is true in labor organizing as in many other regards—as it is also true that globalization has made us all competitors. Unions in the United States once operated with at least the illusion of a closed domestic playing field. Factory workers in the United States now vie for work directly with those in countries where labor costs may be 10 percent or less of what they are here. Those who organize for higher pay and better working conditions face the constant threat that a plant will close down and move overseas if the union drive prevails. Garment workers grapple with this harsh reality daily; so do workers in the electronics industry, in assembly plants, and in most other light manufacturing concerns. From the owner's perspective, there may in fact be some advantages to maintaining plants in the United States: no relocation costs, quick turnaround, the ability to produce in small lots to satisfy local demand, greater quality control, and higher productivity among them. In some industries, such as the garment trade, wages make up a relatively small proportion of the product's final cost, compared to the mark-up for big-name retailer "branding."[47] But contractors compete with each other based on the cost of production, not the final price tag. If the cost of raw materials remains constant, wages matter in deciding which contractor's bid will prevail. And except in the rare niche market where price is no object, the result can be heavy pressure on workers not to ask for more, knowing that someone somewhere would gladly do the work for less.

Labor law offers little in the way of an impediment to job flight. As courts have interpreted the National Labor Relations Act (NLRA), there are circumstances under which it is perfectly legal for an employer to close down shop in one place in retaliation for a union organizing drive and then open again somewhere else. In one of the great exercises in legal hairsplitting, an employer can *predict* that relocation will be the consequence of a union campaign, but cannot *threaten* the same outcome. The only exception courts have found is if the plant's closing would send a chilling message about the prospects for union-building to workers in other plants owned by the same company. But this only applies to that particular employer's workers, and only those inside the country. So if the company closes its U.S. operations entirely, thus putting workers of similar manufacturers in the United States, not to mention its workers in China and Honduras, on notice that organizing will be swiftly punished with job flight, the law stands idle.[48]

Of course, since time immemorial employers have threatened to retaliate against union campaigns by relocating. What difference does it make if the relocation is domestic or overseas? Long before the current wave of globalization, the southern states in this country, with their historically lower wages and their "right to work" legislation permitting workers to elect not to pay union dues even at a workplace where a union contract was in effect, offered similar attractions to companies seeking to avoid unionization and its impact on wages. But there are two key differences between a domestic and a global market in this regard. Imagine an employer in Chicago, considering moving operations to Alabama or Vietnam. The wage differential between a worker in Chicago and one in Alabama is vastly smaller than that between one in Chicago and one in Vietnam. The temptation to move is thus exponentially greater in the global context. And labor and employment laws, including the National Labor Relations Act as well as other laws about wages and working conditions, apply only to workers inside the country or its territories. If the firm decamps for Vietnam, it will escape the grasp of the NLRA, moving into the weaker realm of Vietnamese labor protections and international standards.

What might a creative union do, faced with jobs once held by its members now gone overseas? Move organizing operations overseas also, perhaps, and complement that with an effort to enlist the support of consumers and public interest groups here. And, indeed, that is what a number of unions have tried, either defensively or preemptively. In addition to the more general global solidarity work in which many unions engage, a number of unions have created strategic alliances that they hope will strengthen organizing in their industries in countries that compete directly with the United States for jobs.[49] Important as they are, such efforts face serious obstacles. Unionization on a global scale may be the only grand response that makes sense in the face of globalized production. But a real effort to achieve that would require resources far beyond the imagination of even the richest unions of the AFL-CIO. The idea of taking on the workforce of the world when the workforce of your own backyard barely recognizes you is daunting, to say the least. It is further complicated by restrictive interpretations of labor law, which put limitations on some of the cross-border solidarity that would be essential to the success of such an effort.[50]

Finally, any attempt to extend the support of the U.S. labor movement to other countries also encounters the negative residue of past experiences. The AFL-CIO's earlier efforts to promote its objectives on foreign soil, most notably through its staunchly anticommunist cold war era foreign policy interventions that often sought to repress the most vibrant elements in local trade unionism, did little to inspire confidence among potential allies in other countries.[51] Today's efforts, less politically freighted, nonetheless face the complexity of organizing on an imbalanced global playing field. Although many unions in other countries where U.S. firms have chosen to move production welcome the support of their counterparts in the United States, other foreign unions, workers, and worker advocates have at times interpreted efforts by the U.S. labor movement to build international alliances and set minimum global labor standards as protectionism carried out through a masquerade of solidarity.[52]

Some jobs just can't move. A worker in Bombay can take reservations for a family seeking a hotel room in Miami, but she can't change their sheets or cook their meals long distance. In fact, in Long Island, relatively little of the work that immigrants did faced direct global competition. Most was service work, locally rooted.

Yet locally rooted work has not escaped the effects of globalization. Where work cannot go overseas, overseas comes to the work in the form of a steady flow of mobile laborers unable to make a living in their home countries. Although the global economy is most often measured in terms of mobile capital, mobile labor is both its product and its engine. Faced with the twin impossibilities of making a living in their home countries—or, in the case of those who flee political persecution, of staying in their countries and remaining alive—and of gaining permission to live and work in the United States, millions have entered this country illegally, or have come in as tourists or students but have stayed to work in violation of the conditions of their visas.

While capital's mobility is sanctioned by the trade rules governing the global economy, human mobility is not. Indeed, as capital moves with increasing agility, the United States has taken ever stricter measures to keep would-be mobile laborers from entering the country, reinforcing physical barriers at the borders, militarizing the border patrol, and enacting increasingly punitive laws against immigrants who are in the country without legal status. Those who succeed in entering without being caught, or who remain after their authorized stay is over, know that their lack of legal papers could be detected at any moment, a fact that injects substantial measures of anxiety and evasion into their lives. Necessary tasks of daily living become endlessly complicated: opening a bank account usually requires a tax identification number for which an application must be filed with the Internal Revenue Service (IRS); obtaining a driver's license in many places requires a valid Social Security number, which the government will not issue without proof of authorization to work. Enrolling children in school, although legally protected, can become a logistical nightmare.[53] Reporting robbery, domestic violence, or workplace exploitation to government officials raises the specter of detection and deportation by the U.S. Immigration and Customs Enforcement Bureau, the interior enforcement arm of the agency once called the Immigration and Naturalization Service. Undocumented immigrants do what they have to: they keep their money under their mattresses, pay others for transportation, buy documents on the street, stay quiet about abuse.

Why don't undocumented immigrants just legalize their status? Because most can't. Once it was vastly easier to gain legal admission to the United States than it is now. Until 1921, there were no numerical limits or quotas for the number of immigrants allowed to enter the United States. To be sure, by that date the country already had a history of restrictionist legislation, including the famous Chinese Exclusion Laws and other legislation banning the immigration of all "non-whites." But if immigrants from most places presented themselves at a "port of entry" such as Ellis Island in the early 1900s, and were not ill with a contagious disease, found likely to become a public charge, or excludable under a few other rules (no convicts, no "lunatics"), they were admitted into the United States as legal residents with permission to work. The Irish and the Jews, the Italians and the Greeks faced many problems in their struggle to settle in this country and find decent work, but by and large gaining immigration status was not one of them.

Since the early 1920s, legal status in this country has been available only to those who fit within an increasingly restricted set of categories. To oversimplify somewhat, the average immigrant can gain admission only if she has an adult child, sibling, spouse, or parent who is a citizen (or, in some categories, a "green card" holder); if she can show under a tightening set of rules that she will suffer persecution if returned to her home country; or if she has particular job skills that are in demand by employers and that U.S. citizens are not able to provide.[54] Most undocumented immigrants do not qualify for any of these categories. Even those who do qualify may face long waits before their admission is approved—about thirteen years for a Mexican immigrant with a U.S. citizen brother, for example. And so they risk death by crossing the desert at night, or stay on after their temporary visas have expired.

When it comes to work (and it quickly comes to work), undocumented immigrants' fear of deportation and their lack of legal status make them particularly likely to gravitate toward the underground economy, made up of businesses that operate on cash with little regard for government regulations. The underground or informal economy is technically defined as "income-generation . . . unregulated by the institutions of society, in a legal and social environment in which similar activities are regulated." This lack of regulation may be apparent on many different levels. Underground economy businesses may employ people who are not legally supposed to be working: undocumented immigrants, children, and people receiving benefits such as welfare or unemployment insurance that would be taken away if the government knew they were earning income. They may ignore legal workplace standards such as minimum wage laws and health and safety rules in their relationships with those workers. The business itself may be managed in a way that avoids inter-action with government agencies (for example, by not seeking mandatory licenses or not participating in mandatory insurance programs such as workers' compensation) or seeks to defraud the government (for example, by not paying taxes).[55] Infor-mal economy enterprises span a broad range, from manufactur-ing of various kinds to janitorial, retail, and repair services, land-scaping, childcare, and construction. There is also a parallel, internal underground economy, in which immigrants cook typi-cal foods such as *tamales* or *pupusas* or sweet bread at home and sell them there or on the street to fellow immigrants; look after another immigrant family's children; vend Avon or other catalog products; and bring back cheese, sweets, and other familiar foods from a trip to their country to sell to homesick neigh-bors.[56] Although hard to document, these practices are wide-spread. According to the International Monetary Fund, the U.S. underground economy more than doubled between 1970 and 2000, from an estimated 4 to 9 percent of the gross domestic product (GDP).[57] In immigrant-heavy areas, the numbers are much higher. A 2002 study by the Economic Roundtable esti-mated that over a quarter of Los Angeles's workforce was paid in cash.[58]

"Underground economy" suggests something dank, subterra-nean, completely divorced from our everyday, aboveground lives. But in fact, the underground and aboveground economies are anything but segregated. For one thing, immigrant workers and others move in and out of underground work—sometimes in the same day, if they work two or more jobs; sometimes periodically, as they lose one job and find another. For another, although underground enterprises may rely principally on an undocumented workforce, they often also hire workers who are here legally (and, conversely, some undocumented immigrants work in the formal sector). Furthermore, so-called underground businesses often operate in a relationship of mutual dependence with larger and more formal enterprises. A name-brand garment manufacturer may depend on a chain of informal subcontractors to sew its clothing; a national superstore may contract its groundskeeping or roof repair or janitorial work to a local company that operates in the underground economy. And many enterprises are themselves formal in some regards and informal in others, complying with some but not all laws, paying workers in part on the books and in part under the table. What we label the "informal sector," as if it were neatly contained, then, actually encompasses a complex and varied field, from fine renovations to demolition, homecare to custodial work, sewing sweaters to repairing cars, each with a particular constellation of wages and workers, responding to a particular configuration of local, national, and global pressures and opportunities. Many of the problems of the underground economy are common to formal work, particularly at its low-wage and nontraditional edges. And while many informal jobs are highly exploitive, others offer workers and small entrepreneurs significant opportunities.[59]

Informality itself makes unionizing difficult—in the words of one union representative, "'It's hard to organize someone who for all formal appearances doesn't exist.'"[60] Most of the obstacles to organizing immigrant workers in the underground economy, though, come from factors that cross the formal/informal line:

the small size and high mobility of their employers and workers' vulnerability as undocumented immigrants regardless of the
kind of workplace where they labor. Because the correlation between undocumented status and underground work is high (if
not perfect), one further obstacle deserves attention as we consider the difficulties of organizing in the informal economy: the
way laws that impose penalties for undocumented immigrants
who work serve as tools in the hands of employers seeking to
thwart a union organizing drive.

Under the employer sanctions laws, passed in 1986 as a part of
the Immigration Reform and Control Act (IRCA), employers
who hire immigrants without valid working papers risk fines
and other penalties. But once those workers are on the job, as I
noted above, most government agencies and courts have reached
the conclusion that they are technically entitled to the same
minimum wages, the same health and safety protections, and
the same freedom from sexual harassment as any other worker.
Forbidden from working, yet protected by law if they do? The
logic behind this apparent paradox is simple. Unless employers
are required to obey these laws for whomever they hire, documented or not, their incentive to seek out workers without papers will only increase.[61]

In practice, however, employer sanctions undermine every
workplace protection that undocumented immigrants enjoy on
the books—and organizing protections in particular. Employer
sanctions rules require a new worker to show her employer proof
of her identity and proof that she is authorized to work. In immigrant-heavy sectors, most employers take a minimalist approach to complying with the law, if they acknowledge it at all. If
a worker presents documents that appear reasonably legitimate
when she is hired, the employer records them on the I-9 form de-

signed for the purpose, drops the form in a file, and thinks no more about it—until the day comes when such workers make some demand the employer wants to resist. It may be a simple request for a bathroom break or for overtime wages. More often, it comes as the first stirrings of a union organizing campaign. Suddenly, the employer remembers employer sanctions. If he had never filled out I-9 forms, he gets the urge to comply with the law, forcing all the workers to provide legal papers on the spot. If he has I-9 files, he begins to pay new attention to them, calling the Social Security Administration to check on the validity of numbers, demanding to see new versions of documents that have expired.[62] Employer sanctions has become the perfect cloak under which to carry out an effective campaign of intimidation, sending the clear message that immigrant workers who organize are no longer the kind of immigrant workers who get jobs.

In a sad irony, the labor movement played an important role in securing the passage of employer sanctions in 1986. Only the ILGWU, long an immigrant bastion, dissented from the AFL-CIO position at the time that "illegal workers 'undermine wages and working conditions.'"[63] It took more than a decade of experience with the new law to convince many in the labor movement that their support for the provisions had been a terrible mistake. Union leaders such as John Wilhelm, president of the Hotel Employees and Restaurant Employees International Union (HERE), which had fought for sanctions in 1986, recanted that position: "Those who came before us, who built this labor movement in the great depression, didn't say 'Let me see your papers' to the workers [of that day]. They asked, 'Which side are you on?' And immigrant workers today have the right to ask of us the same question. Which side are we on?"[64] In a dramatic reversal, the AFL-CIO passed a resolution in 2000 not only to fight to repeal sanctions but also to advocate a broad immigrant amnesty that would legalize hundreds of thousands of workers.

But within two years, its impact was eclipsed by two events. One, of course, was of international proportions. The surge in anti-immigrant sentiment after September 11, 2001, derailed promising talks between U.S. President George W. Bush and President Vicente Fox of Mexico and brought the gathering momentum toward legalization to a skidding halt. Years passed before unions and immigrant advocates were able to pick up where they had left off.

The other event, noted by only those closest to the field, was a decision in a legal case. Before the passage of employer sanctions, the Supreme Court had held that undocumented workers were "employees" within the definition of the National Labor Relations Act (NLRA), entitled to its protections when they organized.[65] In 2002, the Court revisited the issue in light of the employer sanctions regime. In a case called *Hoffman Plastics*, it ruled that, although the NLRA still technically covers undocumented workers, the usual remedies of reinstatement and back pay do not apply when employers retaliate against undocumented immigrants for their union support. The *Hoffman Plastics* case eviscerated undocumented immigrants' right to organize. Now an employer who notes that an undocumented worker is wearing a "Union Yes" button, or has attended a single union meeting, can rest assured that if he fires her he will never be fined a penny. Although *Hoffman* was decided in the union organizing context, and most decisions to date limit its holding to the NLRA, it has had a chilling effect on undocumented workers' willingness to come forward on any issue.[66]

Another cluster of phenomena—long present but increasing

over the past forty years—makes labor organizing hard in different ways. Work in the United States since the 1970s has been restructured on a massive scale. Jobs have shifted from manufacturing to service. Direct employment has given way to subcontracting. Long-term relationships between employers and workers have been eroded and replaced by increasingly contingent arrangements. Service work, subcontracting, and short-term employment have long been a part of the economy. But their rise in prominence toward the end of the twentieth century has had an impact on workers at all levels, including those at the bottom of the labor market, where most immigrant workers dwell.

The impact has been particularly severe given the misfit between work thus structured and the industrial model on which the majority of unions in this country still operate. Industrial unionism was born in the 1930s and 1940s as a rejection of the then-dominant—but increasingly ineffective—craft union tradition embodied by the AFL. Craft unions attempted to build power by representing only those within narrow skilled "trades," thus controlling a highly valued labor supply. By contrast, the industrial unions that came to form the CIO sought to bring skilled and unskilled workers within a particular industry together, and to negotiate contracts that covered all of the largest firms in the field: witness the national agreements between major employers and unions in the steel, auto, coal, and freight industries, among others. Industrial unionism had its heyday in the middle of the twentieth century. But from the 1970s on, deregulation and globalization led to the sort of subcontracting and offshore production that decimated many industrial unions' capacity to organize all the work being done in their industry.

Nonetheless, mainstream unions today still work on a modified form of this model. They concentrate their efforts within an industry—or, as they have seen memberships fall in their traditional jurisdictions and have sought more fertile ground, a set of industries. They largely organize one worksite at a time, through "locals," geographically defined branches of national unions. To make this work, they look for places where large numbers of workers are clustered together, all the employees of the same company. Even this approach, though, presumes that it is possible for a union to protect its members from wage competition by those left out. The presence of large numbers of new and unorganized immigrants in many low-wage sectors puts a severe strain on this assumption. Other changes in the economy have challenged the very foundations of this model: among them, the supposition that workers have a long-time attachment to particular jobs; that when they change jobs, they are likely to stay within the industry; and that the people who work *at* a firm also work directly *for* the firm. In many places, as on Long Island, these basic assumptions no longer hold.

Take the challenges posed by the shift to service work. Until public sector workers began to grow as a proportion of the AFL-CIO membership in the 1960s and 1970s, manufacturing long had been the mainstay of U.S. labor union membership. Industrial work remains a critically important pillar of union organizing, and yet because of the shift from manufacturing to service, for unions to survive, they must also aggressively pursue members in the service sector. Service work has proven resistant to organizing. Nonmanufacturing—mostly service—work accounts for 67.8 percent of all work in the United States but only 38.8 percent of union membership. Only 5.7 percent of service workers and a mere 4.4 percent of retail workers belong to a union.[67]

This resistance has many components. Large service corporations often have well-funded union-busting campaigns—Wal-Mart is a notorious example.[68] A significant proportion of the service sector is in personal care—hospitals, childcare centers, nursing homes, and home health services, among others—and these institutions are funded by a mix of public and private sources that makes organizing a particular challenge because of the lack of one clear "employer" with whom to bargain.[69] And the low end of immigrant service work in particular is structured in a way that stymies an industrial approach to labor organizing. In contrast with the large numbers of workers on the average manufacturing shop floor, informal immigrant service work takes place in relative isolation. From the one-on-one interaction of a domestic worker with her employer, to small construction and landscaping firms, to the four or five busboys and dishwashers working in the average restaurant kitchen, workers are divided and dispersed. Even where service companies are large—janitorial conglomerates such as UNICCO come to mind—on a daily basis the workers spend most of their time alone or in small groups. This situation undermines manufacturing-based models of organizing that depend for their success on frequent contacts among large numbers of workers.

The high mobility of workers from job to job and industry to industry, particularly evident among service workers in Long Island's immigrant economy, poses a further challenge to the mainstream organizing model. If immigrant workers are fired in the process of organizing a union at one place of work, they may well not remain within the industry that the union covers for their next job. Workers are thus only irregularly benefiting from the union protection that they must risk so much to gain. And the union is thus constantly losing the people with whom it has begun the organizing process. Under these circumstances, there is little incentive from either the union's or the worker's perspective to put much effort into an alliance that is founded in one industry or one workplace alone.

Then there is the matter of raw bargaining power. Although they in fact require myriad skills, low-wage immigrant service jobs are often "unskilled" in the sense that employers see the workers as fungible and the work as requiring minimal training.[70] As a result, because the barriers to getting a job that exist for "skilled" work are absent here, competition is fierce, wages are low, and work is less likely to be full time or to offer benefits such as health insurance. It hardly needs saying that where competition for jobs is intense and employers see workers as fungible, labor organizing efforts will struggle. Industrial unionism derived much of its ability to benefit low-wage workers from the bargaining power it gained by organizing those at the higher end of the industry. Where demand for labor is high and the majority of skilled workers are affiliated with the union, the union is in a strong position. Where labor supply far outstrips demand and employers see the work they offer as "unskilled," not requiring specialized training or experience, unions are in a weak position. Furthermore, where labor is a high proportion of service businesses' total cost, and where the market for such services is highly competitive, particularly in subcontracted industries such as janitorial firms, profit margins are thin. Thus even where businesses are considerably larger, a union risks sinking the enterprise it organizes unless it can very quickly organize the majority of the industry in a particular geographic area—not an impossible goal, but certainly one that sets the bar higher.[71]

Finally, unions see many small employers as having too few workers to provide a base of dues support that would justify the high level of energy they require to organize. Imagine that a traditional union seeks to organize in landscaping. It will first try to choose a workplace or set of workplaces in which to start, a difficult prospect since most companies are small, family run, and operate at least in part under the table. Once it decides where to begin, it faces the depressing reality that the workers currently at the company are unlikely to be there long, will be gone exponentially more quickly if they support the union, and can easily be replaced by the many more workers who want those jobs. If the employer has seven workers, and four favor the union, the loss of even one will decimate the pro-union majority. If the workers who leave a landscaping job are as likely to take work in a restaurant as to remain in the industry, through its efforts the union will not even necessarily be increasing support for its future campaigns at other landscapers. Objectively, a union campaign conceived this way is unlikely to provide much in the way of a return. The same is true for small restaurants, small retail establishments, small construction firms, and many of the other principal immigrant industries. Recognizing this, few unions venture into this territory.

One last critical change has to do with the way the employment relationship is structured. In the world of industrial work sixty years ago, employment tended to be direct (that is, workers were the legal employees of the company on whose premises they labored) and long term. But increasing numbers of workers today have an *indirect* relationship with the company for which they work. They may be labeled independent contractors, whether they actually consider themselves so (as with many computer consultants) or do not (as with many day laborers). They may be subcontracted, meaning that their legal employer is a company that brokers their services, while they perform work for a second company: think of janitors or security guards. Temp work is a kind of subcontracting, and has expanded far beyond the occasional replacement for an absent secretary. Companies such as Labor Ready offer temporary manual laborers. The catch is that many workplace rights and benefits apply only to direct employees. Only on behalf of direct employees are employers required to contribute to Social Security and pay for state-funded disability and unemployment insurance. Only direct employees are entitled to participate in a firm's health insurance and pension plans.[72] And a number of workplace protections—such as Title VII's antidiscrimination rights and OSHA's workplace safety provisions—principally benefit direct employees.[73]

The right to organize a union is similarly affected. With few exceptions, the National Labor Relations Act now protects only direct employees. Independent contractors are excluded from the NLRA's protections entirely.[74] As subcontracting, the use of temporary workers, and other indirect employment relationships have spread, the impact has been profound. Take the situation of janitors. Most businesses have their wastebaskets emptied and their floors vacuumed not by workers they employ themselves, but by subcontracted cleaning companies hired by the management agent of the building in which they work, frequently selected through a competitive bidding process. Because a janitorial company must price its services low to get contracts, and because wages make up the bulk of each company's costs, wages are under constant pressure in the industry. Who controls those wages? Not primarily the subcontracted cleaning company, which would be out of business if it gave its workers big raises while its competitors held steady. It is the business owner who controls wages, through the bidding process. And yet the NLRA's limits on secondary activity makes it much more difficult for workers to put pressure on a firm other than their direct employer, here the cleaning company. Such workers cannot picket the business owner who contracts for their work.[75] More difficult still, the ban does not work both ways. A business owner can decide not to renew the contract of a janitorial company for the sole reason that its workers have unionized, and can hire a nonunion company as a replacement *because* it is nonunion, without fear of retribution from the law.[76]

Unions in Long Island were not immune to these pressures. They looked at the region's spreading underground economy, and saw workplaces that were impenetrable. They looked at the large numbers of undocumented immigrants, and saw people who were unorganizable. They looked at the high mobility of immigrants, the plethora of small businesses, and the oversupply of labor for jobs labeled "unskilled," and believed that the structure of the economy was incompatible with the way they knew how to organize.

To note that mainstream unionism on the industrial model is a poor fit with the structure of the new sweatshops is not to indict the industrial union model per se, since in some industries, including a number in which many immigrants are employed, it remains a close fit with the structure of work, and offers the best hope for building the power of workers. It is instead to call for a broad concept of a "union," one that is wide enough to encompass industrial unionism where that works but also to foster the growth of other models with other structures and strategies in sectors that demand a different approach.

The new sweatshop is distinguished, and complicated, by the convergence of a number of structural barriers in one place. But workers and unions in other times and places have grappled with many of the separate components of the problem. Subcontracting has been a characteristic of a wide range of industries—from garment making to construction to janitorial work—for a century at least. For women and people of color high mobility between jobs is nothing new, nor is work for a range of small employers.[77] "Low-skilled" workers have long faced serious challenges when they sought to organize. And immigrants have been a perennial part of this country's labor landscape. Although large-scale industrial unionism offers little to the worker in the everyday sweatshop, history provides more than one example of ways that other workers have faced similar obstacles and developed organizing strategies that made sense in their particular contexts.

The story of modern unionism in the United States is often told as the battle in which the CIO model superseded that favored by the AFL. But the reality is far more complex.[78] The period from the late nineteenth century until the New Deal was a time when the labor movement took a variety of forms. In the late 1800s the Knights of Labor and, briefly, the Industrial Workers of the World provided glimpses of what a different labor movement might have looked like. Less well known is the fact that the AFL itself affiliated over 20,000 independently created groups of workers and others concerned about labor conditions between 1888 and 1955.[79] The AFL issued union charters to these groups directly, rather than via the ordinary route of bringing in nascent unions through affiliation with existing "internationals" organized by trade. The labor historian Dorothy Sue Cobble has documented how this direct affiliation process allowed workers to organize themselves along the lines that made the most sense in the context they were facing, from craft associations to industry-wide organizing efforts to others that were organized around geography or community-based affiliation and included members from a variety of industries. It also supported a wide range of experimentation with tactics. Some of these direct AFL affiliates focused on particular workplaces, negotiating contracts with employers on behalf of their members who worked for that firm. Others agreed on work standards for their occupation, and then sought through a variety of means to ensure that employers in that industry hired union members exclusively. Some saw the strike as an important weapon. Others relied more on community-wide protest. Still others pursued local legislation of working conditions. A number had a benevolent function, collecting and administering funds for the well-being of union members.

As a part of this direct-affiliate structure and also emerging from experimentation elsewhere in the labor movement, unions have developed strategies to address particular aspects of the problems workers face in sweatshops today. Where small shops and high turnover are the norm, for example, unions have emphasized attachment to the industry rather than to a particular job. The waitress unions that flourished in the United States before World War II provide a glimpse of one such model.[80] In a situation where waitresses moved frequently between restaurants, an attempt to apply a union model that relied on site-by-site organizing would have been doomed. In response, as Cobble has described, the Hotel Employees and Restaurant Employees International Union organized waitresses into what she calls "occupational unions" from the 1900s to the 1960s. These unions were structured so that the waitresses' primary relationship was with the union and the occupation rather than a particular employer. Members received benefits from the union-administered health and welfare funds, to which restaurant owners contributed but which were allotted independent of affiliation with any particular workplace. The union ran hiring halls, and encouraged employers to hire exclusively through those halls through a combination of closed-shop agreements, solidarity from organized workers with greater bargaining power (for example, chefs and food delivery workers), and community pressure.

Occupational unionism and the union-run hiring hall have been an effective response to the challenge of organizing in any number of industries where workers have a strong occupational identity but change employers frequently. From Hollywood's writers and stars to longshore workers, unions have confronted the mobility problem by enrolling workers independent of an affiliation with a particular employer, setting standards to which union members agree to adhere, and creating pressure for employers to hire their members only.[81] This approach has intrinsic appeal in the face of high mobility. But it is only as effective as the union's ability to control the labor supply. Where there are many unorganized workers and few consequences for the employer who looks to hire from among them rather than within the unionized pool, an occupational union and a hiring-hall structure withers to irrelevance. Unfortunately, many of the strategies that made the waitress union and others similarly structured so effective in their heyday—among them union-only hiring halls and closed-shop agreements that bound employers to hire union members exclusively—were rendered illegal with the passage of the Taft-Hartley amendments to the NLRA in 1947.[82]

A look at what is happening with labor organizing today also reveals some vibrant experiments in organizing immigrants despite difficult conditions. Most often cited in this regard is the SEIU's Justice for Janitors campaign, which has organized over 200,000 building maintenance workers, many of whom are immigrants, since its inception in 1985. Justice for Janitors seeks to win change in the building maintenance industry through active community-labor alliances, large-scale mobilizations of workers and allies, and a strategy that targets all major contractors in a market at once in order to take wages out of competition.[83] Rather than proceeding to organize first the workforce of one contractor, then that of another, a Justice for Janitors campaign puts pressure on all of the building owners in a geographic area to hire unionized contractors only. Although workers march, picket, and strike, much of that pressure comes from the community. The union has found that success in its campaigns comes from the effective mobilization of public pressure, and that there are ways other than pickets to do this.

In part, this strategy is a response to the ways that the prohibition on secondary boycotts in labor law has complicated unions' efforts to press firms to support the unionization of the employees of the subcontractors those firms hire. For example, a Justice for Janitors union's ability to picket is limited to times that janitors are at work in the building, usually at night, when the possibility of conveying a message to building tenants and the broader public is limited. On the other hand, leafleting, putting on informational skits in front of the building, exerting political pressure, garnering media coverage, and organizing community-wide marches are all permitted.[84] But the need to look more broadly for support is also born of the union's recognition that it will prevail only when mobilized religious leaders, students, community organizations, and public officials create an atmosphere in which the union's demands for representation, higher wages, health insurance, and safer working conditions are understood as basic issues of concern to the community at large.

A different SEIU campaign resulted in the largest immigrant

worker victory in recent memory: the union's successful ten-year battle to organize home health aides in southern California. This campaign faced daunting challenges. Like domestic workers, homecare workers were dispersed among thousands of private homes. Further complicating matters was the fact that there was no legal "employer" with which to bargain. In California, disabled and elderly consumers hire their own homecare assistants but it is the state that provides the workers' paychecks. Neither was willing to serve as the employer of record for bargaining purposes. Over the decade of the 1990s, SEIU worked on three fronts simultaneously, organizing the workers, building alliances with the consumers of homecare services and their advocates, and carrying out a legislative campaign that eventually facilitated the creation of county public authorities as employers of record. The union won its biggest victory to date in 1999, when 74,000 home health workers in Los Angeles County chose to be represented by the union, which has since successfully bargained with the county public authority for wage increases and for medical insurance coverage, a first for these workers.[85]

SEIU is not alone in its focus on immigrants. The Hotel Employees and Restaurant Employees Local 2, for example, has brought a remarkable 80 percent of full-service San Francisco hotels under contract through organizing campaigns involving nine thousand immigrants from over two dozen countries.[86] On a much smaller scale, hundreds of union locals around the country are moving forward with campaigns among immigrant workers. In the meatpacking industry, both the Teamsters reform movement, Teamsters for a Democratic Union, and the United Food and Commercial Workers have recently celebrated organizing triumphs in meat-processing plants in the West and Midwest.[87] The United Farm Workers, back in the fields once again after a membership hemorrhage in the 1980s, added 800 new immigrant members to its rosters when workers at Coastal Berry voted for the union in November 2002, and negotiated a contract on their behalf in June 2003. The Laborers Union recently organized over three hundred Latino and Serbo-Croatian asbestos workers in New Jersey, a victory particularly remarkable given the large number of small subcontractors for whom those immigrants worked.[88] Other unions have incorporated or reached out to immigrant bricklayers and deli workers, assembly-line workers and phone operators. If few of these efforts involve substantial workforces, they nonetheless lay the groundwork for future campaigns, building immigrants' knowledge of unions and unions' understanding of what it takes to organize immigrants.

It is important to note, though, that all immigrant work is not the same. Many immigrants work in industries that have traditionally been unionized; the challenge facing unions there is to figure out how to adapt old strategies to new industry structures and to workers with new perspectives and needs. But others—those who are the primary focus of this book—work in industries that have never been organized to any significant extent, or that have changed so significantly because of global competition that they can no longer viably be organized on a domestic basis alone. More dispersed, paid less, employed by smaller businesses, doing jobs that require skills not recognized as such by employers, the immigrants who work in these places are at the very bottom of the labor market. The world of the everyday sweatshop in the underground economy and its lowest-wage environs remains beyond the grasp even of unions committed to leading the way on immigrant work. Few if any unions even try to organize workers in the new sweatshops. The workplaces are too small, the workers too vulnerable, the competition for jobs too stiff. Add all of this to the array of obstacles that unions face in organizing in standard workplaces, and the price is simply too high, the likelihood of meaningful success discouragingly low.

And yet "even harder" may not mean impossible. In the last two decades of the twentieth century, a few small groups of immigrant workers in sweatshop conditions, frustrated by the lack of organizations able to support them in their efforts to win better working conditions, began to form independent organizing efforts. During the 1980s, three or four such local, immigrant-based centers made some headway in improving working conditions for immigrants where unions had been absent or ineffective. These worker centers were organizing among low-wage workers in places as different as New York's Chinatown (Chinese Staff and Workers Association), Oakland, California (Asian Immigrant Women's Advocates), and El Paso, Texas (La Mujer Obrera), to improve wages and working conditions across an ethnic community, rather than in a single industry or workplace. In the early 1990s, perhaps ten new centers were founded, including the Latino Worker Center in New York (initiated by Chinese Staff in 1993 but soon to become independent), Korean Immigrant Worker Advocates in Los Angeles and Long Island's Workplace Project. Worker centers' hallmark is an emphasis on bottom-up organizing, through models in which workers play primary roles in governing the organization and in running its campaigns. Although they focus on labor, they fight for other social justice issues as well. By 2003, there were well over a hundred and thirty worker centers spread throughout the country.[89]

The challenges these worker centers face is more than evident in the story of the Workplace Project. If the Workplace Project was to succeed, it would have to figure out how to bring together a group of disparate newcomers, in competition with each other for jobs that operated below the radar of the government and unions alike, all urgently in need of whatever money they could earn and many desperately afraid of detection by the government.

2

THE WORKPLACE PROJECT STORY

Lilliam Araujo puts the little girl she cares for to bed, and—following negotiations with her employers—leaves to catch the bus. Juan Calderon takes two buses, one to get home to shower after a long day in the warehouse and then another to take him to his destination. José Martinez comes straight from his landscaping job, clothes still covered in specks of grass. Angela Sarmiento comes from home, since her job serving food and cleaning in a high school cafeteria ends mid-afternoon, after the lunch rush. Carmen Lelys Maldonado can come only if he gets the night off from the restaurant where he works, and even then the journey takes over an hour and a half on public transportation, but he makes it often nonetheless. Pedro Hernandez pedals in on his bicycle, directly from the factory, without fail. Sonia Baca, out of work, puts precious cash in the hands of the bus driver, and she comes too.

One by one, they make their way to a shared destination: the Workplace Project in Hempstead, New York. The buzz from inside the office is audible from the hall as they approach. Inside, Latino immigrants stand and sit in small groups, talking about what people who see each other often talk about: work, new jokes, kids, the latest developments on the serial soap operas called *telenovelas*. A TV plays in one corner, the highlights of a soccer match flashing by as the evening news in Spanish concludes. There is food on one table and coffee on another, sticky with spills and sugar. As the clock ticks past 7:00 and a roomful of people have gathered, the group slowly moves its chairs into position, quiets, gains focus. And the work of the evening begins.

One night the topic of discussion is the plans for a weekend picket at the home of a family that owes its former domestic worker over $3,000. Another is the appropriate level of dues for the organization's members. Sometimes the meeting is small, intent, the women's organizing committee working through the details of their campaign to press domestic work placement agencies to sign on to a bill of rights they have written; the cooperative committee reviewing the advertising plan for a landscaping cooperative to be launched within a month. Some nights forty workers come together for a class or debate the next step at a critical moment in an organizing campaign.

There is a lot to talk about. It is 1997, and in the heart of Long Island's suburban sweatshops, an unusual organization has taken root and bloomed. Over the previous five years, the Workplace Project had grown from one desk in a room borrowed from a social service agency into a vibrant membership organization of immigrant workers with the mission of fighting the low wages, high level of injuries, and pervasive abuses of immigrant work in Long Island "through self-organization, supported by community education, leadership training and legal services."[1]

Against the odds, the group had carried out a series of innovative organizing experiments in the underworld of immigrant work. Each was at least a limited success, and some succeeded far beyond the organization's dreams. In its first five years, the Workplace Project and its immigrant leaders raised wages on Long Island day labor streetcorners by over 30 percent—at least most of the time, in most places. They created a domestic worker bill of rights and a model contract for domestic employers, and forced placement agencies to promise to adhere to them—a promise that they sometimes kept. They founded a very small but successful worker-owned landscaping cooperative, and were planning for what would become a much larger housecleaning cooperative. The Workplace Project's legal clinic and its "Justice Committee" pickets of recalcitrant employers collected hundreds of thousands of dollars in unpaid wages for the workers who had earned them. And despite the fact that almost no Workplace Project members could speak fluent English or vote, with training by the Workplace Project staff they changed New York state law, creating and winning passage of a bill that made failure to pay the minimum wage a felony, and raised by 800 percent the civil penalty against employers who did not pay workers in full, from a quarter of the total owed to double the total owed. At any one time, too, a handful of smaller organizing projects were in progress—a shop steward election campaign in a unionized factory to win representation for Latino workers within an existing all-white union structure, an effort to beat back anti-immigrant sentiment in a neighborhood where day laborers waited for work in the morning.

These victories are worthy of celebration. At the same time, they illustrate a set of hurdles that the Workplace Project faced again and again, rarely surmounting them entirely. Raising wages above the minimum was one. The group was much more successful in getting employers to adhere to the inadequate standards set by law than in improving those standards or in organizing for wages and workplace conditions that surpassed the law's requirements. Enforcement of its victories was another sticking point, as is so often the case.[2] Although the group succeeded in achieving its initial demands in several forums, it did not have the resources for the ongoing monitoring campaigns that sustained implementation would have required. Scale was a third obstacle. The Workplace Project's membership hovered in the 500-person range, with perhaps 10–20 percent of those active in the group at any one time. These numbers do not begin to approach the power needed to have significant impact in a labor market the size of Long Island's.

The group's approach to its internal organizing bore far more consistent fruit. The Workplace Project's cardinal principle was that immigrant workers should run their own center and fight their own battles. Creating a democratic and participatory organization is no easy task under the best of circumstances. These were not the best of circumstances. In addition to the exploitation that immigrants on the group's membership rolls faced, they were literally disenfranchised, about 30 percent undocumented and 65 percent either permanent residents or, more likely, holding temporary permission to live and work in the country. They lived scattered over Long Island's 118-mile length, linked only sporadically by public transportation, changing addresses frequently. They came from more than a dozen countries and from every side of the many political, class, and racial divisions within those countries. Few spoke any English. Incentives not to get involved with labor battles were strong. Their potent fear of the INS, coupled with unenforced and ineffective protections for those workers who took the risk of speaking out, convinced many to stay silent. To compound this, many were ambivalent about settling in the United States, their hope of maximizing their earnings in the short term and returning home a persistent counterweight to the increasing stake they held in their life here as the years piled up behind them.

And yet immigrants had become deeply involved in every aspect of the Workplace Project's functioning. A seven-person staff largely made up of Latino immigrants and the children of immigrant families supported and trained immigrant workers as they developed the Workplace Project's campaigns and carried those campaigns out to the streets and into the halls of the legislature. To make such an intensive level of participation possible, the organization had built a path that began with creative community outreach about rights on the job, moved on to an unusual legal clinic that combined organizing and advocacy approaches, and culminated in an intensive nine-week course in Spanish on labor rights and immigration and labor history. Only graduates of the course were eligible to become members. Almost every graduate signed up on the spot. After graduation, members joined the workers' committees that developed and carried out the group's strategies to fight for better working conditions. The most active members were elected to the group's all-immigrant board of directors, which—with intensive training and support from staff—was responsible for running the Workplace Project.

Self-determination, then, was the organization's first core principle. The second was a commitment to constant reflection and discussion in the midst of action. Some of the group's efforts faltered quickly. Many of those that showed early signs of success—for example, the legal clinic—nonetheless generated significant tensions. Whether it was an element of internal structure or the process for developing a new organizing campaign, all of the group's experiments were subject to intense scrutiny by members and staff. The tensions that appeared drove debate at all levels of the organization. Some experiments were scrapped. Others were reformulated, some several times over, in a process that continually crafted the elements of the group's structure so that they remained relevant as the context and the organization itself changed. Whatever the outcome, in ways sometimes immensely frustrating but also deeply generative and alive, the Workplace Project was committed to keeping the question "what works and what doesn't?" on the table.

The Workplace Project *became* a worker-led center. But it did not start as one. It started as a legal clinic with aspirations, and it grew from there. I began to lay the groundwork for the Workplace Project in 1992. My introduction to the world of immigrant work, though, had come years before. As large numbers of Central American immigrants began to arrive in the United States in the 1980s, I joined the many others who opposed the U.S. policy of support for repressive governments in El Salvador and Guatemala by working with immigrants from those countries who were struggling to make a home here. For several years, as I helped lawyers at community organizations prepare political asylum claims in Boston, Texas, and Florida, the main focus of my conversations with Salvadorans and Guatemalans was the persecution they had fled. But as we came to know each other better, life on the job here became a frequent topic of conversation. The immigrants I met were frustrated by how little they earned and how often they were abused—and by the void they found when they sought support in doing something about those problems. The same themes echoed through the discussions I had as I organized with Central American immigrants in Boston in response to changes in immigration law.

Vivid as their stories were, they could not compare to the immediacy of seeing the daily grind of immigrant work with my own eyes. From 1987 to 1989, while based at Centro Presente, a Central American community agency in Cambridge, I visited over a hundred immigrant workplaces in Boston, the casket-building, plush-animal-stuffing, piece-manufacturing, chicken-plucking underbelly of the city. My goal was to teach employers how to protect themselves—and, by extension, their employees—if faced with an enforcement visit from the INS. I also went directly onto the shop floor and spoke with workers about what to do in the case of an INS raid. What I saw there—the chicken carcasses swinging wildly by the faces of workers in a chilly, smelly room; safety guards removed from cutting machines to make the work faster; workers exhausted and in pain from hour upon hour of repetitive line-work in a candy factory; paystubs that spoke baldly of subminimum wages—gave three-dimensional life to all the stories I had heard.

In law school I had immersed myself in public interest offerings. More and more, I found myself drawn back to my earlier experiences. The images and voices from that time seemed to be stamped indelibly on my mind. What I was learning about individual legal services and impact litigation, though, seemed inadequate as a response to the complex and entrenched reality of low-wage immigrant work. I began talking with the immigrants I knew, with union organizers, and with activists around the country about the range of approaches to improving immigrant working conditions that others were trying in different places. A few unions, such as the SEIU's Justice for Janitors, were encountering early successes with their social movement model of unionism. Others such as the ILGWU, now UNITE HERE! had begun to experiment with neighborhood centers that allowed workers to affiliate with the union independent of a relationship with a particular employer. And in places like New York's China-

town and Oakland, California, a few worker centers had developed independent organizing models rooted in a single immigrant community.

With those ideas in mind, I sketched a plan to begin an organization that would take on the morass of Latino sweatshop labor in New York. After I graduated in 1992, I used a seed grant
from the Echoing Green Foundation to explore the possibility
of setting up an immigrant worker center in the rapidly growing community of Salvadorans and other Latino immigrants in
Long Island. On its surface an odd choice given the massive
numbers of immigrants in neighboring New York City, Long
Island actually had a substantially larger Salvadoran population than all of New York's five boroughs put together, but was
home to far fewer service and advocacy groups or to unions that
sought to organize immigrants.[3]

The structure I envisioned for this new organization was
shaped by several experiences. One, ironically, was the short life
of an Amnesty International chapter I initiated as a high school
student. It was the classic one-woman show: I made the posters,
spread the word, did the talking, and copied the letters. My
founder's pride was dashed when the chapter did not survive my
departure for college. In the aftermath of its demise, I began to
grasp a different understanding of leadership, one that relied
less on one person's enthusiasm and more on the genuine involvement of many. As my commitment to work with immigrants took shape over the following decade and I became involved with other organizations, I looked for diverse approaches
to achieving real participation among a wide range of people.

As I began work on the Workplace Project, this commitment
to building a democratic group was intensified by my recognition of the limits of what I could offer as the consummate out-

sider: a white, middle-class lawyer with an elite education, seeking to work in a community of new immigrants of color. My
past work experience with Central American immigrants and my
command of Spanish gave me some legitimacy I would otherwise have lacked. But I was not, nor would I ever be, a community member. What I brought to the organization—my law degree, my skills, my access to foundations and the media and the
advocacy community—represented a double-edged sword. On
the one hand, these attributes were not easy to come by in most
groups of newcomers, and would be concretely useful if immigrants wanted to build an effort to combat the conditions under
which they worked. On the other, they would concentrate power
in my hands, both within the organization and in the eyes of the
outside world. One danger was that I would stay too long, mo-
nopolizing a leadership position in a community not my own.
At the other extreme was the risk that I would walk out on an
organization that needed me, leaving it to collapse when I was
ready to move on to other things. I, and the people I would come
to work with, had both fears simultaneously. The ground between them, the ground of daily collaboration in the face of real
difference and real imbalances of power, was fraught with tensions large and small. Our determination to navigate it as best
we could nonetheless, combined with the deep belief in democratic leadership that I shared with many of the people who became a part of the Workplace Project, became a constant point
of reference as the organization grew. For these reasons, open
discussion, full participation, and sustainability remained for us
critical measures of organizational success, in tandem with the
more usual gauge of the Project's impact on labor conditions.

It would be several years, though, before the Workplace Project even reached a point where it was clear that it would func-

tion as an independent organization. Meanwhile, I spent my first year of the Echoing Green grant learning everything I could about the way immigrant work functioned in Long Island. From a base at the offices of a Central American community organization, CARECEN, I walked and drove around, watching landscapers, construction workers, and restaurant workers on the job. I learned about the established Catholic parishes' efforts to adapt to a whole new set of faces and traditions at mass, and about the collection of small, often storefront evangelical Christian churches to which growing numbers of Latino immigrants belonged. Immigrants had built other networks during their time on Long Island, too, from home-country associations dedicated to using dollars earned in the United States to improve living conditions in the town their members had left behind, to highly competitive Hispanic soccer leagues. I pored over the Spanish-language weeklies, still in their relative youth. I talked with immigrants at churches, on the street, in supermarkets and bus stations about where they worked and how they were treated and what they wanted to change.

Two things were immediately clear. Information about rights was scarce, and very much in demand. And once people knew their rights, they realized they were being violated in spades. In response, I began to teach a basic course about workers' rights, called the Workers Course, which soon drew large numbers of immigrants, and this in turn added to what I was learning about immigrant work, as those who took the course shared information about their working conditions with me and each other. I also started a bare-bones legal clinic, which gave me a direct window into some of the worst working conditions. The clinic offered legal help to Latino immigrants with workplace problems. A few fliers taped in Salvadoran restaurant windows and a few announcements at Spanish-language masses were all the clinic needed before word of mouth took over. A hundred and sixty workers flooded through the clinic's doors in its first six months.

I kept a notebook from the first seven weeks of the clinic. For all that the stories it holds are achingly specific, they would be repeated in their basic details by wave after wave of workers at the Workplace Project. On one of the first pages is pasted a pink message slip in the neat cursive of CARECEN's receptionist: "José Roberto B. worked for Michelle [Michael] as a landscaper from May to November 92. Michelle owes 6 weeks of work $1800."[4] A few pages later, brief notes on another case: "Alan Ramirez (pastor of church) says landscaper owes $520 to Hernandez and admits it. Glen Cove." On another, under the heading "José Antonio S.," are the details about one worker's experience as a rug cleaner and lifter in a hushed and expensive carpet store in a wealthy town. "Blood fr. nose. Eyes burn and tear. Chemicals. No gloves. Headache. Stomach. Hurt back on job, Aug. 92. Emplr. won't pay bills." A different page records the story of Dora Silvia E., who worked at a candy factory where she was eligible to join the union six months after she was hired. On the morning of the six-month mark, she was told she could only take her place on the packing line if she agreed to work under another name, thus relinquishing her right to join the union. Written below the details: *union complicit*. Pain flies from the pages: "$25/day." "Machines: doors slide up and in. So hard to open and close that you have to hit them with hammers. Closing door is how he lost fingertip and so did another man." "$30, 7–4:30, 7 days/wk, cash." "Mike [manager] hit him, pushed him against wall when he fired him." "You work 7 days, he pays you for 5 days." "3 wks owed." "Blisters and rash all over skin."

"Boss owes him $1000." "Sanding paint w/o mask or glasses. Headache. Still gets blood and particles coming from nose. Feels dizzy, drugged." "Not paid *anything*."

As the clinic got under way, this grim landscape of suffering was occasionally brightened by flashes of victory. The state and federal departments of labor were initially of little help. But often, little more than a letter or a call from a lawyer produced payment. If not, a visit to small claims court frequently resulted in a judgment for the worker. In a climate where no private or public agency was making a serious effort to enforce workplace rights for immigrants, these employers were low-hanging fruit. Even undocumented workers were usually able to prevail. Employers might threaten to call the INS to report a worker who sought to recover unpaid wages, but they retreated in the face of the argument that doing so would expose them to penalties under the employer sanctions laws, which imposed fines on employers who knowingly hired undocumented workers or failed to check for valid documents.

But over time—and not very much time—the question of what counted as "victory" became harder to answer. A win in court, for example, did not necessarily translate to wages in hand. The case that the clinic brought in 1993 in state court against Catizone Contracting on behalf of four construction workers for over $11,000 in unpaid wages is typical. The claim plodded its way through the court to a victory for the workers, resulting in a judgment the employer studiously ignored. Weeks of letters and calls to the sheriff yielded a lackadaisical visit to Lee Catizone's home, with a shrug shared all around when he said he had no money. With the help of law student volunteers, I pursued the laborious process of finding and freezing Catizone's bank accounts, tracking down some money but less than what the workers were owed. And those workers were lucky. If an employer was determined to avoid paying, all of the legal tools available were often not enough to find his money and compel him to pay.

At other times, the satisfaction of seeing one group of workers get paid the wages that had been denied them melted away in the face of evidence that the employer planned to stiff his next batch of workers as well. This flew in the face of the clinic's goal of addressing the problems workers faced in the long term. My next notebook, a mere eight weeks into the clinic, records further information about the "Michael" whose worker had left the message at CARECEN when I first opened the clinic. "Every year Michael does this to his employees. They [the original worker and several others who had come to the clinic] only worked one season w/him; he does this each season to a new group of workers. Last yr. paid w/bounced checks." Similarly, two years after Catizone's first four workers walked into the clinic, a new set of his employees were at the clinic doors with their pockets turned inside out. From the point of view of a Michael or a Catizone, an employer repeatedly refusing to pay his workers their wages, what sort of deterrence did the clinic represent? Even if the worker prevailed, all the clinic had forced the employer to do was to pay money he had owed long before: in effect, an interest-free loan from the worker.[5] And he had little reason to suspect that we would catch him all the time. Another sign that the clinic was having minimal long-term impact was the repeat appearance of the same workers, who came in for help year after year as a string of employers abused them.

Then there were the increasing number of situations where a lawyer's intervention could do little without a broader strategy. Day laborers under attack from residents of the neighborhoods where they waited for work, workplaces whose dangers were not abated when one worker was compensated for her injuries, immigrants represented by corrupt or indifferent unions, and groups of workers who wished to organize but had been unable to find anyone to support them—all clearly called for a more complex response.

Although popular, the Workers Course was facing roadblocks of its own. Immigrants were very interested in learning about their rights. Yet what was happening with the new knowledge they acquired? An immigrant who learned that she had a right to overtime pay for hours worked over 40 could approach her employer and demand that he comply with the law. She would likely be shown the door, not a higher paycheck. Doubtless, her stand would be principled. In member Zoila Rodriguez's words, "Perhaps they will fire me for raising my voice or demanding something, but they won't have fired me with my mouth closed. I will have stood up for myself." But her bravery was likely to be less than effective in changing how employers behaved. Immigrant workers' rights were flouted as a part of a thriving economic system that depended on their vulnerability and disorganization. Education strategies could play a role in informing workers, but it was increasingly clear that real change would come only when workers built the power to muster a systemic response to systemic abuse.

A year had passed since I came to Long Island. While the young project had benefited tremendously from volunteer law students and community members, it was time to build a more permanent staff. With these questions in mind, I hired an organizer, Omar Henriquez. Henriquez had immigrated from El Salvador to Long Island more than twenty years before. He had first-hand experience with immigrant work, from construction and landscaping to dishwashing and factories, and his lack of formal experience with labor organizing was more than made up for by his strong sense of injustice, quick mind, and love of a good fight. As the editor of *El Vocero,* the first Spanish-language newspaper in Long Island, he had developed invaluable contacts and media skills. We reshaped the class to focus on organizing and on the history of immigrants and the labor movement in addition to labor rights, and we invited workers with legal cases at the clinic to take the course. Henriquez brought together the graduates of the classes in a workers' committee, which began to provide rudimentary support for workers interested in organizing. The committee, Henriquez, and I began to make plans to move the Workplace Project out of CARECEN, creating an independent worker center.

The idea of such a worker center was not born in a vacuum. In addition to the worker centers that had emerged in the 1980s, the Lower East Side Worker Center (later the Latino Worker Center) had been founded in New York City in early 1993 by the Chinese Staff and Workers Association, in response to the increasing frequency with which it was encountering Latino workers in its efforts to organize formerly all-Chinese restaurant staffs. Henriquez and I and workers' committee members met and spoke often with the staff and members of these two organizations. They strongly encouraged us to consider a membership-based model and to identify the Workplace Project as a worker center that saw organizing as its primary mission. Our concerns about the limits of a purely legal or advocacy-based approach were reflected in our observation of the experiences of these other worker centers. The worker center framework was also particularly appealing for its potential to encourage broad participation.

As we moved toward the transition to an independent worker

center, immigrant workers began playing key roles in the effort. The workers' committee that Henriquez had initiated developed into an all-immigrant board. The graduates of the workers' rights course began to coalesce into a membership. New staff and volunteers came to the organization. And slowly, Long Island's bleak landscape of suburban sweatshops began to witness new life.

While the Project took a great deal from the worker center model, its growth and success came from its ability to create, from the ground up, a flexible response to the needs of immigrants and the structure of work on Long Island. The group welcomed Latino immigrant workers from all occupations. Where it had critical mass in a workplace or a significant number of members in an industry, it developed campaigns at those levels. It also sought to improve wages and working conditions for immigrants across the board. Know-your-rights outreach in the community, the legal clinic, and the Workers Course complemented and fed into these organizing efforts. This array of approaches took shape without a great deal of strategic deliberation in the early days. In retrospect, however, the organic course of the Project's development makes strategic sense.

In a context where workers were highly mobile, focusing on workers in a single industry would have been doomed to failure. Janice Fine's observations of the opening session of a 1997 Workers Course semester in which each participant introduced herself or himself with a few words about her or his work history in this country confirmed what had been evident early on. "Very few of the 28 who spoke that night talked about specializing in one particular type of work. Most had worked in two or three different sectors and had held a number of different jobs. No one mentioned having worked a long time for one employer or in one industry. Almost no one spoke of their work in this country in occupational terms, with a few exceptions—one baker, one mechanic, one carpenter and one painter. In the end, 3 mentioned having performed domestic work, 18 factory employment, 2 car washes, 10 construction work, 10 gardening, 10 restaurant work. The numbers spoke for themselves: 53 different jobs had been held in at least 6 different industries by the 28 students."[6]

The Workplace Project would not have been able to bring this mobile and vulnerable group of workers together without forming an organization open to all Latino workers in Long Island. Such a structure allowed for campaigns at individual worksites or in particular industries where they made sense, but also permitted immigrant workers to work together and with other low-wage workers on issues affecting them across industries. As it happened, Long Island was a reasonable geographical limitation, since while immigrants might travel long distances *within* Long Island to get to work, those who lived on the Island rarely left its borders for work, and those who worked on the Island rarely lived elsewhere. Equally important, this structure provided a way for immigrants to remain active and dues-paying members of the organizing center even as their jobs shifted or in times of unemployment. And it allowed the group to put down deep roots in the Latino community, where shared language and shared experience as immigrant workers helped to hold otherwise very different people together.

The focus on one ethnic group was practical, in a labor organizing sense, because at that time so many of the targeted jobs—domestic work, janitorial jobs, busboy and dishwasher jobs, landscaping jobs, and so on—were held on Long Island predominately by Latinos.[7] Under those circumstances, a Latino organization united rather than divided the workforce. The down side, of course, was that non-Latino immigrants, African-Americans, whites, and other people of color could not join the group, which made it more difficult to tackle the broader ways that employers used race to provoke job competition and stifle organizing, to take on larger issues of racism that a wider base would have made immediately evident, and to respond as the composition of the workforce shifted. The relationships that the Workplace Project built with groups representing African-Americans, other immigrants, and low-wage workers were only a partial solution. They allowed the Project's members to see the connections between their struggles and those of other low-wage workers, and for the groups to support each other's campaigns—Workplace Project members stationing themselves at a voter registration table set up by the predominately African-American local branch of ACORN (Association of Community Organizations for Reform Now) at the Hempstead bus station, ACORN members attending a Workplace Project wage protest—but except for the rapport with other worker centers during the fight for the Unpaid Wages Prohibition Act, the relationship with other groups never developed to the point where the different organizations created and carried out a joint campaign as equal partners, either targeting a particular employer or acting in the political realm.

This core structure did not answer the question the Workplace Project would face later, of how an organization whose members were bound together by ethnicity but who crossed industrial boundaries could effectively exert pressure on their employers. Over time, a variety of issues would emerge. Unless the Workplace Project membership grew so large that it represented a high percentage of workers in *all* the critical industries, how would it be able to gain the leverage necessary to win higher wages and better working conditions? Could such an organization ever use the familiar labor organizing model of an organizing campaign leading to a contract? If not, what would replace it? While the common experience of abuse on the job shared by Latino immigrants would provide the Workplace Project with a starting point, it did not suggest a particular road map for how to answer these questions. Nor did any other local organization have one to offer. The fact was, *no* group had successfully organized Long Island's lowest-wage workers.

Meanwhile, the Workplace Project began to experiment with different possibilities, prompted by the problems that came in its doors. As different workers approached the Project, the organization tried to provide them with the support that their particular situation required. Day laborers being pushed out by the surrounding community? Help the workers pull together a committee and win local government support for a better site. Landscapers denying workers their pay? Gather a group of members to support those affected, and create a picket. Domestic workers isolated and abused? Hire a women's organizer and begin to offer activities designed to draw housecleaners and babysitters in on their day off. On the surface a less than strategic method, in the organization's early days this petri dish approach proved an effective way to cultivate new ideas in the face of a set of challenges that had quashed many old ones, to grasp the skills and resources the Project would need in order to provide organizing support to workers in a broad range of circumstances, and to develop a feel for the sorts of power immigrant workers organized in various ways could—and could not—exert.

It is a late spring Saturday in Lido Beach, a town of faded bathing clubs on Long Island's southern shore.

Suburban homes face each other across the last road before the oceanfront drive. Perhaps twenty immigrant workers march in a loose oval on the sidewalk outside the family home of the owner of Fortune and Frame factory, a man who, the marchers say, owes a group of ten workers tens of thousands of dollars. They are carrying signs that tell their story and chanting, "Pay them now! Pay them now!" When the factory owner arrives, he buzzes the group in his sports car, fast and close. The oval becomes a ball, protecting the children who have come with their parents. Then it reforms, and the chanting begins again. One woman hands out fliers to passing neighbors. The owner walks into his home, and a minute later his lawn sprinklers come on full force, spraying the marchers. With due ceremony, a few people pull out umbrellas, handing them to the kids. The oval bends in the middle to avoid the wettest spot, and continues its circling path.

A few more Saturdays pass, and the game is up. Tired of being embarrassed in front of his neighbors and pilloried in the press, the owner of Fortune and Frame brings a check to the Workplace Project for $35,000.

In its first decade the Project taught thousands of immigrants that they had workplace rights, whatever the job and whatever their immigration status. It helped thousands more to enforce those rights, using a streamlined response that combined organizing with legal representation and, at times, the intervention of state or federal agencies. Its efforts often took the form of a series of pickets combined with media coverage and legal pressure to force the employer to pay, and to make an example of him before other employers who might be inclined to take the same route.

These protests were an effective part of the Workplace Project's arsenal.[8] Members first prepared for them by going with Henriquez to Manhattan to participate in the pickets of fellow worker center Chinese Staff and Workers Association against recalcitrant Chinatown employers. After a few such field trips, the group was ready to transfer what it had learned. In Long Island's staid suburban atmosphere, the sight of fifteen people walking back and forth outside a restaurant with picket signs, shouting in a call-and-response rhythm "No Pay? No Way!" and—in a play on the organizing slogan "No Justice, No Peace"—"No Justice, No Pizza!" or marching in a circle on a Sunday morning outside a large home on a quiet street, distributing fliers informing passersby that their neighbors owed their domestic worker thousands of dollars, drew the sort of attention from customers, neighbors, and the media—and thus from employers—that it never would have gotten in the more raucous city. When the targets of the protests called the police, the officers who responded often asked the picketers to be quieter, but to everyone's surprise they also frequently intervened on the workers' behalf, informing the employer of his or her duty to pay the money owed. The documentary *So Goes A Nation: Lawyers and Communities* caught one such moment on film. As twenty or so Workplace Project members circled outside the home of an employer on a suburban street, carrying signs that asked "Would you work for free?" and stated "Franco Cimieri owes $2,000 in back wages," a police car pulled up. The ensuing negotiation is not captured on film, but in the next frame Henriquez is announcing to the group that an agreement to pay has been reached with the support of the police.[9] Protests were also important from the perspective of

workers, who built camaraderie and strength as they participated. In the process, the clinic and protests together moved
hundreds of thousands of dollars in wages and benefits that
would otherwise have gone unpaid into the pockets of immigrants, where they belonged.

But protests were a last-ditch tactic, a response to employers
who had refused to pay despite the hard proof of bounced
checks or court judgments against them. The legal clinic in
general was similarly reactive, responding to cases as workers brought them in, after the harm had been done. No one
doubted that these strategies were important to individual
workers. And in the minds of most members, they remained a
critical element of what the Workplace Project offered the community. But as evidence accumulated that individual cases had
little impact on how employers behaved in the aggregate or in
the long term, attention within the organization shifted to the
question of how to support workers who wanted to organize
while they remained on the job.

It happened every few months. Working at my desk, which
was just off the waiting room, I would look up to realize that my
door was blocked by a line of workers' backs. Getting up to investigate, I would see that the waiting room was full, the door to
the hall propped open, and more workers had gathered in the
hall. One of the organizers would invite the workers into the
large meeting room. Within minutes, snatches of impassioned
discussion would float into my office: ". . . walked off the job . . ."
". . . treat us like animals . . ." ". . . want to organize . . ." ". . . can
the Workplace Project help?" The answer, invariably, was yes, and
no. The organizer and the clinic staff could usually help the
workers sort out their immediate grievance. But the organization had no consistent strategy to respond to requests that re-

quired longer-term support. At various times, the Project helped immigrants already in unions to organize to run candidates in shop steward elections, and assisted nonunion workers in organizing their coworkers to remedy small problems such as a lack of bathroom breaks. Where workers sought to form a union, the staff would put them in touch with a union that might be interested in organizing and representing them, and often provided linguistic and cultural as well as organizing support to the ensuing campaign. But the resulting grab-bag of efforts had mixed outcomes.

In 1996, the Workplace Project provided support to twenty-five workers fired from the American Tissue company in Hauppauge, whose leaders included Samuel Chavez. The Project helped them carry out a campaign of pickets against their employer, who fired them when they tried to unionize in response to the ways they were mistreated; pursue a discrimination case with the Equal Employment Opportunity Commission (EEOC) and an organizing retaliation case with the NLRA; and make a connection with a more responsive union. Although the workers reached a confidential settlement in the EEOC claim and then won their NLRB hearing, the company appealed the NLRB claim and then declared bankruptcy and went out of business before the case was decided, so the immigrants were ultimately unable to return to work or win their goal of unionization. In that same year, the Workplace Project linked a group of dissatisfied workers at the Seal-It factory with the United Food and Commercial Workers Union, and provided some organizing assistance to the campaign. It was unsuccessful, as were the others in the handful of new union organizing campaigns in which the Project became involved over time, for a variety of reasons: the workers' fear of losing their jobs and, in some cases, of deportation; the employer's superior resources deployed to defeat organizing; the lack of support in labor law for the kind of organizing that would have been necessary to succeed; and, to varying extents, the unions' lack of cultural savvy and dedication to the particular campaigns (a lack of dedication born in part, perhaps, of pessimism about the likelihood of their success) coupled with the Workplace Project's lack of strategy in its approach to collaborative work with unions.[10]

On the other hand, the Workplace Project proved quite capable at a different sort of organizing support within unions—providing assistance to workers who wished to elect Latino shop stewards and union representatives. For example, in 1996 immigrant workers at the Davis Vision company sought the Workplace Project's help in stopping what appeared to be unilateral changes to their contract, after their union was unresponsive to their requests for help. As one outcome of their effort, the workers called for a new shop steward election to be held at the Workplace Project, and elected a Workplace Project member—Benito Estrada—to represent them. A 2000 campaign that sought to replace an unresponsive, monolingual SEIU business agent with a bilingual, more activist representative had similar success. This sort of organizing made good use of the Project's expertise in leadership development and internal organizing, although it did little to improve the Project's institutional relationships with unions that supported the status quo.

At times, members and staff also considered starting the Workplace Project's own independent union. But the problem remained how to define the union's membership. If it was open to workers of all industries, it would face the same problem of diffused power as the Workplace Project as a whole. An effort to organize a smaller independent union, located at a single worksite or in an industry such as car washing, might have been more feasible. Yet independent union campaigns face all the structural obstacles I described earlier, with fewer resources to overcome them. They often fail outright, or falter where an established union would have had the strike funds and other assets that would have allowed it to persist. The experience of the few other worker centers that have succeeded in organizing independent unions has shown them to be massively time consuming, requiring large expenditures of resources to support a union of perhaps one or two dozen workers.[11] And those experiences have been in labor markets where workers have an industry identity that keeps them in the union even if they leave a particular job, a condition conspicuously absent in Long Island.

More common is for a group of workers to begin organizing independently and then to attract the attention of an established union that offers to take over the campaign.[12] But the Workplace Project was reluctant to lead a group of workers down that path without knowing what it had to offer in the long run. As Nadia Marín observed in 1999, "When an individual walks in, we know just what to do, steps 1 through 100, from the intro to the handling of the case to what we ask of them in return. But with a group, other than dealing with their individual cases and doing a protest or two, we don't have any idea what to do. Maybe the group says 'we're tired of being yelled at and abused'—so the Workplace Project says 'Organize!' But into what? An independent union? An existing union? Something else? And how much can we help them? We don't have a vision. We need an organizing strategy first." Thus for groups of workers who approached the Workplace Project for organizing support at a particular worksite, the Project often had less to offer than it—and the workers—liked.[13]

If worksite-level organizing was hard to support, it might seem logical that industry-wide organizing would be inconceivable. Yet in two industries, day labor and domestic work, the Workplace Project sought to identify the elusive points at which immigrant workers could raise their wages, improve their working conditions, and expand their rights rather than just fighting to rectify past abuses.

> It does not look like a historic moment on the day labor corner in Franklin Square, where over a hundred men wait for work on this morning in 1994. It looks like every other spring and summer morning, just after dawn. Men line both sides of the wide and busy commercial street, dressed for work in Payless construction boots and jeans white at the knees with hardwall dust or smeared with green from grass and pesticides, hoping a truck will pull up to offer a job, darting across four lanes of traffic if they sense a better opportunity on the other side. A brown pick-up slows by the curb, and is swamped by men before the driver can roll down his window. The shouting begins. "$50 for the day, get in the truck!" says the driver. Nobody moves. $50 is $10 less than the corner's committee of leaders had voted as the minimum daily wage in a meeting at the Workplace Project a few days before, a vote ratified by the workers on the corner. Sudden silence descends on the usually raucous group. "$55!" shouts the driver. Nobody moves. The truck idles for a few minutes, driver and workers at a standoff. As the truck pulls away empty, the silence is broken by a smattering of jeers and clapping. The driver may go to the day labor corners in Westbury, or Freeport, or

Inwood. But the workers know that all those corners have committees, and that their representatives were at that meeting at the Workplace Project as well. If they can hold the line, $60 is the new limit everywhere. He will be back.

Individual day laborers frequently came into the clinic to get help in recovering unpaid wages or winning workers' compensation for on-the-job injuries. But one day in the spring of 1994, a group of workers from the Inwood day labor site called Henriquez to tell him of a problem brewing that affected all of the workers. Residents in the area were becoming increasingly violent in their efforts to oust the day laborers. White homeowners angry at the presence of growing numbers of Latino men waiting to be picked up by employers began videotaping the immigrants, threatening them with deportation, calling the police. One homeowner had pulled a gun on an immigrant worker. Henriquez and the workers met to discuss possible solutions. He then brokered a deal between workers, residents, and local officials involving a new worksite that the workers chose for its increased visibility and amenities. In the process, he and the workers began to talk about the problem of low wages for the often back-breaking work that day labor required. They formed a committee and considered setting the corner's first minimum daily wage. But there were at least three other big day labor corners in the southern and middle part of Nassau County.[14] If Inwood had a higher daily rate, what was to keep an employer from going to Franklin Square or Westbury or Freeport? The minimum would have to be a matter of agreement between the workers on all the corners. And so the Workplace Project's first day labor organizing initiative was launched.

Within three years, the group's organizing efforts on day labor corners in Nassau County would succeed in raising the base daily wage by 30 percent, from $45 to $60, at least on most of the corners and most of the time. The organizing that led to that outcome had been of the most basic sort: Build a consensus that workers will not accept work for less than the minimum wage they have set, and then hold the line as employers arrive and make lower offers. It had also been supported by a rising economy.

The Workplace Project's day labor campaign was difficult even at its peak. It was a real challenge to build the solidarity necessary to turn away an employer who offered less than the wage the committee had set. Even in high season perhaps only a third of the workers were picked up for jobs on a given day, which made competition fierce for the opportunities that did arise. For this reason, the wage campaign depended on the consistent presence of effective committees on each corners. Yet the workers who were most respected by others and thus were elected to those committees tended to be those who spoke the most English, had been around the longest, and had the most skills—precisely those same workers who were picked first for jobs and left the corner earliest each day, and who were likely to be offered long-term employment and thus abandon the corner as the season wore on. So as the hours passed each morning, the committee dissolved; a parallel but permanent attrition occurred with every week of the season. Meanwhile, new workers were arriving every day, many having set foot on Long Island only days before. The organizer—already monitoring four corners at once and thus stretched far beyond one person's capacity—was forever starting from square one. And the organizer's presence was essential. Because of the constant departure of old workers and the influx of new ones, without the organizer the workers found it very difficult to maintain the $60 minimum.

Further complicating matters was the fact that the corner was not a long-term source of work for most immigrants. There were day labor diehards who preferred the flexibility and independence that the corner offered them, and a few other workers who were usually employed elsewhere but were using the corner to pick up extra days of work or during a layoff. But most day laborers were undocumented newcomers who saw in the street-corner either their best option for entry into the labor market and a lasting relationship with a particular employer, or their best hope to make money on a temporary sojourn in the United States.[15] From the point of view of many in either category of workers, to organize for higher potential wages on a site that they viewed as a temporary stop on the wage ladder was not worth the sacrifices such a campaign entailed.

Finally, while it is not impossible to organize day laborers around wage issues, as the Workplace Project's efforts show, if that organizing goes too far toward formalizing a system whose main attraction is its informality, it risks losing its usefulness for both workers and employers, and finding itself facing competition from a new informal site around the corner. Furthermore, the harder times get, the less likely workers are to adhere to the wages they have set. By 1996, when Congress passed a series of anti-immigrant laws and newcomers feared immediate deportation, a push for still higher wages on the corners was unlikely to succeed.

Viewing this situation, an outsider (particularly an outsider with any experience doing labor organizing) would be strongly tempted to walk away from the corner. Indeed, that was the response of the veteran community and union organizer Bill

Pastreich, who visited the corners in early 1997 to help the Workplace Project think through its approach to day labor. Pastreich bluntly described what he saw in one morning's visit: "There are just too many workers, most of whom are incredibly transient, and too few jobs, and the whole scene is so fluid and uncontrollable. The employers are too small and too varied to make organizing them practical." His conclusion: "give it up and go find an organizing campaign where you have a prayer of success."[16] Janice Fine guided the group through a process of surveying other day labor projects and thinking strategically about the options for new approaches to organizing. The conclusion: Genuine organizing of day laborers to fight for higher wages was almost nonexistent; instead, day labor organizations in other places sought to distribute work fairly, to recover unpaid wages, and/or to defended day laborers' right to work against community efforts to uproot them. But the Workplace Project board, workers committees, and some of the staff were reluctant to abandon the corners. To do so felt like turning away from the most public and most dire face of immigrant work.

This highlighted an undercurrent of tension that snaked through the Workplace Project's organizing approach as a whole. Did the group exist to respond to the needs of the most desperate workers, those who were the most visible embodiment of the exploitation of immigrants? Or was its purpose to identify times and places where workers might strategically be able to exert some power, and to focus its energy on those? With limitless resources, it is conceivable that an organization could do both. But where resources were sharply curtailed, as they were with the Workplace Project, a decision to slot the bulk of the group's organizing resources for the streetcorners was a decision not to take on campaigns at locations where the workers were a little farther up the job ladder and had a more realistic hope of sustaining their victories. The Workplace Project had until that point followed the instincts of its staff and members to offer support to the weakest workers. But history supports the observation that those in the very worst jobs have rarely been in a position to win much in the way of gains through self-organization.[17] The support of other workers with greater leverage has often made a difference, as have those rare moments in which society-wide changes reshape the political, legal, and economic playing field. Neither was on the horizon at the moment the Workplace Project faced this question.

In the end, the Project leadership split the difference. At a retreat of the board, the staff, and key leaders from the workers committees in 1997, it decided not to pursue a campaign to raise wages any further in the absence of strong worker demand for such action. Instead, it made its resources available for less labor-intensive outreach about the organization and its legal clinic and for the distribution of educational materials. As it happened, the surge of anti-immigrant sentiment in Suffolk County in the late 1990s would put day labor squarely back at the top of the organization's agenda. Within two years the group would find itself defending the workers' right to wait for work in public places, winning municipal protection for safe sites, standing up for immigrant laborers' right to live in a community, as well as redressing problems like unpaid wages and injuries. Organizing for higher wages, however, remained an elusive goal.

The large meeting room is hot and stuffy, filled to capacity with immigrant domestic workers, the North American members of congregations and civic groups who are their allies, and local elected officials. The crowd parts as two women enter the room. They are the guests of honor, so to speak, the heads of two domestic work placement agencies that domestic workers have identified for their flagrant violations of the law. They have agreed to attend only to bring an end to weeks of bad publicity, pickets, phone calls, and faxes. As the women take their seats, a series of domestic workers stand up to testify to the illegally high fees that they have been charged by these agencies for the "privilege" of placement in jobs that pay less than the legal minimum wage. Murmurs of outrage and support rise from the crowd.

The domestic workers then present the agency heads with the Workplace Project Domestic Worker Bill of Rights, a document that the Project's women's organizing committee developed after months of research and debate. Among other provisions, it requires that agencies charge only the legal fee of no more than 10 percent of the first month's wages (as opposed to their usual fees of double or triple that amount) and place women in jobs that pay at least the minimum wage, and—a first—includes a detailed contract that the agency, employer, and worker must sign at the time of placement. The workers ask the agency heads to become the first in the county to publicly agree to adhere to the bill of rights. A local African-American elected official rises to give his support to their demand, followed by several homeowners who say that they will not do business with any agencies that do not follow the bill of rights. Within a week, both agency heads sign. Three months and much organizing later, in early 1998, five of the six agencies in Nassau County display a notice: "We respect the Workplace Project Domestic Worker Bill of Rights."

The Workplace Project Domestic Worker Bill of Rights campaign had its roots in the organization's recognition, several
years earlier, that immigrant women had concerns of their own
that a focus on immigrants in general did not address. In the
Project's first few years women were less likely to join the group
than men. Most bore the triple burden of paid work (sometimes
at several jobs), childrearing, and responsibility for housework.
Many also faced their male partners' opposition to their participation in the group. In addition, the structure of the occupation
in which so many of them labored—domestic work—demanded
a different kind of organizing response than most low-wage
jobs. To increase women's participation in the group and to develop strategies appropriate to the private homes where women
cooked, cleaned, and cared for children, in 1995 the Workplace
Project created a women's program and in 1996 hired Esly
Umanzor, a Salvadoran woman with a social work background,
as women's organizer.

Umanzor's outreach and the support she and the women's
committee, Fuerza Laboral Femenina (Female Labor Force), provided to women within the organization considerably increased
the number of women joining the group and taking on leadership roles within it. Providing childcare at every class and meeting, planning social events that families could attend together,
and sponsoring women's discussion groups on issues from self-
esteem to childrearing to breast cancer made the organization a
more welcoming place for many women. New leaders were in-
cubated through the women's organizing committee's debates,
planning sessions, and actions. The goal of having an impact on
women's working conditions, however, proved more elusive. The
women who came in through the program confirmed the importance of domestic work as the entry point to the labor market for many if not most immigrant women, similar to the role

day labor played for men. But repeated attempts to intervene in the one-on-one relationship between domestic workers and their employers generated a great deal of frustration. Although domestic work may be parallel to day labor in that both are typical first jobs, in many other ways the two are nothing alike. Where day labor is often a brief waystation on the road to a better job, many immigrant women remain in live-in domestic positions for a decade or more, often earning minimum wage or less, with little increase in salary or benefits over time. Where day labor provides a public gathering point where workers can share information about work strategies, speak with organizers, and watch public negotiations about wages, the conditions of suburban domestic work are set entirely in private negotiation and the resulting job often isolates the woman from other immigrant workers. Where the essence of day labor is the lack of attachment to any one employer, in the case of domestic workers their success is measured by the extent to which they develop a long-term relationship with their employers.

The stakes in organizing live-in domestic workers were thus much higher, and the challenges in reaching those workers much greater. Domestic workers were isolated in the wealthy homes where they labored, usually unable to drive and without access to regular public transportation. Those who attempted to challenge their working conditions risked not only loss of a job, but eviction as well. This situation was further complicated by the "familial" relationship that employers tended to create with the women who cared for their children.[18] In good times, "she's like family" meant that the domestic worker got extra perks— a birthday gift, the family's cast-off clothes, perhaps an unexpected day off, a television in her bedroom. But often, it was a shield against the worker's request that she be treated like a legal employee—paid legal minimum and overtime wages, covered by workers' compensation, and provided with unemployment insurance in case she lost her job. The fact that live-in domestic workers tended to be the most recent arrivals, with no immigration papers and little command of English, exacerbated the problems.

Organizing domestic workers, the supply side of the labor market, was extraordinarily difficult. Beginning in the late nineteenth century, short-lived domestic worker organizing efforts launched by recently freed slaves in the south and by AFL union locals and the Industrial Workers of the World (IWW) in the north, and later groups such as the depression-era New York–based Domestic Workers Union, the Professional Household Workers Union of New York, and the nationally based Household Technicians of America in the 1960s and 1970s, had focused on enacting basic labor protections through the state and federal legislatures, which had often expressly excluded domestic work from legislation on the minimum wage and other rights, on creating employment agencies that offered better-paying jobs to their members, and on "professionalizing" the industry, giving domestic work a more dignified name and encouraging workers to stand up to their employers on the basis of their expertise and the value they brought to a home.[19] But no domestic workers association succeeded in organizing a stable union that was able to make significant raises in wages. And these earlier efforts had been built largely by African American domestic workers. As civil rights legislation opened up public jobs and other employment with higher wages and less social stigma, many African American women left domestic service.[20] The immigrant domestic workers who replaced them had the added barriers of limited English and fear of deportation, heightening the difficulties posed by atomized workers and long hours. The lack of public gathering places or of adequate public transportation between suburban neighborhoods compounded these women's isolation, making it hard for them to find each other or for an organizing effort to find those who did not make their own way to its doors.

An employer-based demand side strategy to address these problems was also elusive. Unless there was some way to bring employers together into a homeowner-employer association, each negotiation would have to take place individually and in private, with the vast imbalance of power between employer and employee virtually dictating the outcome. Yet other than the pressure of moral suasion exerted through churches and civic organizations, a pressure that was unlikely to sway the most abusive employers, there was no way to require that an individual homeowner join such an association.

It made sense, then, to concentrate the group's energy on the one demand-side point where employers and workers came together in any numbers: the employment agency. In 1997 the Workplace Project's women's organizing committee decided to focus its efforts on the intermediaries, the employment agencies that often advertised domestic workers for placement at less than minimum wage and then charged workers double the legal fee for the privilege of receiving one of those jobs. The resulting campaign for the Workplace Project Domestic Workers Bill of Rights was victorious, at least for a time.[21] But as they evaluated the outcome of the campaign, the women who had been involved in it acknowledged its flaws. Enforcement of the bill of rights in any meaningful way would require ongoing monitoring of the agencies' compliance with the bill of rights.

The group could have made its next step an intensive monitoring campaign, but the participants chose not to. They feared that such an effort would absorb all of the group's energies into a relationship with the agencies. Few new domestic workers had been attracted to the group through the bill of rights campaign, and monitoring seemed likely to attract fewer still. Even more dispiriting was the recognition that, in practice, the agencies lost control over employers once they walked out the door. To ascertain whether employers were actually honoring the contracts they signed, and more important to raise wages above what employers were currently promising, would require a different strategy. While committing to pursuing violations of the bill of rights and of signed contracts that came to their attention, the women's organizing committee began to discuss other ways to increase domestic workers' income and to secure better treatment. In 1998, encouraged by the recent success of the Workplace Project's landscaping cooperative, they decided to explore the idea of launching a cleaning cooperative.

The Workplace Project's cooperative businesses represent a different, complementary approach to impact in an industry. CLIP, the Cooperative Landscape Innovation Project, was the first cooperative business launched by the Workplace Project. Owned and operated by three Workplace Project members, CLIP was far too small to employ enough workers to have any direct effect on the industry. But it stood as a living counter-example to the claims of landscapers who said that there was no way to run such a business *except* as a part of the underground economy. As its business cards promised, tongue in cheek, it offered "A Revolution in Landscaping." In an industry that paid $6 an hour, cash, and generally operated off the books without licenses or insurance, CLIP was fully licensed and insured, and paid a $12 an hour wage. It offered customers pesticide-free landscaping and a variety of specialty services, attracting both those homeowners who were concerned about immigrant working conditions (an early CLIP flier appealed to such families with the slogan "Don't run a sweatshop in your front yard!") and those who wanted to avoid dangerous chemicals. After three years of Workplace Project support, CLIP now operates independently as a successful small business.

While managing a large-scale landscaping cooperative proved too difficult, the Project's recent efforts to build a substantial housecleaning cooperative have been somewhat more successful. UNITY, the domestic workers' cooperative founded after I left the Project, has more than seventy members, all women, about half of whom are active at any one time. Members assign work among themselves through a system that gives points for participation in the cooperative itself as well as seeking to spread the work evenly. UNITY charges $15 an hour. Although its rates are competitive, the cooperative has struggled to attract sufficient numbers of customers to sustain its membership base. It has recognized that it needs to expand beyond the relatively limited numbers of household employers who want to be certain that they are not exploiting workers in the process of getting their house in order, and is beginning to do more aggressive advertising to reach a wider circle of consumers.[22]

The fall morning is misty and the air smells vaguely of salt, one of those reminders that for all its malled-up artifice Long Island is still a real island, subject to the weather of a real sea. Ten immigrant workers and staff from the Workplace Project unfold themselves from a motley assortment of cars outside the nondescript one-story office building in Rockville Centre and begin looking for the office of New York state Senator Dean Skelos, a powerful Long Island Republican. In the past two years, Senator Skelos had voted to deny undocumented children the right to attend public school, require that schools investigate and report suspected illegal aliens, prohibit public hospitals from treating undocumented patients, bar undocumented immigrants from receiving public benefits, and mandate cooperation between local police and the Immigration and Naturalization Service to facilitate immigrant deportations. He also supported the drive to make English the only language of state business. Undaunted, the group is here to ask for not only Skelos's vote but his sponsorship of a frankly pro-immigrant measure, the Unpaid Wages Prohibition Act (later labeled the Illegal Workers Protection Act by a *New York Post* editorial). This bill, created by the Workplace Project together with two other New York–based immigrant worker centers, the Latino Worker Center and the Chinese Staff and Workers Association, would raise eightfold the penalties the Department of Labor could bring to bear against employers who failed to pay minimum wages, and would make willful failure to pay a felony rather than a misdemeanor, among other provisions.

The senator's conference room is too small for the group, and people stand around the edges after the available seats are taken. Waiting for the senator to arrive, they distribute the headphones through which all those not bilingual in Spanish and English will receive simultaneous translation. Senator Skelos is one of that number. As he enters the room and begins polite greetings, someone says "Good morning, Senator. Here's your headphone." Slightly perplexed, he slips it on. With that movement, he enters a world at a noticeable tilt from the one he has long operated in, a new world where immigrants who cannot vote and speak no English talk to him directly, as members of the community he has been elected to represent, and expect his respectful response.

And so the meeting begins. Having rehearsed for several nights beforehand, all members of the group are ready to answer the hard questions that they anticipate the senator will raise. Julio Rocha, a Nicaraguan poet who here works as a day laborer, parries Skelos's question about how businesses to which the senator is indebted have reacted to the legislation. Luz Torres, a factory worker and union member in Colombia, now a domestic worker, responds to his concerns about encouraging illegal immigration.

The seeds sown at this meeting bore fruit six months later. Having interested Senator Skelos in the legislation, the group set about creating a political atmosphere in which his support seemed imperative. They won the endorsement of Long Island business associations as well as labor, religious, and community groups, garnered a firestorm of media attention for the issue of unpaid wages on Long Island, and visited Albany several times. In the spring of 1997, Senator Skelos—and nine of his Republican colleagues—cosponsored the bill in the Senate. In June, the entire New York Senate and Assembly voted unanimously in its favor. When a reluctant but cornered Republican governor signed the bill ten weeks later, he gave New York state the strongest wage-enforcement law in the country.

The act, and its passage, were unusual for several reasons. It was the first in the country to sharply raise penalties for unpaid wages on the theory that only severe deterrents will be effective in breaking the cycle of nonpayment of wages that characterizes the underground economy. The law dramatically increased the penalties the Commissioner of Labor could impose on employers who do not pay their workers, from a 25 percent civil fine to a 200 percent civil fine, and from a misdemeanor with a maximum $10,000 penalty to a felony with a maximum $20,000 penalty. Second, this pro-labor law was passed against great odds in the context of New York's legislative system, in which substantial new legislation is rarely able to survive clashes between the Democrat-controlled Assembly and the Republican-controlled Senate and governorship. Finally, the Unpaid Wages Prohibition Act was designed by nonvoting immigrants in response to a problem that they perceived in their workplaces.

At the same time that it challenged conventional ideas about citizenship and political participation, however, the Unpaid Wages Prohibition Act campaign had limitations. Predictably, the New York Department of Labor did little to enforce the new law. As with the domestic workers' bill of rights campaign, the Project membership decided not to launch an intensive monitoring effort to pressure the Labor Department to do so. In good measure, this decision stemmed from frustration with what a monitoring campaign built on the back of the Unpaid Wages Prohibition Act could hope to achieve. Even when enforced, the law only helped workers to demand a low minimum wage, not to raise their earnings (and its additional penalty went to the state's coffers, not into their own pockets). And yet the law took on new life several years later, in the hands of an activist attorney general and of other organizing efforts by other groups of low-wage workers.

For all the Workplace Project achieved, there is much it found itself unable to do. With wry humor, member Juan Calderon mused, "It makes me angry. Afterward, when we were evaluating ourselves and the [Unpaid Wages Prohibition Act] campaign, some members said we hadn't achieved much. They said it was just like throwing little pails of lukewarm water on a big fire. But what I want to know is, if it wasn't for this, where would we have put all of our lukewarm water?"[23]

The Project has been unable to support itself without substantial contributions of foundation money, upward of 80 percent of its small budget. Without a mechanism to automatically deduct dues from workers' paychecks, collection of the $60 annual dues that members voted themselves is sporadic at best, despite the reminders and envelopes tucked into the monthly mailing from the Project to its members. And foundation funding is notoriously unstable. A small number of foundations are strongly supportive of the group's work, but there are relatively few progressive foundations around the country, and those that exist have limited budgets and tend to fund for a few years at the most. Fundraising is also stunningly time consuming. At one not atypical point in the mid-1990s, the Workplace Project had cobbled together its $400,000 budget out of grants from seventeen foundations, many with their own application procedures and deadlines and their own annual or even quarterly reporting requirements.

The Project has also been unable to build and maintain a substantial membership numbering in the thousands. Part of this is the result of its decision to require all potential members to take the Workers Course before joining, which creates a bottleneck.[24] Many new members might be attracted, too, if the organization was able to define a political position and concrete goals that inspired more immigrants, and thus build the groundswell of a social movement even before it achieved its aims. But most important is the fact that the organization does not yet offer substantial benefits to large numbers of people. If Project membership guaranteed wages of $10 per hour to people now earning $5.50, its rolls would swell dramatically.

This highlights the critical fact that the Project has never been able to develop a strategy to raise and maintain wages above the legal minimum for a large group of workers. Its efforts with day laborers and its cooperative business did deliver higher wages to a few workers. But the majority of its successful work focused on bringing wages up to the legal minimum or on recovering money owed to workers after they had been fired.

One approach to a broad wage raise would have been to seek federal or state legislation. But the business members of the coalition of allies the Project assembled for the Unpaid Wages Prohibition Act would have removed their support immediately had the issue on the table been a *raise* in the minimum wage, rather than compliance with existing minimum-wage laws. Federal or state legislatures could also have raised the income of low-wage workers through a subsidy, but again, the Project was unable to muster the political power to force legislators to agree to such a massive expenditure of funds. Or higher wages could have been achieved through the increasingly common mechanism of a living wage law—but the balkanized power that characterizes politics in Long Island towns, hamlets, and cities made it hard to figure out how to craft an effective local living wage strategy.[25] Such a raise could also have been guaranteed through a contract, as with a union—but as I noted the Project has as yet been unable to figure out how a union with so many members from so many industries would function, or how a worksite-based organizing effort that it sponsored would escape the same obstacles that any union would face in organizing such small workplaces staffed by transient and vulnerable workers.

Where it has won victories, the Project has often also struggled to enforce them. Mustering a potent combination of tactical surprise, public shame, moral persuasion, and economic pressure from workers and consumers, the organization was sometimes able to get employers to agree to its members' demands. But it was not able to exert enough power to preserve those concessions in the form of an enforceable contract. Through a parallel blend of political and economic creativity, it succeeded in convincing the majority of placement agencies in Nassau County to sign the domestic workers bill of rights and, of course, in changing New York State law with the passage of the Unpaid Wages Prohibition Act. But with these as with its more direct economic successes, it was not able to sustain the monitoring or ongoing organizing campaigns necessary to consistently hold the parties to their word.

Part of the problem has been the Workplace Project's lack of experience with deep analysis of labor markets and particular corporations. As a result, it has often undertaken campaigns because they were just, without a good sense until the midway point, if at all, about whether they were achievable. But much of the challenge grows simply from the Project's focus on workers with little social power in a global context. Even one step up on the job ladder, among janitors, home health aides, and factory workers, unions have had more success gaining a toehold. Having chosen to organize workers such as day laborers and domestic workers who work alone or in small groups, and are eminently replaceable, easily deportable, and vulnerable to the worst kinds of abuse without retribution, the Workplace Project is faced with the difficult truth that those workers are not currently in a position to demand that their employers do much of anything beyond the minimum the law requires of them—if that. Nonetheless, the range of ideas both new and old with which the Workplace Project experimented, and the fact that the organization saw some external change and a great deal of internal organizing success flow from its efforts, suggest that there is more possibility for transformation in this difficult context than initially meets the eye.

3

PATHS TO PARTICIPATION

Under harsh circumstances that should have spelled doom for organizing, the Workplace Project built a democratic organization powered by immigrant worker leadership. Here I discuss the processes—the paths to participation—through which this happened, as immigrant workers first encountered the Workplace Project, began to take part in its programs, and became deeply invested in its work over time. I also chart the change over time in the organization itself, from a group largely dependent on me as its founder to one that could thrive without my involvement. Finally, I explore how and when the power generated inside a participatory organizing effort translates to the sort of strength that can shift power outside its doors.

By any measure, the Workplace Project membership was small relative to the problem of suburban sweatshops as a whole. On paper, the Workplace Project by 1998 had about five hundred members. About twenty-five or thirty played leadership roles, with an additional fifty to seventy participating in the organization but less intensively. The rate of member retention was fairly constant. Although almost every graduate of the Workers

Course elected to become a member of the Workplace Project, only 10-20 percent of the graduates—two to four workers per session—actually became active on committees and in the membership as a whole, with some further attrition over time. These are respectable numbers for a local community organization—indeed, in terms of proportion of active members they are respectable numbers for almost any kind of an organization—but in relation to the labor market and the Latino community as a whole, they are paltry.[1] After all, nearly 300,000 Latinos lived and worked in Long Island at the time.

Yet even these small numbers are worth our attention, not least because of all the obstacles immigrants had to overcome in order to become active. For some, the first step was conquering their fear that if they stood up to their bosses or stood out as activists, they were more likely to be detected and, if undocumented, deported by the INS. For others, the most pressing problems were logistical. How could you commit to be at the organization at a particular time on a particular night when your work schedule was subject to the whims of a boss you could not predict, your only childcare ended at 5:00 P.M. when the "señora" who cared for your kids left to work a night shift as a janitor, your home was in one direction from work and the Workplace Project was in the other, you had no car, and public transportation was infrequent and unreliable? Over the long term, there was the problem of staying in touch with the group despite frequent moves and, often, no phone. And then there was the psychological barrier: to commit to the struggle for better working conditions here was tantamount to the difficult admission that life in the United States had not lived up to its promises, that you could not "make it" as quickly as you had once sworn to those you left behind, and that you would not be leaving for home any time soon. In the face of all of this, many would have given up. Many did. But some surmounted these hurdles and stayed.

One logical explanation for the Workplace Project's capacity to attract members despite the hardships they faced would be that membership conferred significant economic benefits.[2] Although joining the Workplace Project membership did entitle an immigrant to some concrete benefits—access to notary services, a monthly newsletter, the right to join one of the group's cooperative businesses, and eventually a card for the discount warehouse Costco—they were small compensations for the sort of time that members contributed to the organization. And most of what the Workplace Project offered was available to the community at large. Any immigrant could get help from the legal clinic on the strength of a promise to take the Workers Course. After completion of the course, membership was wholly voluntary. A day laborer on a streetcorner where the Workplace Project was active would receive the benefits of its support whether he formally affiliated himself with the group or not. A domestic worker whose employment was governed by a contract after the Project's Domestic Workers Bill of Rights campaign did not need membership to avail herself of what it offered—or, for that matter, to enlist the Project's help in enforcing its promises if her employer later violated them. Workers around the state found a new tool in their hands after the passage of the Unpaid Wages Prohibition Act. The vast majority of them were not members either. Those immigrants who became active in the Workplace Project's membership did so because they believed profoundly in the group's mission and because they obtained skills and satisfactions from participation, not primarily because they needed to join in order to get a concrete economic benefit.

How, then, did immigrants come to the Workplace Project, become so deeply involved, and stay to lead? The group put a great deal of thought into building—and tearing up, and rebuilding—its paths to participation, the routes along which immigrants moved as they became more deeply involved with organizing. At bus stations and weekend soccer games, near tortilla stands and on streetcorners, Workplace Project members used plays, comic books, and songs as well as more traditional methods to teach others in the community about workers' rights and the need to organize. From this outreach and from word of mouth, many immigrants came into the Project's legal clinic, a drop-in center that every Monday offered immigrants support in combating violations of workplace rights. The clinic was limited to workplace issues both because of the overwhelming need for such support and on the theory that immigrants who faced concrete difficulties on the job would be most likely to be interested in longer-term organizing to improve the conditions of immigrant work (a problematic assumption, as later became apparent). After initial efforts with a traditional approach, where lawyers solved problems for clients, the clinic evolved so that it asked workers to become active in resolving their cases from the start, using a combination of legal action and organizing. Staff organizers and lawyers helped workers carry out pickets in front of the homes and businesses of employers who had not paid them and reach media interested in their stories. They also went to court and enlisted the help of government agencies.

Solving individual problems was an early step on the journey. To act effectively, Workplace Project members who came in as isolated individuals had to develop a critique of the shared reality that they were living, build a sense of group identity and capacity to act, create meaningful and achievable solutions, carry

them out, and return to evaluate the results. To begin this transformation, immigrants who received help through the clinic—
and others who were simply interested in joining the organization—were asked to take the Workers Course, a nine-week class
about labor law, immigration and labor history, and organizing techniques. Far from a traditional know-your-rights class, in
which a legal expert tells others how the law can solve their
problems, this class was deeply grounded in participants' own
experiences as immigrant workers. It sought to create a common
base of knowledge about history and law, and to provoke immigrants to think critically about the way they were treated at work
and creatively about how to change the situation. Upon graduation, participants were invited to become dues-paying members of the Workplace Project, and to become active in its work
through its network of workers committees. Almost all accepted,
although as I have noted many did not become or ultimately
remain active members. Those who developed the deepest commitment to the group eventually came to govern it. The members of the board, elected to staggered two-year terms from
among the membership and trained intensively by the staff and
others, met at least every three weeks to debate policy, oversee
the budget, fundraise, and carry out their other responsibilities.
And a twenty-person planning committee consisting of the entire board and staff and the head of each workers committee met
twice a year at a weekend-long retreat to evaluate the organization's work and set future directions.

The organization backed up its expectations of active members with intensive training. Every aspect of an immigrant's experience at the Workplace Project, from speaking in public to organizing pickets to running a board meeting, was supported by
formal and informal education. The participatory structure of

the organization itself was a training ground. In staff, board, and membership meetings, facilitation rotated among participants. Agendas were open to whatever items participants wanted to discuss, and were structured to dispense with small issues quickly and reserve as much time as necessary for open debate about larger ones. As problems arose that required further deliberation, they were referred to committees of staff, board members, and general members for investigation, and taken up at special meetings or at the group's biannual retreats. The process was sometimes exhausting. But it created a democratic culture that served the group well. By taking responsibility for running the organization, for making strategic decisions about campaigns, and for carrying out those decisions, immigrants expanded the range of their experience and increased their effectiveness through a constant cycle of action and reflection.

Focusing on a particular path at one moment in the organization's history risks making a "model" out of what is really a set of experiments in a changing context, experiments that worked for a while and then were replaced with other experiments as the organization developed and the environment shifted around it. The path I describe worked reasonably well when the Workplace Project was young, but became less functional over time. In 1999 and 2000, staff and experienced members revamped the path entirely. Now, immigrants with workplace problems come to a weekly workshop where they share their stories with each other, learn the basics of the law, and are invited to join one of three industry committees. Through those committees, workers support each other in resolving their individual problems, and develop broader campaigns as well. To become members, workers can either take the nine-week Workers Course, now retooled, or combine a shorter weekend class with attendance at eight committee

meetings. For the current stage of the organization's development and in its present context, this arrangement works much
better. Although the path has changed, the underlying philosophy remains the same. Activism does not happen overnight. A
critical part of organizing is attention to the development of a
varied set of paths to deeper participation. And to be effective,
a group must remain ever attentive to the complex processes
through which new members are drawn into the organization's
work.

The Workplace Project was able to grow only to the extent
that it could make itself known to large numbers of people in
the community. The organization constantly sought opportunities to reach new immigrants. Spanish-language radio, television, and newspapers were essential. But so were fliers pasted in
the windows and left in piles at grocery stores that sold Hispanic
foods, and at the many small Salvadoran and Honduran restaurants that dotted the Island. So was the time that Project organizers and members spent on the streets and in people's homes,
just talking. And so were the little orange booklets that the
group Xeroxed and handed out to workers at bus stations and
soccer games and laundromats, booklets with spaces to record
wages promised and wages paid, a list of basic workers rights,
and the Project's address and telephone number. With so many
immigrants working for cash, under the table, such booklets often became the only record in wage claims, admissible in court if
regularly filled out by the worker in the manner of a diary. Cases
that otherwise would have been lost were won on the strength of
those booklets.

Churches were a critical link between the Project and new immigrants. It was the rare Catholic church on Long Island that
had not looked up in the late 1980s to find that the complexion

of its congregation had changed dramatically. The nuns and priests who organized the Island's new Spanish-language masses often welcomed the Workplace Project's participation, announcing its presentation about immigrants rights on the job during mass and lending space to carry it out immediately after. These presentations were very popular. For a time there were plays put on by the members, dramatizing common moments in immigrant experience—one even featured firecrackers set off outside to simulate explosives, to what end I cannot remember, other than terrifying many in the audience and earning a harsh reprimand from the priest. Members talked about their experiences on the job and people in the audience added personal testimonies and a Project lawyer gave people information about workplace rights and organizing. People who attended these church presentations often ended up at the legal clinic the following week, or enrolled in the Workers Course for the next session. Increasing numbers of immigrants also belonged to Latino Protestant congregations, some of which were small evangelical storefronts, independent of the established white churches. Many of them, too, opened their arms to the Workplace Project.

A key piece of this outreach was the Workplace Project comic book, *Luchas Laborales (Labor Struggles)*. In 1995, the group invited Hector Valladares, a Honduran political cartoonist in exile in Canada, to spend a week at the Project. After interviewing dozens of workers, he worked with members and staff to develop a storyline interweaving the workplace tribulations of three characters: Rosa, a domestic worker who discovers that her employer is paying her less than the legal minimum wage; her husband, Pedro, a day laborer who becomes depressed after he loses a finger in an accident on the job; and her cousin, Raquel, who along with other coworkers is being sexually harassed by the foreman at the factory where they work. Written in language that workers actually used, set out in the comic book format popular in immigrants' home countries, *Luchas Laborales* gave accurate information about workers' rights, at the same time illustrating through its plot why organizing was often necessary to make those rights real. Very popular when distributed as an outreach tool, the book was also useful as a text for the Workers Course, a starting point to spark discussion about workers' experiences and the difficulties of going beyond knowing rights to enforcing them.

Outreach of all these kinds was critically important for the Project. With time, however, the best outreach for the group came to be word of mouth, workers who had recovered wages through the clinic sending others in with hopes of the same outcome, agencies referring immigrants to the Project, and members talking to family and coworkers about their positive organizing experiences.

Some workers first approached the Workplace Project because they were interested in what they had heard about the organization as a center of political activity and as a way to be helpful to others in their community. Juan Carlos Molina, the young Salvadoran man with experience in El Salvador's revolutionary movement, first learned about the Project from his childhood soccer rival and political comrade, José Martinez. Martinez was one of the first graduates of the Workers Course, and he urged Molina to join him. Molina listened, and soon was drawn deeply into the organization's work. Molina became active in the membership, was a founding member of the organization's landscaping cooperative, briefly held an organizing position on the staff, and remains highly engaged as a member.

Lilliam Araujo had been in the same early class as José Martinez. "In *La Tribuna Hispana* [a local Spanish-language paper] I read the invitation to take the 'labor rights promoters' class. Of course you need to know about your rights for yourself, and at times also to be able to take the message out into the community." Araujo became an active member, was elected to the board of directors and from there to the leadership position of secretary, and after several years as a founding member of the UNITY coop was hired as the Women's Organizer and UNITY's staff coordinator. Carlos Canales, who had worked as an organizer with agricultural workers in El Salvador, came to the Workplace Project in 1993 to apply to become the group's first organizer. In the seven years since he had immigrated, he had dreamed of "going back to my origins," to a job "where my work would not make another man rich." Although he did not get the position, a few years later he returned with a friend to take the Workers Course. "At that time we were both looking to locate ourselves somewhere, to be useful." Canales became active as a member, and in 1999 was hired as an organizer to work with day laborers.

Yet however widespread and creative outreach was, for workers with no past experience with labor organizing or political activism, simply hearing about the Workplace Project was often not enough to bring them in the door. As the active member Eduardo Platero remembers, almost a year passed after he learned of the Project before he signed up for the Workers Course. "I heard they were giving classes—but I wasn't ready yet." Most of these workers got "ready" and approached the Workplace Project when they had an immediate need to know more about their rights or wanted help resolving a problem on the job.

A common entry point for workers seeking help was thus the organization's legal clinic.[3] The Project's legal clinic was the first and last resort for Latino immigrants who had been cheated or hurt on the job, or who had questions about their rights. This clinic had been significantly restructured since the first year in which I provided conventional legal services to all comers. Through the new clinic, workers who came in with a labor issue met first with an organizer, who listened to their problem, introduced them to the Project as a membership organization, and described its collective goals. They were then joined by a lawyer or law student volunteer, who worked with the organizer and workers to develop a strategy to resolve the problem. These strategies incorporated self-help, mutual support, and organizing as well as more traditional legal advocacy. In exchange for the support they received, workers were asked to take the Workers Course. This structure was designed to address individual problems effectively, and simultaneously to invite workers to look critically at the broader causes of those problems and to consider collective action as a response.

The Workplace Project practice of asking workers seeking legal clinic support to take the Workers Course, rather than requiring that they immediately sign up for membership and pay dues, was an unusual one. A more conventional system that restricted services to members would have swelled membership rolls considerably. But the Project board members decided that the group only wanted members who were truly committed to organizing, rather than those who felt forced to profess such a commitment because they desperately needed help. They also decided that it was important that members understand the obligations as well as the benefits of membership before committing to join. Members who had signed up simply to receive services, they reasoned, would be unlikely to participate in campaigns, attend membership meetings, walk picket lines, run for office on committees or the board, all important aspects of active Project membership. They achieved this by postponing the membership decision until after the Workers Course, when participants were both well informed about the meaning of membership and excited about the possibilities of group action.

Some of the workers who came into the Project's legal clinic had suffered terribly. There were the workers who arrived bloody or limping or struggling to breathe as a result of the conditions under which they worked. There were the domestic workers accosted by the man in the home where they worked, and then accused of theft and fired when they refused his advances. There were the landscapers who went unpaid for months while their employer promised them that he was "saving" their money. Then there were, unfortunately, *the usual:* the scores of day laborers unpaid for a few days' work, the dozens of domestic workers earning less than half the minimum wage, the array of injuries in landscaping and factories from speed-ups and lack of training. In all cases, the Project's goals for the legal clinic were the same: to help workers resolve their immediate problems, and to invite them to participate in a longer-term organizing process.

How Rodolfo Sorto and Zoila Rodriguez became involved in the Project illustrates this process. Rodolfo Sorto was one of the first workers I met through the legal clinic. He had come to the Workplace Project a scant month after I began work, to claim harassment from his employer in retaliation for his efforts to organize a union at the janitorial company where he worked. His employer had been contracted by a major manufacturer to clean its laboratories. "Because I tried to organize my coworkers," he recalls, "I was punished, and they sent me to the washing room, where the barrels that held chemicals were washed." He and other subcontracted janitors were also forced to respond to chemical spills without being told what they were. The company's employees who worked with chemicals "had protective clothing that covered them head to toe, and we had absolutely nothing. We were Hispanic, and all of them were white." Within a few months, he was fired. He had been days away from quitting in any case, suffering as he was from dizziness, respiratory problems, headaches, and a spiraling emotional trauma that would eventually land him in the hospital.

What the law had to offer Rodolfo turned out to be limited. The workers' compensation lawyer I referred him to was unable to prove that his illness was a direct result of his working conditions (a not uncommon outcome). OSHA inspected the company, but gave it no more than a slap on the wrist. Sorto was unable to prove that he had been harassed because of his organizing efforts. But what the Workplace Project offered him, even then, appealed greatly to his sense of justice. He became a member and has remained active for ten years, at one time holding a seat on the board of directors.

In 1996, the family for whom Zoila Rodriguez had provided five years of live-in childcare reneged on a promise to give her her first raise. Her sense of injustice was intensified by her status as a virtual shut-in: Her employers forbade her to leave the house during the workweek even if it was night and she had no work left to do. A friend—"the only person I had to talk to"—sent her to the Workplace Project. Speaking on the phone with women's organizer Esly Umanzor, also from El Salvador, Zoila felt a vast sense of relief. "I must have talked for an hour without stopping. I felt like I was with somebody I could really communicate with. Who understood me, who spoke the same Spanish." Umanzor and the Project's legal clinic coordinator, attorney Rhina Ramos, gave her advice about her situation. But they also invited her to join in an upcoming activity. "That was the beginning of the week, and she invited me to come in over the weekend when there would be a protest in front of the home of a woman who also owed money to her housekeeper. And I came in, and we went there, and that's how I began."

Because she was tied to the house during the week, Zoila was unable to take the Workers Course. "That was a tremendous abuse," she says in retrospect, "to shut me up that way, to marginalize me completely." But she started to come to the Workplace Project on weekends, attending regular pickets at the homes of employers who had not paid their workers as well as the workshops and parties, discussion groups and outings that the Project organized on Sundays to bring domestic workers together. Those meetings "were to break down our isolation, and so that we could share our stories and realize that we were not alone in our tragedies." A few years of active membership later, Rodriguez was hired by the Workplace Project as its office administrator and receptionist, her first live-out job in this country after nearly a decade of live-in work.

If outreach and the legal clinic were the broad mouth of the Workplace Project's funnel, the Workers Course was its narrowing point. All immigrants who wanted to become members had to pass through it.

The course began by constructing, through participants' own accounts of their experiences, a broader understanding of how common exploitation was—that low wages, long hours, and abuse were not individual matters, but affected a large part of the community. In one session, immigrant after immigrant drew the health and safety hazards they faced on the job on a huge mural covering the front wall, and then stood before the class and described the burns, falls, dangerous chemicals, and sharp blades to which their work exposed them. In another, each participant recited the long list of industries in which he or she had worked since arriving in the United States, and then the class went back to the list on the blackboard and reconstructed the average wages for such work, discussing the reasons behind the low pay they received. This process simultaneously created a common baseline of knowledge and offered workers the cathartic experience of telling their stories and hearing them echoed and supported in the words of others.

From there the course branched out in many directions. A critical one was discussion of how others had come together through movements and unions to successfully combat similar abuse in the past, putting the struggles of today's immigrants in the context of the labor and immigration history of the United States over the past hundred years. Another was the presentation—and critique—of information about rights. Rather than simply providing information about workplace laws, the course provoked workers to think critically about the problems they faced on the job. In a context of widely unenforced rights, it encouraged participants to move from the reality of their working conditions to an understanding of what the law *said* those conditions should be (whether or not it was enforced), and, going beyond the law, to develop their own sense of what a just system would look like. Yet another technique was practice—through role plays and class-wide strategy sessions—of the skills that organizing required. At times, course participants would also take part in the organization's pickets, protests, public hearings, and other activities, experiences that then fed into classroom discussion. This reflection and analysis, together with practical work on organizing techniques, was designed to move participants from a sense that the abuse they had suffered was an *individual* occurrence, the result of their own ignorance or bad luck, to a broader understanding of exploitation as a *systemic* problem that required a collective solution.

The Workers Course also built a sense of community among participants, and initiated a strong tradition of democratic participation that carried over into the organization as a whole. The course left an indelible impression on many members. For many, the idea that the law protected immigrant (and especially undocumented) workers was a revelation. As Maria Aparicio recalls, before she came to the Workplace Project "I did not know what my labor rights were. I would say that for many people who are outside [the Project]—they are the same as I was. . . . When I began to join the Workplace Project I took the Workers Course. Before, they sometimes used to call me a fighter. Well, knowing my rights, I became more of a fighter still!"

For a smaller number, though, finding out the scope of their labor rights in this country came as a painful shock. Many Latin American countries have stronger protections on the books for nonunionized workers than does the United States, and for immigrants from middle-class backgrounds who had benefited from those protections at home, the difference in the laws was jolting.[4] Carlos Canales remembers what he calls "The Statement," a moment when he had sat in the classroom as I listed the rights workers did *not* have on the job. He imitates me: "At the end of the day, the law only requires that employers pay workers for their forty hours of work, and time and a half at overtime." Canales recalls raising his hand to ask, incredulously, "What about the Christmas bonus?" I had replied, listing the rights I knew many workers had come to expect from their home countries, "*No* Christmas bonus, *no* paid sick days, *no* vacations or personal days, *no* yearly raises, the boss can fire you for almost any reason he wants, *no* right to something after three years, none of that. The only way to win those things is through organizing." Shaking his head, Canales says, "I assumed that if this was a democratic country, then *at least* what is protected in my country should be protected here." The discovery angered him and moved him closer to action.

At the last session of the Workers Course, graduates were formally invited by the board to join the organization, an invitation that almost all accepted. By joining, members took on a series of commitments: to support the Project's organizing efforts, to pay dues of $60 a year, to participate in monthly membership workshops or meetings, to vote in elections, and so on. They also received a variety of concrete benefits, including in addition to those mentioned earlier a photo ID card, ongoing access to the legal clinic, and the right to open a bank account in a local credit union (particularly important for undocumented immigrants, who often carry their money or hide it at home because they cannot open a bank account, thus making them ripe targets for robbery).

That an immigrant graduated from the Workers Course and decided to become a member was no guarantee that she would stay active in the arduous work of organizing as a part of the group. Yet some did, for a variety of reasons. One reason many immigrants stayed beyond the resolution of their individual problems, and remained committed to the organization even in difficult times, was the sense of family and community they drew from the Project. As Carmen Lelys reflects, "I loved the Workplace Project so much because I felt such support . . . more than in my family. I felt so good about being here [at the Project], and therefore I felt committed, and I became involved with the Workplace Project." At the Workplace Project many immigrants found a sense of common purpose, a place to hang out, food, music, jokes—a welcoming culture that combined recreation with the sense of learning new skills and taking on a worthwhile struggle.[5] Sonia Baca, a Peruvian feminist psychologist, recalls that when she joined the Project she had in mind not so much her long activist history as immediate social need. Speaking with Janice Fine in 1997, she said, "At the moment what I needed was a support group, people who could show me how to get around in the city, on Long Island, who could tell me a little about this country, and to meet with women—and I found it. . . . I have made bonds of affection, which for me are so important because of my personality and because I don't have family here."[6]

For those with families already, the Workplace Project had a way of seeping into family life. Zoila Rodriguez often brought her eighteen-year-old daughter, Mónica, and her three-year-old granddaughter, Alex, with her to events and pickets. She laughs, remembering how quickly the culture of the Project became a part of the culture of her family. Alex would chant the latest slogans from her car seat, singsonging, "Wendy, Wendy, You Must Pay!" as they drove to the supermarket. And, as Zoila recalls, Alex "also learned to protest for her rights! One day Mónica punished her, put her in a chair looking at the wall. I was there, and since Grandma was around, she thought Grandma would defend her, right? But I just looked at her, and said, 'Sorry, Mommy has punished you.' So she got up and began to march, chanting 'BAD LADIES, LET ME PLAY! BAD LADIES, LET ME PLAY!'"

A number of immigrants found the motivation to stay in their growing sense of the breadth of the abuse immigrants faced on the job, and with that a belief that the Workplace Project offered part of a solution. This stemmed in part from the Course but in part simply from exposure to others with similar problems.

Rodolfo Sorto, one of the organization's first members, remembers the nights in 1992 and 1993 when he volunteered to answer the phones in the evening when I stayed late to work at CARECEN's offices: "Many workers would call late into the night, to ask for information and see how they could be helped. I began to see that my problem had not been individual. It hadn't been a situation that had only happened to me, but to many people. I saw that the labor problem was immense." In the words of Zoila Rodriguez, "One of the best things that happens at the Workplace Project is that for anyone, their own problem is the biggest one. But when you come up against the problems that have come in here, I start to think, my problem is minimal compared to what that woman has suffered. That gives you strength. These are priceless lessons." Samuel Chavez regards the Workplace Project as "one of the means through which I realized that what we suffered at American Tissue was serious, but that there are much more serious problems elsewhere . . . and at the same time I have learned that people have rights and can organize and defend themselves, put a stop to the situation."

Critical to this belief that something could be done was an understanding of the history of labor and immigrant organizing in the United States. Chavez continues, "When we turned to labor history [in the Workers Course] we could see that the problems that we as new immigrants face are not exclusive to us. That is something that has been happening since this country was founded—as long as immigrants arrived they were looked down on. And I think that's a motivation, in other words, 'Why were these people once badly off, and now they're doing better?' If I take in that information, and it gives me that feeling, I can keep struggling, because I think there is a hope of change. The way that those people changed their situation, we can change ours too."

For some, the Workplace Project represented a first experience with activism. Juan Calderon said that he had never participated in any organizing efforts or in politics—or even belonged to a church—in his native Colombia. "I came to the Center because I had a problem with unpaid wages related to overtime," he recalled. "The Center made me political."[7] For some others, the Project represented an opportunity to resume the organizing work that had been so much a part of their days in their home countries. Moving from a life driven by political commitment and action to one where manual work occupied most of the time and family obligations and the television ate up the rest was disorienting and depressing. In the words of José Martinez, a former student and union activist, "When I was living in El Salvador I used to do a lot of things. [But once I arrived in New York,] before I came to the Center my life was working too many hours and watching television or going around doing nothing. When I came to the Center, my life changed a bit, because the Center made me feel the way I felt back in my home country, which was that I had a sense of purpose other than going to work and coming home." Similarly, the Peruvian theologian and activist Oscar Zúñiga, who spent his early days in Long Island looking for work as a day laborer, recalls: "When I arrived at the corner it was a whole new world and a hard world because of my limitations with English. My work before had been intellectual and now it was manual. My body hurt. I felt alone and far away from my family . . . All human beings feel the need to belong. The Workplace Project is my reference group, I have the opportunity to share my vision as a worker and contribute here as somebody from the street corner."[8]

For immigrants who had emerged from revolutionary movements, the decision to get involved was often based less on their faith that the organization's strategy would yield positive results than on the sense that it had important things to teach them, and they it. Juan Carlos Molina of the Salvadoran revolutionary movement said that he felt himself drawn in during the Workers Course. "It was quite interesting, because it had been years since I had been involved in something that I was engaged in, you know. That would intrigue you so you'd say, wow, interesting." Molina was drawn to the group's strong "organizing culture." The Project's meetings and actions felt alive and open, giving him and other new participants a sense that they could play a real role in shaping the organization's course. Molina recalls many late-night discussions with his friend and political comrade José ("Chele") Martinez, then president of the board. "Chele would say to me, 'I think we ought to participate more, because we have more of an analysis and we can contribute more to the Project.' That's when I began to use that damn daily calendar! I said, there are things in life that a person likes, and I like this; let's give it the time it needs. So I began to get more involved."

Molina's involvement gave him tools that he brought back to the group of Salvadoran activists in exile. Particularly useful was what he describes as the Workplace Project's "organizational methodology"—its practice of deliberation and strategizing, its approach to running meetings and raising funds, and so on. So too was the opportunity to organize in the open, without the fear that had driven the revolutionary movement underground. "Within the group [here] there is dynamic participation, a real attraction. . . . You learn to organize, to do strategy, to put it up for critique and develop it. In El Salvador . . . at times we had to build it all in [snapping fingers] two days. Here there's more often space to build, to analyze and evaluate. There, many times there was no space because of the political situation and the level of conflict. We had two days, we had to have thirty people there, say 'this and this is what we're looking for,' give them tasks and get them going. Maybe it would be a failure. Maybe it would be good. And you don't know which. While it is going on, there's no time to evaluate. Later, yes, but not in the moment. That's different here . . . That's what I liked about the Project." These skills were particularly useful to activists in exile faced with a need to develop an approach that built on the tenacity and commitment they had forged in combat, but that made sense from their changed perspective, now organizing from outside the country to support those still within it.

Finally, there is a new and important category of workers coming to the Workplace Project more recently—those who are attracted not just out of a desire to help others or be active in organizing, or out of the need for help in resolving a labor problem, but because they see the Project as a place that can affirmatively help them to earn more money. Maria Aparicio is one of these. She first heard about the Workplace Project in 1998, when it was launching its UNITY housecleaning cooperative. Her voice, usually faint, becomes strong and proud as she says, "I am among the founding members of the cooperative." After two years of work with other women establishing the cooperative, Aparicio was able to leave her job in a warehouse—a job where "they treated us like animals"—and support her family in part with work distributed through UNITY. "We achieved the goal we set ourselves," she affirms, regarding the seventy-member cooperative with its guarantee of a minimum wage of $15 an hour.

Those members who stayed to become active moved immediately into the Project's workers committees. In addition to the original organizing committee, focusing on educational outreach and work with day laborers, these included the Justice Committee, which carried out pickets at the homes and workplaces of employers who failed to pay their workers; the Women's Organizing Committee (Fuerza Laboral Femenina, or Female Labor Force); and various committees constituted around particular campaigns, events, or projects. Each committee had an elected leadership of members and received staff support. Through these committees, members carried out the Project's organizing campaigns.

Committees met weekly or more often during intensive campaigns. Those meetings served two functions. One, of course, was to plan and carry out the Project's organizing campaigns. But at the same time, the committees acted as intensive leadership training grounds for workers. Through them, workers and staff analyzed problems, debated causes and solutions, created campaigns, worked out the details, and carried the organizing efforts out. The result was an ongoing introduction to the basics of democratic process. Zoila Rodriguez unequivocally states, "Participation is the most important thing that's taught here." "How to organize in small groups, how to talk, how to run an agenda"—all these were skills Juan Carlos Molina attributes to his experience with democratic process at the Project.

In committees, too, workers developed concrete skills in critical analysis, planning, media work, and how to do outreach, carry out protests, and contact elected officials. Staff and experienced members played the critical roles here. Committees took the talk of the Workers Course and slowly, with support, translated it into action. Sorto likened the experience of working on a committee to being taught to drive a car with someone right next to him, foot on the brake. There is another way to teach, he notes humorously. "They could give me the keys to a car and say to me, 'You can drive. Just put the key in, and turn it on.' I can say yes, and they give me the keys. I get in the car and I'm proud to be in there. I put in the keys and turn it on and I'll hear the noise. But then I'm not going to know how to back up, how to get ahead, how to turn on the lights." Only when the organization says, in his words, "we'll train you, and let's see how we can all work together," does real learning take place.

As workers participated in active organizing efforts, the talk and the training came together. Action created commitment; action generated energy. As Zoila Rodriguez remembers, thinking back to the first Workplace Project picket she joined on behalf of a domestic worker, "I had never, ever, ever been to a protest, not even in my country. It changed my idea that we have no rights, right? Because, documented or not, the right to be treated like a human being and with dignity exists, and it can be expressed. That's what I learned at that protest. It gave me energy to go on, and I said, *this* is what I've wanted. This is what I wanted to do, to defend people's rights as human beings." Protests had a similar effect on Angela Sarmiento, a Venezuelan school principal who was upper middle class and active in a conservative political party in her home country. She had never attended a protest there, much less in the United States. She describes her first Justice Committee protest: "The first protest, I think it was in Glen Cove, a landscape worker, an Italian [boss]. He owed money to a group of people. So this was my first protest and I didn't know how things worked with the police . . . I said, 'And what if they take us to jail?' And the [board] president, who at that point was Mr. José Martinez . . . was joking with me, saying, 'Look, we've got vinegar here for the tear gas,' and I believed him. 'And here we have our bulletproof vests.' And I said, 'But I didn't bring any of that stuff.' 'Don't worry,' he says, 'we'll give it to you.'" She laughs. That day, she watched with trepidation as the police cars pulled up in front of the group of marchers. But rather than telling the group to be quiet (as they often did) or arresting them (as she had feared), the police had gone into the employer's house with the worker and the Workplace Project organizer to demand payment. Sarmiento became a protest regular. For other workers, an effort relating to their own workplace rather than protest on someone else's behalf galvanized them. The Salvadoran Eduardo Platero speaks of the effect on him as a janitor of seeing his union, the cleaning company that was his direct employer, and *Newsday,* the business that contracted the company's services, respond to the campaign he and coworkers carried out with the Workplace Project's support in 2000. Where "none of them [the campaign's targets] thought it was important when I spoke alone," he recalls, he was inspired to see the way the group's demands were recognized because of the pressure the campaign generated.

For still others, it was work on the campaign for the Unpaid Wages Prohibition Act that proved crucial in spurring their commitment to organizing. It was not that Workplace Project members saw their ability to meet with a state senator as proof of the openness of political debate in the United States, or of the ease of access to power. Many had been politically active in their home countries and were critical of U.S. politics; even those who were not saw the difference between being granted a visit with an elected official and actually having a range of viewpoints debated and heard within a political system. But the fact that they were able to sit across a table with, as one worker put it, "esos viejones" (those big old guys), make a series of demands, respond to the objections that arose, and gain the support of people in power who had otherwise been unsympathetic to the cause of immigrants and workers, made them rethink their notions of their own inability to exercise political power within the

U.S. system. Juan Calderon described the resulting feeling: "In Colombia, I always thought of politics as for politicians and of myself as a worker who—whoever's in power—is going to have to work every day to earn my bread. I couldn't change that. But I feel like now I may have a chance to participate in a process of making changes." Raul Lopez echoed him: "It never occurred to me that we could do something like this. It has awakened something in me: we can keep going on with this."[9]

Beyond the work of the committees, immigrant workers participated in deliberation and decision-making at the Workplace Project through membership meetings. The monthly meetings alternated between workshops about key issues such as globalization or an immigrant's rights if she was stopped by the police, and debate-and-decision-making meetings at major points in campaigns or of organizational change. Decisions about where to compromise on the Unpaid Wages Prohibition Act, about whether to create a new category of membership that did not require passage through the Workers Course, and about whether to undertake a campaign around immigration issues, among many others, were all debated in that forum. Membership meetings were an important form of participation for some members. Lilliam Araujo reflects: "As a member you feel, 'I am the voice of the organization.' To have the power to decide the course of the organization makes you feel strong . . . because what you're seeking is that the organization move forward. So that work that you're doing for others is part of yourself." For the most involved, serving on the board of directors was one more step toward leadership.

The path to participation was intended to feed new members into a democratic institution. But in the beginning the Workplace Project was run by staff rather than members, and real democracy represented little more than an aspiration. The transition toward deeper participation was slow, but over time the idea of a genuine member-run center took on weight and meaning, in a process that has continued and intensified in the years since my departure.

The first visible change was at the staff level, as my central role as founder—intensified by my status as a white outsider with connections to foundations and the media appeal that comes with a Harvard degree—gave way to a broader sharing of responsibility for decision-making among staff, almost all immigrants or the children of immigrant families. At the same time, underneath the public radar, the workers committees and board were beginning to take on strength and independence. This was no accident. Staff and more experienced members gave the board and committees training, support, and room to experiment gradually with greater independence. Members attended conferences and trainings so that they could meet other workers and learn about different organizing strategies; the board became increasingly involved in fundraising, not just from the Latino community but with foundations and individual major donors; and the staff stepped back and members stepped forward in situations where someone spoke for the organization, whether to a foundation, an elected representative, or the press. As a result, by 1997 and 1998, members had more experience in handling difficult decisions and more power within the organization.

The shift in power and control is reflected in the change in how particular questions were handled. For example, when in late 1994 the group shifted from a traditional legal clinic model to the organizing-oriented approach I described earlier, the real conversations and decision-making happened among the staff and legal clinic volunteers. By 1998, the organization's planning committee, consisting of the entire board and staff and the head of each workers committee, was the forum for extended conversations about the role of the legal clinic in the organization, with the board itself making the final decision about the direction the clinic was to take in relation to other organizing goals. The change can also be seen in a matter as simple as the handling of testimony as a part of the Unpaid Wages Prohibition Act campaign. At a large public hearing in early 1996, I gave the principal testimony and fielded all questions, with supporting testimony from two Project members. Later that year, a committee of workers was responsible for fielding legislators' questions when the group visited them, although I still made the introductory presentation. By the spring of 1997, members carried out legislative visits alone, with staff functioning primarily as translators. When the legislature passed the bill, I was away on a month's leave, and the organization coordinated the campaign to press the governor to sign without me.

A particularly clear example of how the Project shifted power and knowledge comes in the area of fundraising. When the organization began, I had all of the foundation contacts, and all of the individual donors came through me. As the staff began to grow, first Henriquez and then others began meeting with foundation representatives; staff and volunteers both brought potential donors in contact with the organization. By 1996, the Project had begun to give the board intensive training in community, foundation, and private donor fundraising, and board members began to accompany me and other staff to foundation visits and donor meetings. In 1997, the organization hired Randy Jackson as a fundraiser. Jackson, at the time a recent college graduate, intuitively understood raising money as an organizing process. With his support, seeking financial support for the group's work became yet another opportunity for member involvement and control. The staff wrote proposals and did the groundwork to set up meetings with potential donors. But board members and others active in the membership took on the primary responsibility for speaking on behalf of the organization. With the staff doing simultaneous translation, board members spoke and fielded questions about the organization during house parties at the homes of individual donors. Foundations that came to visit the organization met with from ten to twenty members from the board and committees, not as an adjunct to meetings with staff but as their principal opportunity to ask questions about the Project. By the organization's sixth year, if I participated in these meetings at all, it was only as a translator. Where once I had been the only voice in the money-raising room, now my voice was limited to translating for the organization's members as they spoke about their work.

The growing ability of the board, heads of workers committees, and the staff to function collectively to run the organization and its campaigns made it possible for me to decide to leave the organization in the summer of 1998. By that time, the board had become strong enough to make important decisions over opposition from me or the staff—and the organization had become strong enough to continue functioning when this happened, with me or the staff carrying out the board's directions. This was critical to the organization's survival during the rocky period following my departure, when the board chose a candidate to succeed me over the staff's preference for another finalist. That candidate took the position, but left for personal reasons within six months, returning to El Salvador so his wife could be near her family. He was followed by Nadia Marín (now Marín-Molina, having married Juan Carlos Molina), who has ably led the organization since then. Marín-Molina had begun work at the Workplace Project as a law student intern, received an Echoing Green fellowship to start the organization's cooperatives program in 1996, and had thereafter become a member of the staff.

The Workplace Project was founded on the premise that dedication to participatory organizing would lead to a strong worker center. Part of this commitment to an arduous process of member development grew from a deep political and moral belief in democratic organizing. But part of it stemmed from the view that such an approach was also pragmatic. The organization was founded on the premise that immigrants themselves would have to take leadership roles in the organizing for it to be successful. This was so because they were the ones who would have to do the hard work of collective action, day in and day out; because they knew most intimately about the conditions under which they worked and therefore had the major contribution to make in terms of strategy; and because funding for staff to support such an enterprise could not be guaranteed for any length of time. An active membership backed up by an all-worker governing board, the group believed, would be the Workplace Project's best chance at successful organizing.

This is an appealing proposition. But is it true? Does an internally democratic structure actually make a group any more powerful and likely to succeed than the alternatives?[10]

On the one hand, the power of the immigrant workers who do the worst jobs is severely restricted by the social, political, and economic circumstances in which they labor. Global competition, for example, is a phenomenon made up of many converging forces, over very few of which immigrant workers in one location can conceivably exert any meaningful control. No matter how they come together in their neighborhoods or their workplaces, most immigrant garment workers in the United States do not have the power to keep their employers from moving elsewhere—or simply replacing them from the long lines of others in the same city who would like their jobs—if they organize for higher wages. Even where jobs cannot move, most worker centers do not have anywhere near the critical mass of members required to put pressure on most individual employers, much less across an industry. In ways I have already detailed, the law is arrayed against all workers who want to organize, against immigrants with tenuous or undocumented legal status even more so. When the economy falters and political winds blow hard against immigrants, the situation gets worse.[11] In the short term, it is hard to imagine how participatory organizing is going to change these limiting factors.

In the face of such evident obstacles to the effective exercise of power by immigrant workers, it is tempting to shift to the contention that participatory democracy is meaningful not (or not just) for instrumental reasons, but because it has inherent value. Building member-led institutions of immigrant workers is important, that argument runs, because a democratic and participatory structure replicates within the group the sort of society that it struggles to create in the outside world, one that respects the dignity of its members, thrives on a broad range of contributions, and is controlled by those it purports to represent. It is important because it helps people who are often demeaned and isolated in the outside world to come into their own in the process of building communities of mutual support and respect.

The learning and growth that participatory organizations generate is meaningful for the individual transformations it supports and for the collective spirit it creates, independent of its impact on the outside world.[12]

All of these things, I believe, are true. And yet democracy is *also* important because it builds "internal power" among immigrant workers. By internal power I mean the growth in organizing capacity both on the individual and the group level that occurs when people build a shared sense of identity and develop a common purpose, when they strategize together and reflect together on the work they have done.[13] That internal power can then be exercised to shift power in the outside world.

As history has so often taught us, power is elastic in surprising ways. The amount of power any group of workers have is the result of the complex interaction between economic circumstances, the political setting, law at a variety of levels, their level of solidarity and their strategic creativity, the amount of activism already under way in the community, the legitimacy the group has in the eyes of the public, and so on. By influencing any one of these elements, workers have the capacity both to build power directly (as, for example, when day laborers refuse to work for less than a set amount) and indirectly (as, for example, when home health care workers win a change in the law that creates a state-run board with which they can bargain, thus reshaping the field on which their power is deployed).[14]

Internal power is an important route to this kind of change. As Workplace Project members attested above, the experience of building and running an organization, of debating key decisions and carrying out campaigns, transforms those who go through it. The process of reflecting on their own reality, examining the causes of the problems they faced, thinking strategically about possible solutions, applying those solutions, and evaluating the results as a precursor to further action, expanded not only the range of what immigrant workers could imagine, but of what they felt able to do.[15] They developed or deepened their critical analysis, bolstered their courage, and had a taste of what it is like to stand together in the face of those who did not believe they could stand at all. Many developed not just what is sometimes called "voice"—the capacity to speak out and be heard—but a fundamental shift in orientation toward strategic and collective approaches to solving problems.

The result is a variety of new resources that strengthen a group's capacity to take on external battles. One is the solidarity that springs from the fact that "giving people a stake in the decision gives them a stake in the success of the action and in the survival of the group,"[16] rendering them more willing to put themselves on the line when the moment arrives. Another is leadership, an essential element of any organizing effort. And immigrant worker leadership is not only critical to the future of worker centers. The survival of the labor movement as a whole depends on unions' ability to organize women, people of color, and immigrants. That goal would be facilitated by having women, people of color, and immigrants represented in the movement's leadership to a far greater extent than they are today. This is only in small part because of the symbolic message that a diverse staff and leadership sends. Real diversity at all levels is instrumental to the sort of shift in organizational culture that is required for unions to become genuinely responsive to the interests and expectations of these new members.[17]

Seen as a potential resource for the future, when members of worker centers may work elsewhere and find other opportunities to organize, such a process of personal transformation also has the potential to have far more of a collective impact than we can measure by looking at one slice of time. In the long term, the organization itself may also undergo a transition into a broad social movement or a new form of labor organizing, one that is capable of shifting the landscape in such a way that it generates power on a broad scale.

Although there will be times when the leadership that worker centers develop among their members does not come to fruition through successful collective action at the workplaces where they labor, in other arenas it may play out in a wide range of ways beneficial to the community—at their children's schools, in the run-down apartment complexes in which they live, or through continuing involvement with politics in their countries of origin. Workplace Project members credited their capacity to undertake a wide range of organizing efforts wholly or in part to what they had learned at the organization. One member started a Hispanic cultural center in the North Shore town where she lived. Another group of members provided tactical and financial support to the election campaign of a mayoral candidate in their Salvadoran hometown. And Carmen Lelys Maldonado brought together hundreds of former residents of Cañas, his Honduran village, now living in Long Island—by his estimate, half of the population of the village as a whole—and founded an association that raised enough money to fund the construction of Cañas's first highway, among other development projects.

Yet another product of participatory organizing is tactical resourcefulness, a critical source of strength for groups seeking to make change at times and in places where the standard repertoire of strategies does not work.[18] Democratic organizing brings many minds to bear on a problem, minds of people who have intimate experience with the problem in their daily lives.

The result can be just the sort of innovative ideas about strategy that crack old molds of thinking that fit poorly with a changed world. Small organizations like worker centers are in an excellent position to translate those ideas into experimentation with new strategies in a variety of contexts, strategies that larger and more established organizations might deem too much of a long shot, too small scale, too resource intensive, or too particular to one location. In turn, when such strategies succeed in several locations simultaneously, their impact has the potential to be greater than the sum of their parts. Scattered local victories may not significantly change the power landscape in those areas, much less have a national impact. But as word spreads of the ways that participatory approaches to organizing have generated successful efforts to tackle daunting obstacles, participatory practices become more interesting to a range of organizations that have traditionally adhered to top-down approaches, from advocacy groups to unions.

In the worker center context, it is also important to recognize that even in one small geographic region, the amount and kinds of power groups of immigrant workers can exert vary widely. Outside of the most dire contexts there are pockets where immigrant workers have more capacity to make demands on their employers than a first glance reveals. Where work is locally rooted and immigrant workers have a fairly stable relationship to jobs and industries, democratic organizing can have direct impact on workers' ability to build and exercise power. For a time, at least, with the support of the Workplace Project day laborers in Long Island were able to enforce a higher daily minimum rate than they had previously received by withholding their labor from employers who offered less, clearly an example of workers' direct economic power in action. This does not mean that all day laborers in all places and at all times can do this. The question is location-specific and dependent on a wealth of other factors as well, and can be answered only through in-depth research and analysis.[19]

Building a participatory membership organization of immigrant workers is no guarantee that the powerful change such a group generates within its boundaries will translate to transformation in the world at large. If internal power is understood merely as an emphasis on cooperation and personal growth, and cultivated in isolation from the question of how the group can challenge the existing balance of power, it is unlikely to result in structural change, because structural change requires engagement with structural power. Rather than resting on the considerable satisfactions of democratic participation for its own sake, the challenge is to continually seek out ways to transform internal power into external strategy and action.

4

RIGHTS TALK AND COLLECTIVE ACTION

Although the story of the Workplace Project is, above all, about the formidable task of tackling suburban sweatshops, its history speaks richly of another challenge as well: that of navigating the relationship between law and organizing. How do law and rights relate to the practice of building power and making change through collective action?

It is not immediately obvious why this should be a difficult issue. After all, organizing efforts often need lawyers to represent people in court. Lawyers also teach people about their rights, seek change in the laws, and do transactional work such as preparing nonprofit incorporations, all useful to communities and movements doing social change work. But the two traditions are founded on very different assumptions. In the sort of organizing I am discussing here, people with a problem come together to develop their own vision of justice and their own voice, and seek to realize their goals by acting together. That process is rife with tensions in ways a brief description cannot convey, but nonetheless holds the principle of self-determination at its core. In law, people with a problem come to trained professionals who tell them what they are likely to be entitled to under the state's vision of justice, and then speak for them as the legal process proceeds. Little wonder, then, that when law is asked to function in the service of organizing, sparks often fly.

The Workplace Project used a variety of legal strategies—rights education, legal services, and lobbying among them—as tools to build the power of immigrant workers. Immigrant workers' desire to learn their rights was the Greek chorus that ran through the Workplace Project. For those immigrants mired in the underworld of informal work, where abuse ran rampant and rights on the books were broadly ignored, the idea that the law promised redress was a powerful one. Language barriers and persistent rumors that undocumented immigrants were not covered by labor laws made accurate and intelligible information particularly valuable. The Project responded to this need in spades, teaching about rights through its outreach, in the Workers Course, and as a part of the legal clinic. Talk about rights was woven through its membership discussions and its organizing campaigns as well. Even its name in Spanish—Centro de Derechos Laborales, the Workplace Rights Center—emphasized *rights* as the organization's central purpose.

Rights education is most often imagined as a group process with individual outcomes: people may come together in one room to learn about the law, but they scatter to the winds (or to lawyers' offices) when the time comes to put the new knowledge to use in resolving their problems. Some scholars have further argued that even when it happens within a social movement, talking about rights actively undermines the possibility of meaningful collective action for social change, because of the ways that a quest to win individual rights can atomize movement participants, because a battle for rights channels a movement's energy from the streets to the courts, and because of the way a focus on winning new rights leads to passive reliance on the state to grant those rights rather than a broad struggle for justice, among other concerns.[1] The Workplace Project's experience challenges these images, painting a much more complex picture of how talk about rights interacts with organizing.

The Workplace Project sought to teach about rights in a way that supported collective action, and its vision was largely realized. The Project began providing information about labor laws because workers urgently wanted it, because it was hard to find elsewhere, and because knowledge about rights was a critical component of the effort to improve working conditions. But over time, talk about rights came to serve broader purposes within the organization. For many members, learning about their rights was a first step toward feeling that they had the capacity to act to challenge the conditions under which they worked. Beyond this individual transformation, talk about rights became a kind of "story" that drew the group's members together, motivated them to organize, and explained their struggle to the public. And discussions of rights became a springboard that launched a vision of justice that went far beyond the law's provisions. In these internal ways, rights talk—a phrase that encompasses all the ways people develop their identities in relation to rights and use rights to frame their claims on others—was a strong complement to organizing. Once the group turned to action to enforce or win rights, more tensions with organizing came to the fore. These tensions were particularly evident when rights talk translated into individual legal representation, as with the legal clinic, and when the organization sought to establish rights through the legislature, as with the Unpaid Wages Prohibition Act.

What does it mean to teach about rights, especially in a way that supports collective action?[2] In a damp church basement, in a legal services office's conference room, in a public school classroom as the janitors sweep the halls in the evening, a typical presentation about the law goes something like this. An expert stands up and says, *These are your rights.* People in the audience raise their hands and say, *This is my problem. How can I fix my problem?* The expert says, *This is what you need to do to vindicate your rights; I and others like me can help you.*

In some situations, this approach may give people all the information they need. But for immigrant workers seeking to improve their working conditions, the standard presentation poses problems. Despite its underlying message about reliance on experts, community education about rights is often described as a tool for "empowerment." Its vision of empowerment is an individual one. In hearing about their rights on the job, participants may be "empowered" to know and advocate for their rights, to "stand up for themselves." Yet violations of the law in the underground economy are structural. They are not anomalous problems; instead they define how business is done. In this context, individual action to resolve individual problems is unlikely to get far. Individual legal action may result in temporary relief (although it just as likely may not), but it will do little or nothing to keep the problem from happening again within weeks or months.

A second problem is the more subtle suggestion inherent in such a presentation that the outer limit of what those in attendance should seek is defined by the substantive rights already on the books. In the labor context, as in most contexts, there are both substantive and procedural rights. Substantive rights—found in laws like the Fair Labor Standards Act and the Occupational Safety and Health Act—set basic floors on workplace conditions, naming a minimum wage, requiring payment at time-and-a-half for hours worked over 40, listing a set of standards for a safe workplace, and so on. Procedural rights—found in the National Labor Relations Act, among other places—establish the rules of the game that come into play when workers wish to organize to demand higher wages, more benefits, and stricter safety standards than those the substantive laws require.[3]

Procedural rights are essential to any effort to raise wages and improve working conditions beyond the minimums prescribed by law. Yet most know-your-rights presentations for immigrants (and others) concentrate on substantive laws. The reason is simple: If those laws are the floor, many immigrant workers labor in the basement. Their employers honor minimum wage, overtime, and health and safety protections only in the breach. But the result is a focus on enforcement of what may be baldly inadequate existing minimums. Take, for example, wages. The minimum wage leaves a family of three dangling far below the poverty level even when a parent works full time. In this context, the emphasis of a traditional know-your-rights session on minimum wage risks reinforcing the message that workers should see the minimum wage as an acceptable level of pay.

The Workplace Project thus found that a standard approach to rights education that emphasized individual substantive rights left unsaid much that was important, short-circuiting creative thinking about organizing rather than encouraging it. Over time, the Project developed a method of teaching about rights through its outreach and its Workers Course that sought to open up organizing possibilities, rather than close them off. This approach at once provided accurate information about what the law said it did, and turned a critical eye on its promises. It began by mapping the reality of participants' work lives. It then moved on to a comparison between that reality and the law on the books, both substantive and procedural. In discussions about those laws, it asked critical questions about how they had come to be, how they actually worked in practice, and whose interests they served. Finally, it left current laws behind, working with participants to develop a vision of a more just system and the rules that would govern it.[4]

This approach to teaching about rights recognized that poor people's lives rarely reflected the full range of rights and benefits that they are guaranteed by law. It acknowledged that the law itself falls short of a complete vision of justice. Rather than being taught as facts, rights became a lens through which to map and critique the gaps between reality and law, and between law and a broader vision of justice. In this context, the question of *why* those gaps exist, and of what kind of power and vision it would take to close them, moved to center stage. This question was taken up again in the context of concrete problems as graduates of the Workers Course moved on to active participation in the Workplace Project.

The contrast between the standard approach to teaching about rights and the critical method becomes sharper by example. The classroom quiets instantly when the OSHA inspector walks in the door. He stands at the front of the room as an assistant distributes copies of the Occupational Safety and Health Act. Holding the pamphlet up, he begins. "This Act guarantees your safety on the job. As a worker, you have a right to the following." He turns to the board and sketches out the basic areas that the law protects. He emphasizes that OSHA inspections occur without notice to the employer. He describes the process through which employers are fined. And he opens the floor to questions. "There are unlabeled chemicals in the factory where I work," says one woman. "Call OSHA, here is the number," he replies. "The scaffolding on my construction job is not secure," says a man. "OSHA will inspect the site. Call that number," the official answers. And so on. The unspoken lesson in this session is: The people in this workshop have individual problems that they can fix now that they know about the law. If the purpose of providing the information is seen as "empowerment," it is empowerment on an individual level, reliant on state intervention to achieve its goals: participants are "empowered" to appeal to authorities to enforce a legal remedy.

Compare this to the Workplace Project Workers Course session on health and safety as it was taught from 1995 to 1998. That safety session began with a wall covered by blank paper. As participants came in they were asked to draw a picture of the worst safety hazard at their current job, producing a graphic mural of workplace danger: lawnmowers without safety guards, unlabeled chemicals, collapsing scaffolds. They then described their drawings to the class. This exercise created a visual and spoken record of the group's shared experience, which set the context for the discussion to follow. As the discussion began, the teacher asked, "Does anyone here know about a law covering some of these problems?" Eventually someone would suggest that there was one; the teacher identified and briefly described OSHA, but few in the class had ever seen an OSHA inspector at their workplace. Class discussion then turned to the political and economic question of why such hazards might be common despite the protections that exist on the books.

At this point, an OSHA official would arrive. Standing in front of the mural, she gave a standard "know-your-rights" presentation. Rather than seeing the official as "the authority who will tell us how to solve our problems," participants—fresh from a discussion of their own reality—were often critical of her claims. In addition to queries about individual cases, she was met with a series of thoughtful questions about why OSHA so rarely appeared—and why OSHA rights are so rarely respected—at participants' workplaces. The underlying lesson was: Individual ignorance of the law is not the issue; unsafe working conditions are a systemic problem. To address the violations there must be structural changes, which will come about only when workers as a group use their reality as a base from which to challenge the proclamations of government and the evasions of their employers.

When the OSHA inspector left, the teacher talked with the class about the gaps in OSHA coverage that the inspector regularly failed to mention—for example, the lack of any right to heat in the workplace. Tracing that hole back to the lobbying influence of the meatpacking industry on Congress, she guided the class to a discussion of the political process out of which laws are born. She then asked participants to imagine that they worked together in an unheated workplace (as some inevitably did), and to create a model campaign for how they would organize together to force their employer to provide heat in winter, a campaign that did not have the law to fall back on.

Rather than starting with the assumption that *participants* in such a discussion had a problem, then, the Project began from the belief that the *system* had a problem, of which individual's experiences of unenforced laws were merely a symptom. And rather than starting with what the law said, the course began with participants' own experience as workers and immigrants. When the

Workplace Project grounded its health and safety class in the starting point of participants' reality, it quickly become clear that participants had many experiences of workplace danger and injury in common, regardless of their particular job or industry. Unsafe working conditions were a problem endemic to whatever work low-wage immigrants did. When this reality was compared to the law on the books, a system-wide gap appeared. This gap became the entry-point into a deeper discussion of power and politics. The class moved on to analyze where laws come from, why the law often failed to protect workers in practice, and how participants might make paper rights real in their workplaces. The course encouraged workers to move beyond the assumption that what was legal defined what was just, and to ask instead what justice in the workplace would look like and what strategies they might use to achieve it.

Why did the Workplace Project place such an emphasis on rights? Rights offered its membership a tool in its struggle for better wages and working conditions. Critically, though, rights were also important because they became a point of unity in an often divided community. Since the Workers Course was the first place most Workplace Project members came together, it bore a heavy burden for forging a group identity that could carry the Project's organizing work forward.

An outsider looking at the crowd of Latino immigrant workers at any Workplace Project event, almost all new to the United States within the past decade, 70 percent of them from El Salvador, working at the same low rungs of the same suburban economy, might assume that among them such a shared identity was a given, that their organizing together emerged naturally from the easy solidarity of people with similar lives and experiences. The outsider would be mistaken. The Workplace Project membership was in fact riven with divisions of national allegiance, of political alliance, of religion and of class, as well as divided along the more visible lines of gender and race.

It is the first Monday of the month, membership meeting night at the Workplace Project. Coffee in hand, Juan Carlos Molina and Eduardo Platero, two longtime Project members, sit talking to each other before the meeting begins. Molina, now a thirty-five-year-old with a ponytail, had been a university student with a major in international relations in the mid-1980s when he became active in the Salvadoran student left. Becoming increasingly committed to the goal of overthrowing El Salvador's repressive government, he forsook his studies to join the revolutionary movement, the FMLN. After the movement's massive urban offensive intended to pressure the government to the negotiating table drew to a close in the fall of 1989, and when the government and paramilitary groups detained and tortured many of the people with whom he had worked for years, Molina left El Salvador.

On the next chair is his countryman Platero, now fifty-seven. When Molina was still a young boy in private school, Platero was finishing his second decade as a government telecommunications employee. His family had longtime allegiance to the government, and he staunchly opposed the guerrilla movement. As the civil war began, small town telecommunications offices, where Platero went to replace workers on vacation, became frequent targets for guerrilla dynamite. Platero joined a notorious paramilitary group responsible for many beatings and killings of suspected guerrillas and "sympathizers," and was trained as an oreja, or "ear," to report any sign of antigovernment activity. He woke one morning to find his family's home plastered with the slogan "Afuera Burguesia Criolla" ("Out with the National Bourgeoisie"). Fearing that he had become an obvious target, he fled to the United States in 1979.[5]

Across the room from Molina and Platero, Maria Aparicio and Angela Sarmiento are also talking. Aparicio refers to her childhood in rural Ecuador as "my hell." Her mother, a farm laborer, incurred so much debt by the time Maria was seven that she had become enslaved to a local hacienda, laboring night and day with animals, in the fields, and in the owners' large home. She pulled Aparicio out of the second grade, never to return to school, and Aparicio began to work around the clock by her mother's side. At fourteen, when her father died, she was sent to cook and clean for a bishop and the nuns who lived with him. They beat her and her mother had to petition a court to free her after two years. She then began work as a live-in maid for a wealthy family in the city of Cuenca, returning home when she had a baby at the age of twenty-three. She was soon back in Cuenca, however, this time doing domestic work for a less well-off family. A single mother, unable to buy food and medicine for her daughter on the wages she earned, she sent the one-year-old girl to live with her mother, and left in 1988 for the long journey to Long Island.

Angela Sarmiento talks about her childhood as a paradise, and about the transition from her life in the Venezuelan city of Maracay to Long Island as "falling from heaven to earth." The daughter of a wealthy landowner, Sarmiento spent twenty years as a classroom teacher and eight years as the principal of a public school before immigrating at the age of forty-six with her husband, a fifty-nine-year-old university professor, and their eleven-year-old daughter in 1989. Their home in Maracay was large, with a beautiful garden and patio. They had servants and three cars. Each year in Venezuela, they saved their money and then spent the two months of school vacation traveling around the United States as tourists, visiting relatives and sightseeing. But strikes at the university had slowed education to a crawl, and wanting to put their daughter through college before they got too old, they uprooted themselves and moved to Uniondale, New York. Here, Angela has now worked for more than a decade in a high school cafeteria; her husband labored as a security guard until his death in 2002.

The Workplace Project membership split along many other axes as well. Members came from over a dozen countries, some of which—like Peru and Ecuador, or Honduras and El Salvador—had recently been at war with each other. They had lived in the United States as little as six weeks or as much as twenty years or more. They had spent lifetimes of work before immigrating in jobs as far-ranging as tenant farmers or truck drivers or teachers or engineers. They were of African, indigenous, or Spanish descent—or, much more often, some "mestizo" blend of the three. The gender division was sharp, with men often immigrating alone while the women came with or soon had children and struggled to bear the triple responsibility of work, home, and childcare. For some who had experienced earlier moves from rural areas to the city or to export processing zones within their country, the journey to the United States was just the latest in a series of migrations. For others, Long Island was the first place they had lived outside the villages where their families had made a home for generations.

If the Workplace Project was going to organize among immigrants from such diverse backgrounds, it would need to work

hard to develop a shared understanding of who the group members were and what they had in common—a sort of narrative
that would explain and critique members' present circumstances
and fuel their collective work to set and achieve goals for change.
But what kind of story could put all these disparate people on
the same page?

Certainly the very similar circumstances in which immigrants
found themselves was a good starting place. Wherever they came
from, whatever they believed, all had left home and landed in
Long Island. Each journey had been different, with the sharpest
divide between those wealthy enough to obtain a legal tourist
visa and enter the country by airplane, and those who had been
forced to travel across the treacherous and increasingly milita-
rized border on foot or in the trunk of a smuggler's car. But the
demands of immigrant life after settlement on Long Island, its
deprivation and its isolation, the endless work, and the relent-
lessly homogenizing lens through which others saw immigrants
—these were shared experiences. Shared, too, was the pernicious
hold of the two-year myth and the dashing of that glittering chi-
mera, the American Dream.

An outside observer might assume that such shared disillusionment would provoke a kind of automatic we're-in-the-
same-boat-now kind of fellowship. Instead, immigrants as often
blamed each other or similarly situated groups (such as Puerto
Ricans or African-Americans) for the problems they faced as they
sought to develop a more profound analysis, and as often felt
paralyzed or helpless as they felt empowered to act. The intensity
of blame of fellow immigrants was particularly striking. Because
it proved impossible to make enough money through formal
work to live and save at the same time, immigrants turned to
making money from fellow immigrants, charging each other for

rides, food, childcare, and housing that in the home country would have been given freely as a part of a reciprocal friendship or family relationship.[6] Immigrants' resulting disillusionment with each other was intense.

Even at the Workplace Project, it was rare to have a discussion in which members did not lament the way that "we, the Hispanics," undercut each other for jobs, make money off of each other, mistreat each other once in possession of a little power, and generally "don't know how to stand together." José Ramirez reflected that "in the United States there are so many Hispanics and no solidarity. If a Hispanic gets to be a boss, he treats other Hispanics like dogs. And I ask myself, how will we ever get ahead?" His sentiment was commonplace. Lilliam Araujo, too, expressed a widely held belief when she lamented that Latino immigrants are "not accustomed to being participatory or to supporting one another, even if they have the same problems. They don't get involved." Despite the churches and the hometown aid associations, the soccer teams and the informal loan pools—all examples of collaboration and mutual support—many Workplace Project members talked about other Latino immigrant workers with resentment and competitiveness, rather than with what might be called solidarity.[7]

Despite these obstacles, Latino immigrant identity came to be an important common theme for the organization. In part this was an identity thrust on the group. In my experience, immigrants identified strongly with their country of origin ("I am Ecuadorian," "I am Salvadoran") and weakly, if at all, with the group label "Latino."[8] But the outside world often saw them as an undifferentiated group. This was true in a negative sense, with generic "Hispanics" often blamed for, say, problems in the schools or overcrowded housing; it was also true more positively, as advocates and supporters characterized the Workplace Project's mission as an "immigrants' rights struggle." Over time, however, Latino immigrant identity became something that the group claimed from within, woven from its members' shared experiences as newcomers in this country and as low-wage workers in and on the fringes of the underground economy.

Taken alone, though, immigrant identity was not enough of an impetus to organize. It described what people had been through and what they continued to suffer and to strive for, but did not offer a clear way out of the morass. It was still fragile, vulnerable to shattering when immigrants blamed each other for their troubles rather than their employers or the broader economic system. It was not enough simply to bring Latino immigrant workers into the same room or even for each to build within himself or herself a sense of agency to act according to a private conception of his or her self-interest. The challenge was to recognize the real differences among participants, and to create a process through which they could talk openly about their conflicts and about their competing assumptions of how the world worked, and from that painful starting point craft a common way of understanding their struggle, a lens through which they could interpret their shared past, their current suffering, and the hope of future change. This group story had to be strong enough not only to unite them at the outset, building on their shared Latino immigrant identity, but to move them into action and keep them together in times of defeat.

One possibility was to turn to a religious framework. Many organizing narratives start with faith traditions: Think of the role of the church in the black civil rights movement, the mass meetings held in churches and the sermons preached to send people off to march in the streets; think of Cesar Chavez and the strong

Catholic streak running through the United Farm Workers, with its fasts and its rebel priests and its pilgrimage marches; think of Dorothy Day and the Catholic Workers. A religious narrative at the Workplace Project might have emphasized both general themes of struggle and the ultimate righteousness of the fight for justice, and the Bible's more specific stories about sojourners and the trials of the exile.[9] Given that many Workplace Project members were deeply religious and understood their own lives in relation to a Christian story, it is worth wondering why the organization did not talk more about God. The answer is quite simple: its first storytellers were a Salvadoran lapsed Catholic and a Jewish atheist with a law degree. To begin by talking about the Lord would have rung false in the ears of those who believed as the two of us did not, never mind its rank instrumentality. Over time, many members and other staff drew on their religious beliefs to support and explain their work with the organization, but this story remained more private than public.

Another possible story would have emphasized a critique of capitalism, a political and economic perspective that argued for class solidarity. To a great extent, the Workplace Project did construct such a story. The thrust of the Workers Course and much of the foundation for the group's work was that immigrant labor was part of a larger system of economic exploitation and needed to be dealt with systemically. The course traced the parallels between the treatment its members experienced on the job and the labor histories of previous waves of immigrants. Building solidarity with other low-wage workers across barriers of race and ethnicity was a consistent goal of the organization, one that it promoted by learning from, supporting, and joining forces with organizations of African-Americans, low-wage white workers, and immigrants of different ethnicities, even as it explored the ways that racism had a particular impact on the exploitation of workers of color. Sporadic membership workshops also discussed questions like the effects of globalization and free trade zones on immigrants' home countries and the role of global economic institutions in provoking people to immigrate.

In the context of a group with such mixed class identity and political beliefs, though, shaping a central story primarily around class was not easy. Members often continued to identify with the class from which they came in their home country, with former school principals and business-owners and engineers retaining a sense of themselves as middle- or upper-class even as they worked here as landscapers and busboys and construction workers. As the contrasting stories above of Juan Carlos Molina and Eduardo Platero illustrate, some members brought with them deeply held political beliefs, often forged indelibly in times of war. Even those who had not fought on one side or the other were often marked by having witnessed fierce repression of those who argued for leftist politics. As Juan Carlos Molina says, reflecting on the reaction of many Workplace Project members to his and others' efforts to inject critical political and economic analysis into the group's debates, "It's a fear of the Project's membership that when you talk about a 'political perspective' you're talking about going against the government . . . Many of the people come from countries—some have suffered at the hands of one side, others at the hands of the other. When they hear this they think that the Project is going to become a red bastion with the face of Che [Guevara, the revolutionary] on its flag."

In the face of these challenges, the Workplace Project talked a little about history, a little about religion, a little about race, and a lot about the economic and political systems of which immigrants were a part. But most of all, it turned to talking about rights. A narrative of rights could not pave over the vast differences. What it could do, however, was to bring people together on a shared project and a shared vision for at least one purpose: grappling with the conditions under which they worked in this country.

This talking took place on several planes: the internal process members went through of telling and understanding their story *for themselves,* and the external processes of relaying that story to others in order to foment change in ways both small and large.[10] The former is essentially a narrative process, a process that reflects (and itself shapes) the identity, values, and ultimate goals of the participants. When it works, it can be transformative: People come to a shared understanding of the common aspects of their experience, one that provides them with a new sense of standing to challenge the suffering they had previously felt most intensely as individuals. The latter is essentially a strategic process.[11] It can take place on a number of levels, from an individual member of the group confronting her employer in an effort to negotiate different working conditions, to a cluster of members demanding a set of rights from their employers and/or from employment agencies, to the group as a whole seeking institutional change. It grows out of the normative framework described in the story, but must build a bridge of power and persuasion between that internal vision and the different economic, political, and social frameworks that must be moved for change to happen. Its success thus depends on a close analysis of the context in which the group is organizing.

This country has a long history of rights talk as the starting point for mobilization and collective action for social change. Rights talk and rights consciousness played critical roles in the early upswelling of the women's suffrage movement during the mid-nineteenth century, and in the antislavery movement and during Reconstruction after the Civil War.[12] Labor organizing, too, has emphasized rights as a call to organizing. Some of this activity bypassed state intervention entirely. In the late nineteenth and early twentieth centuries, for example, workers "legislated" their own rights through union-determined work rules, which they then used as rallying cries in their organizing efforts to require that employers adhere to those rules.[13] Other upswellings of rights talk sought more explicitly to inspire organizing in the face of restrictive official interpretations of rights. William Forbath and James Pope have argued that organized labor in the early decades of the twentieth century had its own constitutional vision, one that saw a worker's right to organize and to strike as essential to emancipation and continued freedom from slavery.[14] This view opposed—and was galvanized by—the vision offered by employers, who argued that the law should protect freedom of contract over all other freedoms. The employers' version was for years broadly accepted by judges, who imposed injunctions on workers when they sought to strike. "Labor's constitution of freedom" (the phrase is Pope's) supported the decades of union activism that set the stage for the negotiation of the rights enshrined in the National Labor Relations Act.[15]

Each new wave of rights talk has drawn on those that came before, creating the galvanizing quality of a demand that was built on the base of a long tradition, and yet pressed for its extension. Labor's vision, for example, drew explicitly on rights rhetoric from the fight against slavery and from Reconstruction.[16] The religious resonance of the message of equal rights so prominent in the antislavery battle—the delivery from bondage into full personhood—would echo down the decades to the 1950s and 1960s, when rights talk once again melded with biblical images to galvanize a new movement for civil rights.[17] As the civil rights movement inspired other identity-based movements, rights talk sparked and fed demands for the extension of existing rights to different groups of people: women, disabled people, gays and lesbians, and so on.[18]

A call for "immigrants' rights" is both consonant and dissonant with this tradition. On the one hand, when immigrants call for respect for their work and recognition of their right to political participation, their claims too are resonant with the overtones of those who have come before. On the other, immigrants—and in particular undocumented immigrants—do not have the same basic political rights in the United States as citizens. This shapes both how they see themselves in relation to rights, and how others respond when they use rights talk.

As an internal narrative, rights as the Workplace Project taught and talked about them did several things. Talk about rights supported a shift in individual identity that was particularly notable in undocumented workers. The life of an undocumented immigrant is lived in the uneasy space where physical presence meets legal denial of that presence. Despite the popular organizing slogan "No human being is illegal," many undocumented immigrant workers assume that their "illegality" extends to all aspects of their experience, that there is no harm that they could suffer that the law would recognize and remedy. This assumption often extends to immigrants who have temporary permission to work, who take the same jobs and are treated in much the same way as their undocumented neighbors.

Many immigrants are unaware that the law covers them. As María Aparicio relates, when after a decade in Long Island she first heard about the Workplace Project, she wondered: "workplace rights—what might those be?" Similarly, when I asked Carmen Lelys Maldonado whether prior to coming to the Workplace Project he had known that he had rights on the job, he replied "I knew I had none. I *knew* I had none." Or they may know they have rights, but believe them irrelevant because they suspect that to file any sort of claim would provoke firing or, worse, deportation. Employers, street rumor, and the media often reinforce the idea that the law does not protect an immigrant who is abused.

Even an immigrant who seeks help has no guarantee that she will find it. As an office worker in El Salvador, Zoila Rodriguez had a keen awareness of her rights, but the confidence that this knowledge gave her vanished when she crossed national and class borders. "In a strange country, where you don't know your rights, where you think you have no rights . . . and you're alone, and there's the language . . . your self-esteem goes all the way down . . . When my boss said something to me I would just hang my head or cry." Rodriguez's sense of no recourse was confirmed one day five years after she immigrated, when she walked into a storefront agency she had noticed on the street and asked whether the law offered her any support in her relationship with the family that employed her as a domestic worker. "The woman there asked me if I had filed my taxes. I told her no. She said, 'If you don't file your income tax declaration, you don't exist. So you have no right to anything.'" Rodriguez resisted: "I told that woman, 'I am here. *I exist.* I buy things, I contribute to this country's economy.'" But the confirmation of her legal nonpresence left Rodriguez paralyzed. She worked for a year under increasingly oppressive and humiliating conditions before asking the question again.

To someone who is constantly told that she has no standing

in this country, talk about rights is particularly powerful.[19] As Patricia Williams reflects about the experience of African-Americans in the United States, "The black experience of anonymity, the estrangement of being without a name, has been one of living in the oblivion of society's inverse, beyond the dimension of any consideration at all. Thus, the experience of rights-assertion has been one of both solidarity and freedom, of empowerment of an internal and very personal sort; it has been a process of finding the self."[20] The power of rights in this sense goes beyond whatever specific benefit the right promises and beyond the question of whether the right is actually enforced or not. For immigrants, it is the jolt of a change in how others see you: If I have rights then the government recognizes me as being here after all. If I have rights then I exist here in a way I did not when I thought I had no rights. More profoundly still, it is a change in how you perceive yourself. Being seen as a person with rights opens the possibility of seeing yourself differently, and then of acting differently—of acting like the sort of person who has rights.[21]

This possibility is an open one. There are a lot of ways "a person who has rights" might act. Zoila Rodriguez illustrates a common progression when she recounts the difference in her reaction to a work problem before and after she joined the Workplace Project. Before she became a member, the family for whom she had worked as an off-the-books live-in childcare provider for five years promised her a raise in an unconventional form: they would put her on the books but pay her income tax for her, and when her rebate check came at the end of the year they would give it to her. Months later, the rebate arrived, but her employers made her sign the check over to them. Zoila complied, saying nothing.

But the following year, after months of involvement with the Workplace Project and a newfound confidence in her rights, Zoila was adamant. She refused to hand over the rebate check to the woman in the couple she worked for when it came. "I told her, no, this is *my* money. I worked for it." She continued to argue with the husband when he came home and told her that she wasn't taking into account the value of what they had given her—such as the car she drove the children around in. "I told him, when I leave the car stays with you. It's your car not mine." In the end, she prevailed, insisting "I've never seen that raise you promised me, and that's not just." She ascribes the difference in her actions to "everything I had learned at the Workplace Project, the workshops I had been in, the documentation [of rights] I had gotten in writing." What is worth noting is that there is no "right to a raise," much less a right to retain your rebate check when your employer has paid your taxes. What Rodriguez stood up for was not a legal right, but what she saw as a question of justice. Knowing her rights, she mustered the self-respect and confidence necessary to confront her employers and hold them to their word in a deal that went beyond the law's promises. Her success bolstered her growing sense of herself as someone who could stand up for herself—and for others.

This is a positive story. But it is also quintessentially an individualistic one: woman learns rights, woman stands up to boss, woman gets a raise (although it is in fact less individual than it sounds, because it was enabled by the group context in which it took place). Indeed, most of the scholarship on rights, identity, and action focuses on this individual level.[22] At the Workplace Project, though, it was not enough for *individual* immigrants to experience a shift in their identity and develop a sense of agency. For those individuals to come together in a group, they had to have a parallel experience of developing a sense of *collective* identity and collective capacity to act. A further question about the Workplace Project's experience with talk about rights, then, is how it related to the organization's goal of forging a membership that could identify the problems they faced as a group, talk about them critically, and develop the capacity to strategize and act as a group to challenge the conditions under which they worked.

The individual shift in identity had its parallel at the group level. Rights were powerful in crafting a shared identity in part because they began with the shared conditions under which all members labored as relatively recent immigrants, but offered an alternative explanation for the discouragement and resentment that immigrants had largely turned on each other in the face of the impossibility of "making it" as they had imagined they would before they emigrated. If the American Dream had proven a disappointment, as it did for almost everyone, if the first years in this country came and went and (as the Workplace Project landscaper joke went) the closest anyone got to picking the gold that grew on trees was raking the leaves that fell incessantly on suburban lawns, who was to blame, and what was to be done?

For the workers, the idea that employers were violating the laws of their own country when they paid pitiful wages and worked their employees to the bone was the first step in identifying what they had lived through as a problem, rather than an inevitable condition of immigrant work. The idea that employers were *supposed* to be acting differently—that in paying so little and demanding so much they were ignoring a set of established norms, codified as rights—suggested a less individualized, more systemic explanation of the problems immigrants faced in trying to earn enough money to support themselves and their families, and offered a different, outward target for their resentment. If the problem was systemic, immigrants would need to respond in kind. In the discussions that grew from the organization's critical approach to talking about rights, Workplace Project members imagined the forms group unity and action to build power might take—and simultaneously reinforced a sense of group identity through their deliberations.

Beyond their interpretive value, rights gave the story forward momentum. In a very practical sense, if rights existed, and they were being violated, and those violations explained some of the organization's members' past suffering, then the group had its mission in hand. Furthermore, rights stood for the possibility of government support in a context where government was otherwise notably absent, in an underground economy ruled by the market and by personal relationships in a situation of unmitigated power imbalance.[23]

The Workplace Project's way of talking about rights opened out onto an imaginative process as well. In their book *Minding the Law,* Tony Amsterdam and Jerome Bruner describe a group's imagining of "possible worlds" as essential to the process of social change. They talk about the importance in all cultures of "contests for control over conceptions of reality. In any culture," they note, "there are both canonical versions of how things really are and should be and countervailing visions about what is alternatively possible." As a first step, they argue that "to replace or reconstruct the familiar world, you must first defamiliarize what you would replace—make what was familiar or obvious seem strange again."[24]

The Workplace Project's way of talking about reality, law, and justice is a part of this defamiliarization process. It begins by challenging the idea that law is an accurate representation of "the way things should be," replacing it with a description of participants' actual lived reality, a description that often exposes the way legal protections fail. It calls into question the idea that the laws that we have are "natural" background rules for how we act, bringing the way law itself is politically constructed into the foreground. Approaching rights in this way reveals them as historically and politically contingent choices that judges and legislators have made, rather than accurate representations of reality, incarnations of absolute principles, or markers of the just. And it opens the door to a fuller discussion of the alternative possibilities, ones that take power and politics into account. As Patricia Williams has noted, this process can create a narrative of equality, a story about what human beings are entitled to that stands in contrast to participants' actual lives and that raises both their expectations and their determination to win change.[25] By asking its members to start by imagining the world in which they want to live, in which they deserve to live, a group can free itself if only for a moment from the daily grip of poverty and the limitations of law. In the space created by this freedom, they can build their own vision of the solutions to the problems that they face.

It is the first night of a new semester of the Workers Course in the middle of winter. The large meeting room at the center of the Workplace Project has been transformed into a classroom, a brightly lit cell suspended between the dark cold outside and the noisy warmth of the Project's work that continues on the other side of the doorway. The room is full beyond capacity, forty immigrants sitting and standing, pressing up against the table bearing coffee and sweet Salvadoran bread. Despite the exhaustion of many participants, who have already worked ten- or twelve-hour days on top of their family responsibilities by the time they arrive, the feeling inside the classroom is focused, intent.

At the request of the teacher, the men and women stand up one by one, introducing themselves by saying their name and home country and how long they have been in the United States, and listing the work they have done since arriving here. The board fills up quickly with jobs: babysitter, landscaper, dishwasher, construction, housecleaner, mechanic, factory worker, their accumulated weight a testimony to years of hard labor. *Let's talk about wages,* the teacher says. *What do people earn for each of these jobs?* "People? It depends on what people," says one woman. "Right," says a short muscled man. "White people in unions make $20 an hour or more for construction work. I got paid $6 an hour for the drywall job I did last week." Starting, then, with construction, the teacher moves with the class through each occupation on the board, debating and deciding on the range of wages paid for each, noting on a separate list the factors the class suggests will determine what a worker earns in that range: the number of other workers looking for jobs, the presence of unions, the color of the worker's skin, her related experience, her ability to speak English, whether or not she has legal documentation, and so on. That list is the starting point for a conversation on wages as a product of power—and on how workers might be able to build more power and thus earn higher wages.

It is at this point that the teacher brings up the "minimum wage." With the prior discussion as a backdrop, the minimum wage—$4.75 at the time—is easy to see as a point on a continuum that represents not some normative "just wage" but the product of the relative power of business and labor interests in the political process at a particular point in time. The class talks about the minimum wage, about overtime wages, about how to calculate if you have been cheated, and about the different ways to enforce the law, from court to the Department of Labor to a picket. For some workers this is new and useful information. For others, the minimum is set too low to be much help. The teacher points this out but does not try to resolve it. The threads in this discussion—the concrete grounding in participants' reality, the discussion of power, the presentation of practical information about rights coupled with recognition of those rights' political origins and limited reach—are the raw materials for participants' future work as members of the Workplace Project.

Shaping organizing around rights is not without risk. So far I have used the Workplace Project's experience as a counterpoint to those who claim that rights inevitably derail collective action. I hope I have convincingly illustrated that they do not, at least on the level of an interpretive narrative that is internal to the group. But matters become more complex when we turn to the question of the sorts of strategies and external narratives, or stories told to the public, that rights talk generates. If rights give an internal narrative forward momentum, what kind of road do they plot out of the quagmire?

For all their potential connection to social change, rights talk may also lead to strategies that are in tension with transformative struggles. As I have noted, one danger is that talk about rights will translate to an emphasis on vindicating individual rights. Where the group is able to maintain a collective focus, it is still worth wondering whether the strategies that it develops will tend to emphasize rights enforcement over more ambitious or creative goals, when initial discussions about injustice have leaned heavily on rights. Do people who talk a lot about rights come to think only in terms of rights—"rights violations" as the blanket explanation for what has gone wrong; "rights enforcement" as the blanket solution?[26]

The Workplace Project's experience suggests that the answer will depend to a large extent on the setting in which the rights talk takes place and the approach used. The tendency of a rights-based approach to lead to a fixation on individual rights claims was most obvious in the legal clinic, where the tension between individual case resolution and collective action created a dynamic of constant conflict that I explore in the next chapter. In the Workers Course, and in discussions about rights within the organization, however, the Workplace Project's method of talking about rights eased some of the pull toward individualization. Most members unquestionably came in with an individual view of rights. Individual rights were the starting point for the workers who took the course in exchange for the legal clinic's support in resolving their individual cases. In the class, workers' desire to vindicate their individual rights consistently accompanied—and sometimes restrained—any more aspirational conversation about systemic justice. But the group transcended the individual level at the moments when it used rights as a way to ask questions about participants' shared reality, about politics and about power.

Before I move on to consider whether a similar phenomenon was at work with regard to enforcement, it is worth pausing to question my intimation that an enforcement focus is necessarily a problem. In the setting in which the Workplace Project's members labored, successful rights enforcement strategies would have been no small achievement. In a very practical sense, if rights exist, and they are being violated, and those violations explain some of the organization's members' suffering, then a fight for rights enforcement is a logical and worthwhile next step. For those Workplace Project members whose basic rights were disregarded daily, who were paid $3.00 an hour and worked around the clock in dangerous conditions, achieving enforcement of laws on the books would have represented a meaningful improvement in wages and working conditions. Enforcement of existing laws thus remains a critically important role for any group working in the underground economy, rather than representing a flaw in strategy produced by using rights as a starting point. Furthermore, whether enshrined in a negotiated agreement, a judge's ruling, or a law, new victories won through organizing always require further organizing to make sure that they do not wither in the implementation stage.[27] This kind of enforcement work is a predictable and necessary part of a cycle of collective action.

If enforcement had been the *sole* direction of the Workplace Project's approach, however, it would indeed have been problematic in the context of immigrant work in Long Island. As I have noted, employers' disregard for the law was only a symptom of the problems of the underground economy, not a cause. Complicating matters further, when Workplace Project members sought the enforcement of existing laws they risked reinforcing the tendency among members of the public to consider whatever protections were on the books as a marker of reasonableness (a tendency manifested in the common question "Well, is she being paid minimum wage?" as the litmus test for whether a worker was adequately compensated). If they then sought to win higher wages and better working conditions in the political arena by talking about rights, they had to overcome the barrier they had strengthened. And then there were the many immigrants who worked for employers who complied, at least in part, with basic workplace laws. The problem for them—and, eventually, for all workers—was the inadequacy of existing rights. To attempt only to enforce laws on the book would thus have been to concede far too much.[28]

At the Workplace Project, then, it remains important to ask the question of whether the group became irretrievably mired in enforcement strategies as a product of its initial emphasis on rights. Certainly much of the Project's work, from the legal clinic to the passage of the Unpaid Wages Prohibition Act, took place with the goal of enforcing existing laws. But the group's approach to rights also supported consideration of systemic explanations for problems and a wide variety of solutions beyond rights enforcement. The Workplace Project proved, in other words, able to devote some of its collective imagination to enforcement strategies without becoming consumed by them. The conversation about wages begun in the session I described above flowed into later conversations in membership meetings and committees about whether the minimum wage was adequate to meet workers' needs. In many instances, the Project membership generated and carried out ideas for solutions that put in place standards that went beyond rights on the books (as with the day labor wage organizing campaign), or sidestepped a state enforcement approach entirely (as with the development of cooperative businesses). Although the Unpaid Wages Prohibition Act was purely an effort to enforce existing laws, it was conceived as one prong of a campaign that had winning higher wages as its other goal.

The Workplace Project's method of talking about rights facilitated this process of opening out. The Project used its members' own experiences, needs, and sense of justice as a measuring stick rather than the standards set by law; focused on the limitations of rights on the books as well as their benefits; and integrated talk about rights with talk about political and economic power. By discussing together what they had lived through and observed as immigrant workers, the group found that rights were broadly unenforced. By exploring what they felt they needed to live decent lives, they concluded that, even if respected, current rights would be inadequate to ensure safe work with adequate pay to provide a family with food and shelter and medical care and childcare. To feel that you had the *right* to a decent life, to have come to that feeling in the context of the Workplace Project, and to believe that work together with others in the Project offered you the best hope of realizing them, forged a powerful sense of shared possibility and determination that was able, at times, to transcend its ties to rights on the books.[29]

Even when a group talks intensively about rights internally, the "story" that participants come to tell the public about the possible world they see, a world that represents their vision of the just, does not *have* to be based on law. But discussion that begins with rights clearly encourages a group to understand its vision of justice in a particular way. A process that begins with the observation that current laws are inadequate leans strongly toward a new vision expressed in terms of an alternative scheme of rights. And rights can make for powerful rhetoric. When you talk about rights—as opposed to "needs" or "moral responsibilities" or "biblical guarantees"—you speak a language that resonates across our culture. Rights have the stamp of legitimacy, of rules that must be obeyed by all, unlike personal morality or religious beliefs. If something is your right, then others should respect it. If something is your right, the state should guarantee it and defend it against encroachers.

Critically important for immigrant workers, talking about rights is a way of both demanding and demonstrating inclusion within the broader community. Martha Minow argues, "By invoking rights, an individual or group claims the attention of the larger community and its authorities. At the same time, this claim acknowledges the claimant's membership in the larger group, her participation in its traditions, and her observation of its forms . . . Those who exercise rights signal and strengthen their relationship to a community. Those who are claiming rights implicitly agree to abide by the community's response, and to accord similar regard to the claims of others."[30] Rights talk is useful in communicating with a broader public not just for the demands it does make, but for those it does not. As sociologist Francesca Polletta notes, "We usually think of rights as claims backed up by the force of law—or *potentially* done so. This allows for innovation but not wild invention. What makes legal rights claims powerful is the conjunction of moral principle and the force of the state."[31] Basic substantive laws mark a political consensus at a particular time about what constituted minimal justice. Violations of those laws then become something that the public and politicians can be mobilized around.

Thinking in terms of rights further implies some limitation on the imagination—a limitation that Bruner and Amsterdam argue is not only not harmful, but wholly necessary. Constraints, they argue, are as important as freedom. And rights talk operates within a public framework of recognized constraints.[32] In this sense, rights talk is powerful *because* it is constrained. The limits within which it operates make it familiar, allowing us to relate this claim to others made in the past.

In other ways, though, those same constraints on how far the discourse can stretch, and on who has the power to decide about whether a new claim will be enacted and enforced, limit how innovative a group can be within the rubric of a rights narrative. When the group presents its justice claims to the outside world as a narrative of rights, it moves onto terrain quite different from its internal discussions, terrain on which it can no longer control the meaning of the story it offers up. As Martha Minow points out, "The rhetoric of rights draws those who use it inside the community, and urges the community to pay attention to the individual claimants, but underscores the power of the established order to respond or withhold response to the individuals' claims."[33] The canon of rights claims can exclude the alternative formulations of rights that the group has developed, imposing the din of too many echoes of past claims, crowding out the new meanings the group proposes. The group may find that the freedom it found internally to shape the way a rights claim resonates has evaporated—or that its alternative understanding of what rights should be is trumped by another group's formulation. In the early labor organizing examples I offered above, for example, workers were committed to the belief that the right to collective action on the job was a right fundamental to human freedom. But when they sought to act on that belief in the workplace, they encountered employers' opposing claim to a property right in their labor. For many decades, courts flatly rejected the workers' interpretation of rights and validated the employers' version through injunctions on strikes.[34]

A group that seeks to advance its new understanding of rights publicly also risks becoming mired in an endless round of court and legislative battles to win those rights, turned toward the state as the only possible source of victory. None of these concerns obviates what is useful about rights talk—or about litigation and legislative change. They coexist with it. Elizabeth Schneider has used the phrase "the dialectic of rights" to capture this perpetual sense of interaction between positive and negative possibilities that rights work generates.[35] Finally, the constraints generated by rights talk can be detrimental in other ways as well. An argument about rights may begin broadly, but when it is translated to a program or policy, the question of *rights for whom?* becomes paramount. The same categories that have been so helpful in generating a sense of group identity can become walls that protect the right for that limited group at the cost of excluding others.

The Workplace Project recognized the force of rights in public debate, and spoke amply about rights and in terms of rights in almost all of its efforts for change. And yet if the problems that rights talk as an internal narrative pose were largely conquered by the Workplace Project's critical approach to teaching about rights, the limitations of external rights talk were much harder to overcome. When Workplace Project members talked about rights among themselves, they could create their own idiom. But when the Project ventured into the external political arena, the ways of talking about rights and the meanings rights held could only be suggested by the Project, not controlled.[36] In the outside world, there are others who will claim rights of their own that stand in opposition to the rights you seek, and who will offer opposing interpretations of the rights you have so carefully crafted. Furthermore, undocumented immigrants were easily—if inaccurately—dismissed as outside the realm of those entitled to invoke rights in the United States. Even when the group surmounted the hurdle of convincing those it sought to sway that immigrants were entitled to protection of the laws, it faced the challenge of shifting the public understanding of "the just," in order to create new laws that reflected that justice.

Rights were an important part of the way the Workplace Project staff talked with immigrants and the way that members talked with staff and each other, but they were only one part. It was not talk about rights alone that moved people toward a sense of group identity, toward belief in the possibility of change, and into collective action. No class on rights, no matter how carefully crafted, can alone be the vehicle that takes people from atomized passivity to organized movement. In a globalized world, the question of what to do about the problems immigrant workers face necessarily involves a broadening spectrum of perspectives, from the microcosm of the workplace, to the local labor market, through the state, national, and international levels. It involves multiple lenses, critiques of the workings of power and race and economics and politics.

The Workers Course worked as a part of the overall Workplace Project strategy because it was tailored to the economic and political context in which it was set, a context in which rights resonated; and because it was structured as a part of an institution with a strong organizing culture and a framework to support the move from rights talk to collective action. Given that its role was a supporting one, what made the Workplace Project's way of talking about rights effective in enabling the creation of a group rather than individual relationship to rights, of an active and fluid response rather than a passive and restricted one?

At its best, the organization approached rights not as "facts to be learned" but as "data to be analyzed"—understood as products of specific political times and constellations of power, discussed in relation to workers' own experiences, and considered as potential targets for change. The Workplace Project's approach to talk about rights thus started with the individual but soon led to discussion of group strategies to tackle systemic problems. Talk about rights moved toward work only to enforce minimum substantive rights when the context made such work meaningful. Even so, the organization's approach was collective and often unconventional. Talk about rights also transcended discussion of substantive rights on the books to become a springboard to developing the group's vision of justice—and then to acting on strategies to achieve that vision.

Through this process, Workplace Project members developed a new consciousness of several specific things—of how immigrant workers fit into the much larger economic system, of how widespread the abuse they faced was, of the need to build power in order to make change, of how others had done and were doing so. The result, for many participants, was the shaping of a new element of their identity, a sense that the term "immigrant workers" not only described the fact of their exile and their labor but represented a fuller story about themselves, a story that linked them to other immigrants and to other workers, a story that involved membership in the Workplace Project and implied a commitment to action. This consciousness and identity deepened as members began to participate actively in organizing work, and provided them with some sustenance through that work's inevitable hard times. Yet talk about rights had more complex and sometimes less effective results when members carried it to the outside world.

5

A LEGAL CLINIC AND ORGANIZING

If rights *talk* can support people as they dream—and act—beyond the limits of current law, it makes sense to talk about rights as a part of an organizing effort. But what about rights *enforcement*, traditionally understood as the plodding process of pursuing a case through the courts or a government agency? Such legal claims tend to be deeply individual, dependent on a lawyer as an intermediary, tightly scripted in terms of how the "client" can behave and what she can demand, and limited in outcome to the law's definition of justice. Much of this is antithetical to organizing's belief in self-reliance and collective action. It would seem that offering members legal representation to enforce individual rights would have little positive role to play in organizing.

And yet, under some conditions a legal clinic can be shaped to work in tandem with an organizing effort, to serve collective goals even as it vindicates individual rights. In the process of helping people in the community solve the kinds of pressing individual problems that a longer-term collective approach may not reach, a legal clinic draws to the organization new people who might otherwise never have come to its door. If the clinic provides effective help in a respectful way, and does a good job of explaining the link between individual issues and the systemic problem of which they are symptoms, some people who come in that way may consider staying to become involved in the organization's collective strategies for change. The group's reputation in the community as a trustworthy and committed organization will grow. And the group will gain invaluable information about the range of problems community members face.

All is not so simple, of course. When a legal clinic seeks to further the goals of an organizing effort as well as of its individual clients, there are always tensions. Some grow from the contrast between individual legal representation, with its emphasis on a lawyer's winning the case for the client, and collective action, with its focus on a community working together to resolve its collective problems. Much can go astray in the attempt to make a single claim bear the burden of these two very different sets of expectations. Other tensions, easier to avoid with forewarning, arise from missteps in the planning of the clinic or the organizing effort or the amalgam of the two.

It is Monday, clinic day at the Workplace Project in the mid-1990s. In the large and sunny meeting room, clusters of people gather around mismatched tables. At one, a small group of women tell a volunteer law student how each was told to "put a plug in it" when she asked to use the bathroom at the factory where they worked. At another, a day laborer, knit cap pulled down over his head and two-year-old son on his knee, bends over a small notepad on which he has recorded the days he worked for a man in a blue truck and the days he was paid—or, more often, stiffed. He explains his notation system to the Project member who sits at his side holding a calculator. At a third table, a woman in her twenties holds her mother's hand as the older woman, in evident pain, explains to another organizer how she was forced to clean up chemical spills with no protective gloves while working as a janitor at a cosmetic company.

Intermittently, volunteers and members and organizers rise to look for the lawyer and other organizers around the office. Here the conversation draws on collective memory: "Did we report that factory to the Department of Labor last year? "Is this the same guy in the blue truck that didn't pay Wilfredo—what happened when we picketed him?" "What happened with the other chemical case that we turned in to OSHA?" And, as other staff and members and volunteers are drawn into the discussions at the tables, memory moves toward strategy. "Can you get other workers to come to a meeting?" "We can ask Project members to join you to visit that employer and demand that the owner pay you." "You should get workers' compensation. But here's how to get a doctor to take care of you first." Then a refrain, rising from each of the tables at some point, from the organizer and the volunteer and the member: "If we support you in your case, we will ask you to support us in fighting for better working conditions for others."

Is this a legal aid center? Is it a union? What exactly is being offered, and what asked in return? The answer is complicated. The workers come for help. And the clinic is there to help them. But it is also there as a way to introduce them to the Workplace Project, a place that strives to be "a center of immigrant workers, not a lawyer's office," and to draw them into its work. These are not necessarily confluent goals. Indeed, they feel contradictory: the one seeking to resolve problems quickly for workers, the other insisting that there are no quick solutions, that workers must act together to resolve problems for themselves.

The Workplace Project had a legal clinic before it had a name. I started offering legal services for labor issues during my first weeks on Long Island as a way of filling a need in the community and of learning more about the problems immigrants faced on the job. As those initial explorations coalesced into an independent center with a focus on organizing, the legal clinic continued to seem relevant. A clinic that offered assistance with wage claims and other violations of workers' rights would clearly be useful to immigrants in and of itself. Many employers of immigrants violated wage and labor laws with impunity. The traditional mechanisms for redress—government agencies, unions, social services—were not addressing the problem.

Such a clinic's services would be of greatest interest to those workers the Workplace Project most wanted to draw in: low-wage Latino immigrants with active complaints about their treatment on the job. Presumably, some number of those workers would be interested in organizing. The defense of immigrant workers' rights through the clinic promised to launch an opening salvo toward exploitive employers, announcing that immigrants would no longer tolerate unpaid wages and dangerous working conditions. Finally, such a clinic held out the promise of amassing information about what was happening in workplaces, thus providing critical data to inform future campaigns.

And so, a more formal clinic took shape, open for drop-in intake on Mondays. Workers came in and were seen as they arrived by a lawyer or by law student or community volunteer counselors. The workers described their problem; the counselors informed them about their legal rights and, with the support of the supervising attorney, described the range of legal options for redress. If possible, the case was taken; if not (usually because of case overload) the workers received self-help advice and referral information. Once a case was accepted, the Workplace Project volunteers and staff worked with the client and employer to negotiate a solution. If negotiation failed, staff members would take the case to court or to the appropriate administrative agency.

Consider a typical case: It is 11:00 A.M. on a Monday, late November 1993. The CARECEN receptionist sticks her head in my office—a man is in the waiting room, and he wants to see me about a problem on the job. My hours are punctuated by these arrivals, workers I have never met coming in with bandaged hands, or fired hours before, or anxious about a payday that never came. I go to get the man, and find him sitting tensely, folding a flier for an upcoming party into ever smaller squares. In my office he tells me what has become an achingly familiar story: Hired late in the season, he had worked for a landscaping company for two months. At first he had been paid regularly, a cash envelope containing $6 for every hour worked handed over by the foreman on Friday. But for the past three weeks he has been given nothing but promises. Finally, this morning, he was fired. He is owed—and here he pulls out a moist scrap of paper from the wallet he keeps in his back pocket and consults it—$672.

I write down what he tells me, gathering all the information I will need to make the claim. I tell him the law supports his claim to the wages, even though, as he has informed me, he is undocumented. I promise to call his employer, write a letter if there is no response, and to look into other avenues—perhaps small claims court, perhaps the Department of Labor—if necessary. He has no phone, so I ask him to call me from a pay phone or to drop by in two days to see how things went. He thanks me and leaves.

A few weeks later, he is a much happier man. I had reached the employer, and the threat of going to the government had been enough to induce him to scrape together the money. After several missed meetings, the employer finally comes forward with the cash. The worker gets his money. He tells me, "I feel so much better. Now I know if I have a problem at work, I can come to you and you can take care of it." He tells friends and neighbors what happened. Over the following months, some of them also come in to the clinic seeking help.

And so it goes, with minor or major variations—the worker was hurt or sexually harassed, she was paid on time but less than minimum wage, four workers came forward instead of one, the employer did not respond to my calls and had to be taken to court. It was sometimes more difficult to prevail than in this landscaping case, and even a formal victory in a court or administrative agency often did not lead to payment. But the legal clinic had some clear advantages for workers and for the organization. When workers' problems were seen from an individual perspective and in a short time frame, legal representation was often successful. Five hundred and fifty workers passed through the clinic's doors in its first two years, and the Workplace Project recovered over $120,000 on behalf of more than a hundred of them.[1] As those numbers illustrate, in certain cases legal services were the swiftest and least costly way to vindicate a worker's rights. Where few workers were involved in the dispute or where the employer was not responsive to low-cost public pressure, such as pickets or a media campaign; where workers were denied unemployment benefits; where a worker was injured on the job but did not receive workers' compensation, individual representation was almost always the fastest, if not the only, way to solve the problem. The Workplace Project benefited as well. Many immigrants came to trust the organization in the process of resolving their cases. They talked to friends and neighbors about the help they had received and those who heard often came in as well. The group developed a strong reputation in the community. A few workers began hanging around to see if they could help others; a few became curious about rights and work and change in the broad sense.

And yet the clinic was also providing a crash course in what could go wrong in the melding of legal services and organizing. There were limitations on what the law could do. In a number of cases, legal services alone were often not enough even to achieve short-term victories. A lawyer alone often could not collect the money a judge determined an employer owed a worker, or force the state Department of Labor to do its job on behalf of immigrant workers. The clinic seemed even weaker measured against the organization's long-term goal of improving wages and working conditions in Long Island's suburban sweatshops. A number of employers proved to be repeat offenders who did not consider one experience of being forced to comply with the law's minimal penalties a deterrent to future violations. And then there were the ways that the clinic seemed to be working *against* the possibility of collective action.

The light filters through the dusty windows of the rabbi's study in the old Hempstead synagogue where Workplace Project legal intern Rhina Ramos and her then-husband live and work as caretakers. It is autumn 1994. Ramos, Omar Henriquez, and I have retreated to the synagogue to talk through the thickening tension that we are feeling between us and in the work as we try valiantly to run the legal clinic and the organizing efforts as parallel "programs" of the Workplace Project.

"The legal clinic undermines everything I'm trying to do as an organizer," says Henriquez, frustration evident in the tightness of his jaw and in his body, half turned away from the table where we sit. "People come, win their cases, and leave. Everybody thinks this place is a lawyer's office. It's no good to have a clinic that attracts people if it doesn't keep them around, if it teaches them only that they should look for us again the next time they have a problem." Ramos is young and new to this sort of conversation, but she has deeply held feelings about the clinic, motivated by her religious beliefs, by her capacity for empathy, and by her growing abilities as an advocate. Ramos struggles visibly with Henriquez's perspective, with the idea that the clinic should be measured not by the immediate relief it offers workers but by whether they remain with the organization. Speaking quietly, she says, "Immigrant workers really need the help we are offering. If we don't do this work, there is no one else who will. And if we are going to say that we help people, we have to be sincere in our efforts to help them, do a good and honest job." After a time, she adds: "Why are people going to trust us if we don't offer them concrete help? Will workers come in at all if we have no legal clinic?"

I bring up the problem that some individual cases have actively impeded our ability to do effective organizing work. "Remember the busboy who came to the clinic after being paid less than the minimum wage for years? We asked him to find out if other busboys at the restaurant had been underpaid for years, the way he was. When he came back and said that no one wanted to come forward, we took his case. And negotiated for a decent amount of money, remember? Five thousand dollars. But the boss demanded a confidentiality agreement, and the busboy agreed. So he took his money, and left the restaurant, and neither he nor we could tell the other workers about it. And they are still being paid less than the minimum wage." Henriquez mutters, ". . . and we never saw him again either."

Over the next few hours, we develop a consensus about the core conflicts we are facing. For the clinic to draw in new workers and build trust in the community for the organization, it was critical that it be effective in resolving cases and that it publicize its victories widely. It was furthermore not clear that workers would come to the organization if it did not offer them something concrete that they needed. But for all its usefulness both to the organization and to workers, the clinic had a complicated impact on the group's organizing efforts.

It was increasingly evident that the successful provision of legal services in the employment context often coopted potential leaders. The workers who brought their problems to the legal clinic were at the very least determined to find redress for their own problems. At best, they were leaders in their workplaces. They had figured out who could help them and had taken the risk of coming forward. Often, these individuals were in a position to provide critical leadership for a future organizing campaign. Yet once the clinic won their lawsuit and they received their money, these workers frequently left to find other jobs (if they had not already been fired). The rest of the workers, who would have benefited from their leadership had they stayed, were left to suffer. Such workers also rarely remained active in the Workplace Project after their cases were resolved. By "paying off" the bravest and most determined workers with a settlement or an award, the Workplace Project's legal program was unwittingly playing the role of the employer who decapitates an organizing effort by making a deal with its leaders.

Even when the clinic staff and volunteers were successful in brainstorming organizing solutions with the worker or the group, workers often preferred litigation to carrying out these creative strategies involving group action. It is easy to understand why. Organizing as an immigrant worker is a frightening and risky proposition. For workers from countries such as El Salvador who have seen worker organizing result in brutal repression, traditional legal services may be the most appealing alternative.[2] In the United States, the chances that the worker will lose her job as a result of organizing are high, the protections are low, and the payoff is unpredictable at best. Finding a lawyer to resolve the problem presents the least risk and the biggest possible benefit. If the worker wins her lawsuit, she reaps the reward; if she loses, at least she has not gone out on a fragile limb. Finally, organizing takes a considerable commitment of time, time which most immigrants do not feel they have.

Finally, for the Workplace Project to be known as a place where lawyers won cases for workers created a service-oriented, "agency" public image for the organization, one at odds with its goal of becoming known as an organizing center. And the more effectively a clinic lawyer worked on a worker's behalf, the more her efforts deepened the worker's reliance on a professional's support and the more the result undermined the organization's message that long-term change required immigrants to work collectively to resolve their own problems. The worker who benefits from the legal action has not learned the skills that she will need to fight back the next time she is exploited; instead, she has learned that she should seek out a lawyer to solve her problems. The entrenched societal belief that a lawyer, doctor, or accountant knows how to solve problems better than the layperson also encourages this response.

And yet the simple solution to the challenges posed by the first version of the Workplace Project clinic—eliminating lawyers to eliminate the dependence—seems naive. As the workers who came to the clinic recognized, a lawyer's expertise can be uniquely useful in solving some kinds of problems. And there are real questions about how much of what a lawyer offers can in fact be reproduced by an individual worker even once that worker is aware of his or her rights. Combined with the clear need for a clinic such as ours and our recognition of the value of the clinic in attracting new workers to the organization, these questions acted as a counter-pull whenever we thought of eliminating the legal clinic entirely.

A related factor that we did not discuss at the time, but about which I have come to think a great deal since, was that many of the workers who frustrated us by failing to stay with the Project to organize were simply behaving rationally in response to their objective reality. Most waited until they were fired or quit before coming into the clinic with their claims. By the time they encountered the Workplace Project, they thus no longer had roots in a workplace where they could use a legal clinic victory as a steppingstone to broader organizing. Although the Project's definition of organizing was not tied to a particular workplace, it had little concrete to offer workers by way of an alternate framework that could explain in any but the most general, long-run terms how fired workers could hope to benefit by the group's broader campaigns. Furthermore, the wages that the Workplace Project recovered through the first two incarnations of its legal clinic consistently represented more money than its systemic organizing was likely to put in any worker's hands in the near future. As a result, the Project found itself in the perverse position of trying to persuade workers who had been successfully represented by the clinic that what they had just observed about the efficacy of lawyers was untrue, or at least not as true as the efficacy of collective action—with all evidence being to the contrary.

We had begun, then, with the intuition that the moment when a person faces a legal violation that reflects a larger systemic problem is a moment ripe for organizing; a clinic is attractive because it draws in potential members just at that juncture. But the legal clinic was foundering on the essential contradiction that the initial intuition conceals. Although the need for legal help and a desire to organize logically *could* arise at the same time, in practice the provision of legal help tended to obviate any perception of the need to organize, rather than encourage it. Once a lawyer solved the immediate problem the person had little incentive to consider longer-term organizing solutions. And the next time he had a problem, he returned for the lawyer to take care of it for him. In the bluntest terms, a successful experience with legal services taught the worker nothing more than reliance on legal services. At the same time, recognizing what lawyers can offer to immigrant workers, we were not ready to declare defeat in our effort to link law and organizing. Legal services attracted significant numbers of people to the *organization;* the question was what more work was needed for them to begin *organizing.* What approach might build a bridge that workers could cross from getting help through the clinic to participating in the organization and its collective efforts to make change?

A week later, on a gray and windy day, Ramos, Henriquez, and

I return to the same room. During that meeting, and several
more over the next month, we develop a rough plan to weave our
legal clinic into the fabric of our organizing. We decide that if we
ask people to take the Workers Course in exchange for legal services, we will increase the likelihood that the clinic will be a
bridge as well as a draw. In this sense legal services will become
the Project's half of a bargain in which a worker "pays back" in
time what she receives in legal representation. Equally important, we decide to incorporate organizing and self-help into our
legal approaches to the problems people bring to the clinic
where organizing and self-help are appropriate, because we hope
that doing so will make case resolution more effective, because it
will introduce people to the practice of organizing, and because
it seems likely to reduce the dissonance between a clinic where
the lawyer does everything for people and organizing, where people do things together for each other. In this sense we will try to
make the experience of getting help through the legal clinic itself a source of changed consciousness about the need for organizing and of new confidence about the possibility of achieving
change through collective action, as well as an encounter that
embodies the respect and dignity that the Project is organizing
to achieve for immigrant workers more broadly. In both conceptions, the legal clinic is the first step on the Project's "bridge" to
active participation in organizing. We present the plan to the
embryonic board, and its members approve it without serious
discussion.

The basic structure of the new clinic worked like this. An immigrant who came in with a problem on the job first met with a

Project organizer. The organizer described the Workplace Project as an organization of workers, run by the membership and dedicated to collective action, in contrast to a legal services center. The organizer also explained that, although the Workplace Project would readily provide free legal counseling, for actual services the "client" must commit to giving back to the organization. The organizer then provided an overview of the Project's programs and gave examples of ways in which the worker could participate, culminating with the Workers Course.

Workers responded to this approach in a variety of ways. Some accepted it, but others offered to pay the center to take their cases, believing that the organizer was asking them to participate in the organization because he thought they could not afford the lawyer's services. Nevertheless, in the end, few workers balked at this commitment. Only about one in ten workers chose the "counseling" alternative, rather than choosing to participate in the organization, possibly because the requirements were not particularly onerous. Another possibility is that workers felt they had no choice but to commit. Other workers agreed initially and then did not comply, if their case was resolved by the time they were required to fulfill their responsibilities to the Project.

After the orientation, the worker met with a counselor. If the problem was a simple question—for example, do I qualify for unemployment benefits or workers' compensation?—the counselor, in consultation with the Project's lawyer, helped the worker figure out the answer. If the problem was more complex, the counselor, joined by the organizer and often the lawyer, discussed the problem with the worker. The group talked about general conditions at the workplace, the number of workers involved, and past efforts to improve conditions. The team explained the relevant

law to the worker, and described how the organization incorporated organizing into its problem-solving when organizing
could increase the chances of victory. Some cases, such as denials
of unemployment benefits, did not involve collective action, although Ramos for two years trained such workers in self-repre-
sentation and established a buddy system for workers who had
been through the process to accompany new claimants to hearings. But other cases—largely wage claims—routinely did. At this
point, the worker had to decide if she was willing to fight collectively for better working conditions. If she was, the Project's staff
asked her to return later with other workers who had the same
problem, if there were any, so that the group could strategize
and decide whether and how they wanted to take action. When
groups of workers were involved, a series of meetings often took
place.

When it became clear that legal services were going to be a
part of the strategy, the worker or workers were asked to sign a
contract. Through the contract, the Workplace Project committed to providing legal support on a particular issue. In exchange,
in addition to paying a $20 retainer and agreeing to a 7 percent
contingency fee, the worker committed to participating actively
in her own case—gathering information, finding and interviewing witnesses, preparing cross-examination questions, playing
the role of the employer in mock negotiations or trials, and preparing the first draft of an affidavit or complaint—and in the organization. As a condition of receiving legal services, the worker
had to agree to take the Workers Course, or if that was not possible to participate in the Project's committees and campaigns in
some other way. Workers for whom the participation requirements imposed an undue hardship—those with jobs that conflicted with the course, those with no access to transportation,

those with disabilities or sick children or who faced domestic violence—were simply given assistance. All other workers were offered counseling and referrals if they did not want to make this commitment, but were not given legal representation.

Once a case was accepted, the team (including the worker(s), an organizer, a counselor, and, when necessary, a lawyer) began work. Case strategy was formed around the idea that the *experience of service*—the experience that individuals had while resolving the problems that had brought them to the legal clinic—should, to the extent practical and useful to the resolution of the case, be an experience of organizing. To that end, legal clinic staff and volunteers discussed with workers the limitations of legal remedies, identifying the points at which they might be able to achieve their goals only through organizing. For a worker with an individual problem—say, a domestic worker or day laborer who had not been paid—the first step was usually a confrontation or negotiation with her employer. Accompanied by the organizer, and often by other workers as a sign of support, the worker would go to the employer's home or workplace to demand payment. If she was not successful, the lawyer would follow up with a letter. If these contacts failed to produce results, workers developed a group strategy to bring pressure to bear on their employer. As a part of this strategy, the staff would initiate a lawsuit or file a complaint with the Department of Labor and other appropriate agencies. Simultaneously, workers, members, supporters, and staff frequently picketed employers' workplaces and homes to force them to pay the wages they owed. For bigger cases, these legal tactics were part of a larger campaign against the employer, waged through the press, leaflets, and other organizing techniques.

The case of the Be-Bop Bagel workers, although larger than

most in terms of the amount owed, was typical of this clinic in terms of the process followed. The owners of Be-Bop Bagels in Hempstead hired an immigrant woman and man to do a variety of tasks in their deli and bagel shop. The workers' court papers assert that they regularly labored 66 and 1/2 hours a week, but were paid considerably less than the minimum wage, with no overtime wages: the woman earned $170 a week, the man $200. By the time the workers left their jobs and came to the clinic in December 1996, the unpaid wages they were seeking had grown to well over $10,000. The workers agreed to take the Workers Course, and Ramos began the process of contacting their employers to demand payment. When she reached the owner, Ramos remembers him acknowledging that the wages he paid them were below minimum, but he refused to make up the difference on the grounds that the workers were undocumented and inexperienced. In response to his intransigence, the workers decided to picket, and—joined by other Project members and staff—they carried out two protests in May of 1997 on the busy sidewalk outside the shop. When the owners did not respond to the protests, the Project followed up with a lawsuit in New York State Supreme Court in August of 1997. The lawsuit brought an offer of $5,000, which the workers were not willing to accept. When the owner refused to raise the amount, the group carried out five more protests in September and October, handing out fliers that said things like "Q: Are Be-Bop Bagels part of a balanced diet? A: You'll have to ask a nutritionist. But common sense tells us that working 66 and 1/2 hours a week for less than minimum wage is not healthy for anybody." To end those protests, the owner offered $6,000, and the workers took the offer, afraid that the evidence they had of the hours they had worked would not stand up in court.

For perhaps two years, the Workplace Project ran the clinic in this way, working out the kinks, building up experience, turning the group's critical attention to other programs and campaigns. During that time, the clinic proved successful in several areas. First, the new clinic did a better job than the old of resolving workers' problems. As the Be-Bop case illustrates, the combination of legal pressure and protest was often more effective than a lawsuit alone in settling cases. Second, it continued to be effective as a draw. Building on the track record of the previous version of the clinic, it attracted new immigrants to the Project each week by demonstrating to them that the organization was willing to fight with them and on their behalf and that challenges to employers could succeed. It filled a serious and otherwise unmet need in the community, and thus brought in 250 to 300 people each year who otherwise might not have approached the Workplace Project. Through the clinic, hundreds of thousands of dollars flowed into the pockets of workers who had not been paid or whose rights had otherwise been violated, and word-of-mouth and media publicity about these victories built the organization's reputation as a center that cared about the community's problems and was effective in resolving them. Of course, the clinic had been a good draw before it was retooled. Perhaps what is more notable here, then, is that the addition of the organizing requirements did not undermine the clinic's power to attract new members. The clinic did not experience any decrease in use after the new requirements were put into place.

Third, the clinic was a useful benefit for ongoing members, providing easy access to legal and organizing support when they encountered problems on the job. In the words of the long-time member Carmen Lelys Maldonado, "I felt supported because this center had a lawyer. Many times I called you [Jennifer] and you called my boss . . . and that helped me a lot." Meanwhile, Maldonado continued to work on the organization's campaigns and serve on its board of directors, receiving services and contributing to organizing at the same time. Because that support was (ideally) given in the context of the member's ongoing participation in the Project's internal governance and external organizing campaigns, there was much less danger of service usurping organizing than in the case of the legal clinic as the point of entry into the organization. Use of a lawyer's services could and often did coexist with active participation in organizing.

Fourth, the clinic brought new resources into the organization. It proved an excellent way to recruit and incorporate volunteers into the Workplace Project.[3] It provided learning opportunities for members, college and law students, and others in the community (the clinic's most dedicated volunteer over the years was a retired teacher and union representative)—and in turn trained a cadre of lawyers-to-be, many of whom went on to do important work in the immigration, labor, and community organizing fields. It allowed the organization to produce the "numbers served" and "amounts recovered" that reassure individual donors and more traditional foundations that real work is being done, reassurance that can be difficult to provide in the context of long-term organizing campaigns. It brought in small amounts of money through legal fees, both those paid by workers and the occasional payments from opponents ordered by a judge to cover the Workplace Project's legal costs, and larger amounts through grants earmarked for legal services.[4]

Fifth, the flow of workers through the clinic also allowed the organization to monitor what was happening in the community and in workplaces around Long Island. The legal clinic generated an extensive database on employers, common workplace

problems, wages, and characteristics such as gender, immigration status, and country of origin of the workers it served. Clinic
staff kept detailed records on each worker in a database that had
reached over 2,000 entries by the year 2000. The database and related clinic documentation pointed both to clusters of problems
in particular industries and to breakdowns in the labor-law enforcement system.[5] This information was invaluable—although,
as I explain below, not without complication—in designing organizing campaigns to attack these issues. It also provided the organization with ample ammunition to back up its claims, both
in terms of statistics from the database and in the form of individuals willing to talk with the media about problems that
typified larger trends.

For all of its advantages, this version of the legal clinic drew
fire from both outside and inside the organization. From the
outside, lawyers expressed concern that a clinic structured in
this way violated legal ethics. From the inside, some members
and staff argued that the reconfigured clinic was still inadequate
as a bridge to organizing.

During presentations about the legal clinic, law students or
lawyers frequently raised two objections. First, they argued that
the clinic represented a form of bait and switch. People who
arrived at the clinic came with urgent needs and a genuine ex-
pectation—generated by the clinic's own reputation and advertising—that they would be helped. And yet the assistance they
received was made conditional on their agreeing to become
members of an organization, or was offered in a format designed
to teach them a lesson about collective action rather than to
solve their problem quickly. If they did not want to agree to the
terms the organization set, they were turned away. One reprov-
ing observer said, "It's as if a church opens a soup kitchen and

advertises that it will feed all comers, but then makes hungry people swear they believe in Jesus before they are allowed to eat." It would be different, some said, if the demand was made in the context of ample options for representation on a wage claim. Most often, though, the Workplace Project could suggest nowhere else that would take a worker's case, not legal services, often not any private attorney. If under these circumstances the worker "chose" to walk away from the Project because of what it asked of her, she was choosing to jettison her one chance of representation on her claim. A business executive doesn't have to go through an obstacle course to reach a lawyer, the questioner might conclude; why should a much more vulnerable immigrant worker?

The response was blunt: she shouldn't. In the ideal world, there would be resources to provide free legal representation to all workers cheated on the job. Workers interested in going beyond their individual cases could join organizations such as the Workplace Project; others could simply walk in to a local legal services office, sign up, and have a competent attorney bring the matter to court. In the world where the Workplace Project was situated, however, there were not nearly enough lawyers to do this. The Project had to triage its cases somehow. For everyone other than those whose life circumstances made compliance too difficult, triage was done by presenting workers with the choice: take the Workers Course (or participate in some other way) and get assistance; refuse to take it and we cannot help you.

By rationing legal services on the basis of an analysis of which clients were most likely to become active participants and leaders, the Project hoped to be able to serve its long-term goals while preserving the legal clinic as a source of short-term assistance. When Habitat for Humanity asks those who will live in the houses it builds to contribute sweat equity to their construction, it is doing the same thing. Where the membership and board of an organization of immigrant workers concur that organizing offers the greatest hope of bringing about substantive change in their lives, and where legal services are scarce resources, it seems a logical and quite reasonable decision to ration them in this way.

There is no rule of legal ethics that prohibits a lawyer from refusing to represent a client who will not comply with an organization's requirement that she participate in its activities or become a member to get legal services. Those that come closest are provisions forbidding a lawyer to take her own interests and beliefs or the demands of third parties into account when representing a client, and prohibiting a lawyer from soliciting business under certain circumstances.[6] The former does not strictly come into play at the moment of deciding to take a client. With regard to the latter, in a series of cases in the 1960s the Supreme Court established that conditioning legal services on organizational membership fell within the bounds of legal ethics.[7]

Nevertheless, in most legal services offices, triage is done through an uncontroversial combination of first-come, first-served, and selection based on the merits of the case. The center's board of directors or staff establish basic areas of practice: public benefits, housing, family law, and so on. Depending on the lawyers' caseload, the office may interview only the first twenty clients who arrive on Monday morning, and offer representation to all those in that group with legally actionable claims. This approach has the advantage of looking "neutral," not "biased" or "political" as a process. But it is not neutral. It privileges people who rise early on Mondays; it privileges the unemployed, or those who can take time off from their jobs to seek legal help. It also privileges, it is worth noting, those with legally actionable claims, which is not concurrent with the set of people who have been treated unjustly. Beyond our belief that it does not ration legal services in a "political" way, what does such a system achieve? Only to keep the caseload at manageable levels; not to attack a problem strategically.[8]

Furthermore, the Workplace Project would point out to those who made the church soup kitchen analogy, it did not ask workers to pledge allegiance to a cause in exchange for whatever help they received. The Project never asked people to *join* in order to become members. It asked them to take the Workers Course. In the course they got useful information about rights and (depending on their level of participation in the class) helped develop or were exposed to a critical analysis of the problems immigrant workers faced—an analysis they were free to accept or reject. At the end of the class, people who were not interested simply walked away, while those who were signed on for membership. Either way, they received representation. They had fulfilled the requirement, which was to take the course, not to become active participants in the organization. Although workers were asked to take action as a part of the class, supporting other workers at protests, attending demonstrations in Albany and Washington, or participating in strategy sessions, many chose not to.

The second set of objections of law students and lawyers sprang directly from the code of legal ethics that governs lawyers' behavior, but raised broader questions as well. These concerns focused on the relationship between the individual client and her lawyer in the context of a clinic run by an organizing center. The rules of legal ethics, although endlessly debated, are quite clear on a few points, and one is: a lawyer's responsibility is to her client. No third party can make demands on how she handles the case or seek to influence her strategy so that it favors its ends over the client's. In trying to shape a legal clinic "in the service of organizing," the Workplace Project, with its institutional goals of improving wages and working conditions across suburban sweatshops, appeared to be meddling in the resolution of individual cases.[9]

The problem is clearest where the interests of the client and the organization diverge. Say a car wash attendant comes in to a legal clinic affiliated with an organizing effort to report that he and his fellow workers are being paid $1.50 an hour. He is unable to convince any other workers to join him. The clinic sues his employer for $10,000 in back wages. The employer offers that worker $10,000, on condition that he not discuss the fact of the settlement, the amount he received, or the general problem of subminimum wages at the car wash with the press or any of the other workers, and that his lawyer remain equally silent. The worker wants to accept. The organization is planning a campaign to raise wages to legal levels at local car washes, where the problem of subminimum wages is endemic, and wants to use the settlement as a way to illustrate to workers that they stand to gain by becoming involved with the campaign.

If the lawyer and client have not discussed this issue in advance, under the rules of legal ethics the lawyer must defer to her client's decision, and sign the agreement. There is, however, an alternative that a group can implement as a matter of policy. If the lawyer advises all clients in advance of agreeing to represent them that the organization will not itself consent to be bound by confidentiality agreements if they arise, and explains the situation fully to the client, and the client still decides to pursue the case through the organization, he has consented to these terms.

Of course, this comfortable fiction masks the fact that, first, the worker has nowhere else to go, and, second, he has not yet lived through the experience of his employer offering him cold cash on conditions that he would like to agree to but his lawyer refuses to accept. To simply present the technical solution as though it were enough is to shy away from the real tension. However the objections are phrased, the queasy fear that underlies them is that in harnessing a legal clinic to an organizing effort the immediate needs of individuals will be sacrificed to the larger—but far more uncertain—aims of the group. It is very hard to ask a worker who has put months of sweat into a job to turn down money on the table, money for which he has already worked.

Let's sharpen the scenario. In the 1960s and 1970s, the United Farm Workers (UFW) had a powerful legal department. At its peak in the late 1970s, the legal team consisted of seventeen lawyers and up to forty-four paralegals, a department of remarkable size in a union renowned overall for its lean staffing.[10] Although most of the legal department's energy went to representing the union as an entity, lawyers not infrequently also agreed to represent individual workers on cases against growers in ranches where the union was organizing. UFW lawyers filed claims on behalf of injured workers, brought lawsuits when workers were sickened by pesticides, and fought for unpaid wages and overtime in court and with administrative agencies, both to help the workers and as "bee stings in the battle" against employers. The UFW's lawyers pursued those claims until the union reached an agreement with the grower. Then, as part of the accord that led to a contract, the union dropped the individual claims. Sometimes the contract or a side agreement addressed the worker's individual problem. Often, it did not. It is hard to find a clearer example of the trade-off between the interests of the individual and the interests of the group.

UFW General Counsel Jerry Cohen was well aware of the concern that trading lawsuits for contract clauses harmed the individual worker, who would be better served by an individual resolution of his or her individual case. Cohen's first response was practical. "When you think about the chances of winning a good judgment in Kern County Superior Court, as opposed to getting something in a contract you can actually enforce, the individual workers didn't seem to think [they were harmed by the trade], and the union didn't seem to think so." "But," he acknowledges, "there *was* a tension there . . . you had to be very clear up front [about] what you were doing."[11]

Thus in order to fulfill his ethical obligations, Cohen would talk with workers at length about the context of suits against growers and their possible outcomes. "You'd say, 'Look, we're going to file this thing. The chances of winning it in Kern County aren't that great. We're going to use it publicly. We're going to use it to help generate power.' People *loved* it . . . The folks that were attracted to the union were really sophisticated people and they understood the game pretty well. 'And ultimately, if we ever get to a position . . . of negotiating [a contract], you've got to know that one of the conditions to getting a contract is that they're probably going to want these suits dropped.' The workers would say, 'Whatever you want to do.'" At the end of the day, with regard to the ethical issues that representation of individuals to achieve group ends brings up, Cohen concludes, "those are legitimate questions to ask. But, on the other hand, if you're generating some power, and people know it, and everybody is on the same page, I never had a problem with it."

Such solutions allow formal compliance with the rule, but they do little that is meaningful to protect the individual worker. This is a sacrifice, and from the point of view of legal ethics, it is a slippery slope. But if we stick to the principle that we must always gear our representation to the desires of the individual, we will make a greater sacrifice of the possibility of meaningful change in situations where collective action is imperative.[12] For organizing to be successful, there will be times when the individual will be less important than the group. Furthermore, our preoccupation with the presumed self-interest of the individual fails to take into account the complexities in people's understandings of their self-interest or the transformations in those understandings that take place though education and action. As Cohen points out, the "sophisticated people" who make up the membership of a movement such as the UFW or an organization like the Workplace Project may see beyond their personal case to a goal whose achievement would raise their wages and improve their working conditions, and may value that outcome more highly than individual compensation.

Although the concerns Workplace Project staff and members raised were very different from those voiced by outside lawyers, by 1997 internal debate had put the "legal clinic question" back on the agenda. The focus once again was on tensions between the clinic and the group's organizing focus: Could the legal clinic act as a bridge to organizing? This time, the discussions would not be held among three staff members in an off-site room. The organization had grown into itself over those intervening years. A vibrant membership, a much stronger board, active workers committees, and a full-fledged staff all had a stake in the matter. The legal clinic debates would be hashed out in conversations at many levels, in all-organization retreats and in large weekend and evening meetings at the office, involving many members as well as staff.

For all the changes the group had made since the first version of the clinic, the issues on the table were remarkably similar to those that had led to the changes in 1994. On one side were those who believed that the reconfigured clinic still failed to attract workers who would stay to organize, and that it sent the wrong message about the group's purpose and method. Juan Carlos Molina remembers his late-night discussions with his friend, José Martinez, then the board's president, about the legal clinic's role within the organization. "I would say to him, 'What's the benefit of Rhina's work [the clinic]?' We would argue about that. 'The benefit of Rhina's work is that it's a mechanism to attract people, but they don't always stay.' . . . The work is done, it's developed, it used a lot of time, and they didn't stay." Molina, Henriquez, and others argued that the Project continued to have a social service agency reputation in the community because of the clinic. And within the group, they said, the focus on case resolution—however organizing-rich—continued to be a problem. As the current director Nadia Marín-Molina would reflect in retrospect: "Once you create a situation where someone has a case and the Workplace Project is handling it, all the focus is on the case. That's why the person calls, comes in, etc. It gets hard to maintain any other dynamic."[13]

Members and staff pointed to examples of workers who had come in through the clinic and continued to see the organization's lawyers as the professionals who would resolve their problems for them even after the initial case was resolved. Adding insult to injury, many workers still left the organization entirely once their case was resolved, whether they ignored or fulfilled their commitment to take the course. In a broader sense, because the clinic attracted a stream of workers with urgent problems, and because the organization's resources were limited, addressing their needs often absorbed energy that might otherwise have turned to broader strategizing and thinking. The underlying assumption of this group was that the organization did not need its legal clinic in order to attract new members, and that those who came in for other reasons would be more likely than clinic clients to remain active over time.

Other members and staff argued that the legal clinic built the organization's good reputation in the community and provided a critically necessary service, one available nowhere else. Some believed it should be maintained independent of its relationship to organizing. As Zoila Rodriguez later said, speaking for many who held this view, "What I have always admired about this organization is how it defends the rights of the person, of the individual, as a human being. And when I come to believe that it's failing completely in this, I'll go get involved in something else." Others argued that the clinic was valuable as a bridge to organizing, and should not be condemned as a bridge because *all* those who passed through it did not stay to organize. They pointed out that to have even 10 percent of the workers who started the process in the clinic stay to become active members was a success, given how little time, money, or stability most immigrant workers had in their lives. They offered the fact that a third of the organization's active members had come in through the clinic as proof. They also pointed out that some of the "bridge" failings had to do not with the clinic, but with what happened afterward: the length of time people had to wait for the next session of the Workers Course to begin, or the periods when the committees had little engaging work for newcomers to do. These gaps, as much as anything in the clinic itself, were to blame when workers drifted away.

Certainly, this group argued, this clinic had eased the tension between the we-do-it-for-you service that the first version of the clinic provided and the you-do-it-for-yourself organizing gospel to which it was intended to lead. The organization may have had a reputation as a legal service center, but when workers encountered a different reality they often shifted their expectations as well. As Samuel Chavez recalls, thinking about the day he and more than twenty-eight other workers first walked into the Workplace Project clinic, referred by the Division of Human Rights, "The first impression we had was that here were people who were going to translate and make it easier for the Human Rights Division to communicate with us. But once we were here and they explained to us what kind of organization it was, I think obviously we could perceive all that from the way in which we started to work. I remember that we began to make picket signs; we were going to do some demonstrations." This group acknowledged the tensions between the clinic and organizing, but saw the support it provided as an important first step. Among other benefits, the clinic alleviated the urgent need that kept people from having the time or energy to consider organizing. As Lilliam Araujo reminded everyone, "People come in desperate." It is not enough to say to someone "the important thing is that in the future you learn to resolve your own problems, and help others resolve theirs." The first step was to say "Here we will fix your problem." Then, once they were able to listen, "you try and get them to stay, to keep working, continue in the struggle."

After a lengthy debate, the first group prevailed. Saru Jayaraman, a recent law graduate hired to replace Ramos in 2000, designed a new approach to resolving the problems immigrant workers brought to the Workplace Project called the Alianza para la Justicia, or the Alliance for Justice.

Jayaraman describes the Alianza para la Justicia—instituted a year and a half after I left the Workplace Project, and still in effect in a modified version—as "a new law and organizing model in which we eliminated the legal clinic and its problematic lawyer-client relationship altogether, and instituted an entirely new process of member entry."[14] The Alianza, now referred to by the organization as "the committees," emphasizes the clinic's role as a bridge to organizing, rather than its role as a draw or as a way to resolve individual problems. The new approach offers individual workers organizing assistance in vindicating their rights through a structure of industry-based workers committees.

The first change is in what happens when a worker arrives. No longer are workers seen individually on Mondays. Nor is the staff available for new workers or members to consult with about labor problems during the week, except in emergencies. Instead, all workers who call with problems are invited to a weekly evening workshop. At that workshop, facilitated by Project volunteers with no attorney present, workers learn about the Workplace Project and hear about their rights. They are told that the Project "used to have a legal clinic but workers were not learning how to resolve their own cases . . . [and] were becoming dependent on the attorney. So we stopped providing legal services and started to work in teams."[15] They tell each other about the problems they are facing, as the facilitator notes on the board the nature of the abuse and the number of other workers affected by it, the rising tally a constant reminder that there are more people "in the room" than the number visibly present at the workshop.[16] And they hear about the Project's structure of industry-based committees, one each for day labor, factories, and cleaning, in which they can participate and through which they can receive support in resolving their problem. Additional committees devoted to collecting unpaid wages have been created since this version's inception. These teams include workers from the relevant industry and an organizer, as well as other worker volunteers and students. At the workshop, volunteers demonstrate the method of group problem-solving that the committees use. Those workers who emerge from the workshop with a desire for individual legal representation are given a referral list of lawyers and government agencies. Those whose cases are not amenable to group resolution—those with unemployment benefits issues, for example—are always referred out, because the organization now assists only those whose claims can be addressed collectively. Those who fit that description and want the support of the Workplace Project in resolving their case are invited to the next meeting of the relevant committee.

The second change is in the method of handling cases. New workers present their workplace problems to the committee. The group then develops an organizing strategy to address the problem. No step in the strategy is taken unless the worker is present and participating. In addition, at least three committee members must be present to take any action.[17] All actions are carried out in the name of the committee—no phone calls made, as they would have been in the past, by a lawyer on the workers' behalf, no demand letters written on an attorney's letterhead. A common approach to a case of unpaid wages is to begin with team members accompanying the new worker as she seeks support from fellow workers from her workplace. The committee then writes a letter to the employer: "We, the _____ committee of the Workplace Project, have learned that . . ." If there is no response, committee members visit the employer to make the demand in person. If these steps do not result in payment, they again go to the employer's home or place of business and hand out fliers informing customers, neighbors, and passersby. That failing to produce positive results, they organize a picket or demonstration. Only as a last resort is a lawsuit or claim with the Department of Labor filed, and then with representation provided not by the Workplace Project, but by a pro-bono attorney or law school clinic.[18]

Since this form of the clinic was designed and implemented after my departure, I do not have the personal experience with it that I bring to my analysis of the previous two versions. Observed from the outside and through conversations with those who remain at the Project, such an arrangement seems to have some arguable advantages. But the clinic's determination to put lawyers at a greater remove sharpens my questions about how much organizing is served by denying legal support or delaying it considerably.

The principal advantage of the committee structure is that it focuses on group strategies from the beginning, lessening considerably the tension caused by using a clinic that solves individual problems individually as the conduit to membership in a group that works collectively for systemic change. "With the committees," Marín-Molina observes, "from the first moment a worker's contact with the organization is in a group, through the workshop, and then in the committee, another group. There's never an individual consultation." The collective setting and approach, she argues, are more effective than either of the previous versions of the clinic as a bridge to active membership in the organization.[19] "Before," she notes, "we talked about organizing, but we were giving an individual consultation . . . Now, people are immediately channeled into organizing."[20] The absence of lawyers on staff has also eased the concerns about organizational identity and philosophy. Not having staff lawyers in the clinic sends a clearer message that the group is wholly dedicated to collective action; those who want individual representation will have to look outside its bounds.

Despite this focus on organizing, the clinic turns out to have retained two features of its predecessors. Interestingly, although the committees no longer decide which cases they take by whether they present a viable legal claim, and therefore they could decide to pressure an employer to rectify an injustice not recognized as a rights violation by law, in fact the claims they have pursued have remained as tied to the enforcement of basic workplace rights as before. Most of the committees' time is still spent resolving individual wage claims. Notes Marín-Molina, "when a worker comes into the workshop angry after being fired and is told that the law doesn't give him a right to his job back, we offer committee support, but people become discouraged." As a result, "the committees still fight for the enforcement of legal rights—it's just that the fight itself is more collective." And legal claims—although now delayed until group action has been given a serious chance to succeed on its own—have remained important as leverage in resolving cases. Many of the stories of success-through-organizing in the committee structure have somewhere in them the filing of a lawsuit that provided the threat that brought the other side to the table. Thus although lawyers no longer staff the clinic, law has remained important in shaping the claims that get made through the committee structure and, through outside attorneys, in putting pressure on recalcitrant employers.

"Organizing" can mean many things: individual empowerment, institution-building, collective action to resolve a short-term problem, or long-term campaigns with more systemic goals. Various versions of the clinic supported different kinds of organizing. Through its role as a draw and a bridge to the organization, the clinic built the Workplace Project as an institution. The data it generated was another important source of strategic support for collective action. In addition, organizing supported individual case resolution: experience with the clinic over time showed that collective action combined with legal interventions resolved some kinds of cases more quickly than legal intervention alone.

In one way, however, the clinic did not—and I would argue could not—do a good job of supporting organizing. That was when it came to generating the organization's forward-looking organizing campaigns. The clinic came under a steady stream of criticism when the individual cases that workers brought into its doors failed to blossom into long-term organizing. Several of the restructuring efforts sought to remedy this problem by making case resolution more and more about organizing. But as the Workplace Project's experience illustrates, expecting clinic cases to turn into organizing campaigns—and dedicating much of the group's organizing capacity to those efforts—can misfire, committing limited resources to work that is reactive rather than proactive and focusing the group on winning legal minimums rather than higher standards.

At the Workplace Project, a proactive, justice-oriented organizing strategy would have shared at least some of the following characteristics. It would have involved workers who remained in their jobs while they organized—who were organizing over live and ongoing issues, not simply over redress for past exploitation. It would have raised wages and working conditions to the legal minimum where they had been substantially below it, and well beyond the legal minimum where they had been at or near it. It would have had meaningful impact beyond a small group of workers or a single workplace, building the organization by attracting new members through their interest in its campaigns and the vision they represented. It would have emphasized the leadership of the workers themselves in the organizing effort. And it would have been chosen to maximize the pressure workers could exert on their employers and the likelihood that they could win the change they sought.

A discussion of ideal strategies brings us directly back to the structural challenges to organizing low-wage immigrant workers. Figuring out where this vision might be realized would have required a clear-eyed analysis of the numerous labor markets in which Project members worked. In which of those contexts were the possibilities greatest for building and exercising power? If its investigation revealed one or more sectors with organizing potential, the organization would have had to face some difficult choices. How much of its limited resources was it willing to dedicate to campaigns selected not on the basis of which workers were worst off or which community needs were unmet, but which efforts were most likely to succeed? As the group's debate in 1997 about its work with day laborers showed, its members and staff were reluctant to consider turning away from those immigrants in the worst circumstances in order to help those slightly better off. In addition, the more strategic its analysis, the more the campaigns the group chose were likely to overlap with existing union efforts. Would the Project work out some collaborative arrangement with those unions? Set up an independent campaign that took advantage of the group's deep roots in the community, its tactical flexibility and its participatory leadership? Limit itself to targets not already in the union realm?

The organization never squarely faced these issues because of its dependence on two flawed methods of generating campaigns. One was strategizing-by-outrage. In this approach, the membership builds consensus that a particular issue represents a serious injustice, and decides to take it on in its entirety, without look-ing carefully at its components, its political and economic con-text, or the ways it can expect to exert power for change on that issue. The result is a campaign that decries something that is clearly harmful to workers—"down with employment at will!"—without a realistic strategy for achieving its abolishment.

The other was strategizing-by-what-presents-itself. Here, the group sinks its organizing resources into the problems workers bring in the door; in the Workplace Project, this largely meant the cases that came through the clinic. The problem is that few cases workers brought into the clinic were capable of generating organizing that fit the criteria I outlined above. The group's ini-tial intuition had been that a clinic would draw in workers with "live" workplace issues, in situations that were ripe for organiz-ing. Yet in truth, the great majority of the workers who came to the clinic had already been fired or had quit—a common experi-ence among groups that seek to help workers address the prob-lem of unpaid wages.[21] They suffered a violation of their rights—they were not paid, they were injured, they were discriminated against or abused—and they bore it until the job was over, at which time they sought help. From the workers' perspective, this was a logical response to a difficult situation. But from the Pro-ject's perspective, it meant that the group invested an inordinate amount of time into organizing-for-individual-redress in situa-tions where the workers were no longer on the job, consuming resources that might more fruitfully have been used to organize around ongoing conditions in workplaces where participants continued to labor.[22] Whether a lawyer intervened or the workers themselves pressured the employer into making good, the end result was a settlement that rectified past harms, not an agree-ment that governed future contact.

Furthermore, because the minimum legal standards for

worker protections fell far below what the organization's membership considered adequate, much less fair, a legal clinic proved flawed as an entry point to organizing because it overlooked the group of workers who felt they were being treated *unjustly* but not *illegally*. The law has no remedies for the worker who needs $12 an hour to support her family but makes only the legal minimum, less than half of that; for the worker fired in the many cases where the law provides no guarantee of continued employment; or for the worker who needs health insurance but cannot afford his employer's plan. Some people who feel these issues intensely may never come into the clinic. Others may come only to be sent away. Or, following a discussion with an organizer or advocate, they may shift their anger away from the injustice that brought them in, one that did not correspond to a legal wrong, toward a different one that had a legal remedy. In either case, situations that might have become good organizing campaigns because they represented a strongly felt injustice are lost because they are not also good legal cases.

Two restaurant dishwashers from the same hometown in El Salvador who came into the second version of the clinic are a case in point. They sit down and begin to tell their story to an organizer, a law student, and a member volunteer. The owner of the restaurant where they have worked for eight months, always a volatile man, has been increasingly abusive over the past few weeks. He calls them "idiot" and tells them they are lazy bastards. His insults are unrelenting. Last night, toward the end of a long shift, the owner walked into the kitchen where they were immersed to the elbows in lukewarm greasy water and said, without preamble: "You're fired." The workers are angry that they have been treated disrespectfully, and furious that they have been dismissed without explanation after working hard and well.

After explaining that the Workplace Project is a membership organization and so on, the organizer asks what the workers want. "We want our jobs back," they say, "and we want the boss to stop insulting us." Turning to the law student—they have come, after all to a legal clinic—they ask, "What are our rights?" After consulting the supervising lawyer, the law student tells them with regret that workers who have no union can be fired for any reason or no reason at all under New York's "employment at will" doctrine, so long as the reason is not in violation of laws against race, gender, age discrimination, and so on—which it does not appear to be in their case. Unless the employer's conduct is "outrageous," there is no law that prohibits employers from speaking abusively to their workers, so long as that abuse does not include racial slurs or other signs of prohibited discrimination. They are both undocumented, and so they are not entitled to collect unemployment insurance. They probably have no right to redress. The workers are taken aback, certain that they have been wronged and equally sure that the law's role is to avenge wrongs such as these.

"But," the organizer adds, "there are some other questions we have. Tell us a little about the hours you worked and the amount you were paid." His hunch is fueled by years of talk about wages with dishwashers and busboys, who are rarely paid according to the legal minimum. Indeed, once these workers begin to describe their average income and hours, it is clear that they were underpaid. The member begins writing down the details as the workers speak. The law student explains minimum wage and overtime law to them and asks if they are interested in trying to recover the money they are owed. "Of course," they answer. One has kept a small notebook with a record of the hours he worked each week and the amount he was paid. The other has nothing but his memory. For the next two hours, they sit with the member and the law student and reconstruct a record of their schedules and wages, finally arriving at a figure for back pay due.

The organizer returns to the table. The conversation turns to ways to recover these wages (through protests, through small claims court, through the Department of Labor), to whether other workers are similarly affected (they are), to whether those others might be interested in doing something about the problem (as it almost always turns out, they will not be, not so long as they are still working). He explains what the Project asks in exchange for the support it offers if the workers want to pursue the claim: that they work actively on their own case and that they take the Workers Course. The workers agree. They decide on a strategy: first go with the organizer to confront the boss, then if that bears no fruit send a lawyer's letter, then file in small claims court, then picket to collect the wages. The workers leave after setting up a time later that day to meet the organizer at the restaurant and confront their boss about the money they are owed.

What has happened here? The workers came in full of anger and a sense that an injustice had been done to them. They learned that their anger did not arise from a legally recognized harm: being sworn at and fired was unjust, but it was not illegal. As they were digesting this, they were offered a substitute: the way they had been paid—which they had understood as legitimate—did violate the law. Their desire to right an injustice was channeled toward fixing a legal problem. In the process, their perceptions were adjusted away from their own intuitions: Dignity and livelihood—not a right. A minimal level of pay—a right. As Marín-Molina noted above, although the third version of the clinic did not use the same process, it continued to generate the same kind of outcomes, in which workers pursued the claims validated by law and dropped those that were not.

One final effect of this relationship between the clinic and the Workplace Project's organizing goals was to skew the membership, about a third of which came through the legal clinic, toward the very bottom of the labor market, because it was in that sector where violations of the law were most frequent. These workplaces often were the most chaotic, the most informal, and the hardest to organize—not the ideal focus for the membership from a strategic perspective. Many other potential members—indeed, most of those with whom organizing might have been easier, because they were less mobile, less afraid, and had slightly more of a financial cushion—worked in jobs that paid at or more than the minimum wage. Most factory, janitorial, retail, mechanic, and live-out domestic jobs paid the minimum wage or more. Workers in those jobs were much less likely to approach the clinic for help recovering wages.

The third version of the clinic sought to build a stronger bridge to organizing and create a closer match with the group's organizing goals by removing lawyers from the resolution of workers' problems. This change indeed seems to have better helped workers to develop a belief in their capacity to act on their own behalf and in support of others, the opposite of the lawyer-dependence that a clinic so often generates. But it leaves two core questions unanswered. One is why a worker should forgo a lawyer's representation when it would be helpful to her. The absence of a lawyer did not change the fundamental nature of the issues that most immigrants brought to the clinic: post-firing claims for wages due and on-the-job injuries. Under those circumstances, a lawyer's help, in combination with protests, often remains the fastest way to resolving the problem. In such cases, refusing to provide people with legal help sends a clear prescriptive message: thou shalt organize. But the pragmatic response for someone with an individual problem (why shall I not also sue, if suing works) is hard to answer unless the group has an effective long-term organizing strategy that addresses that person's problem.

This in turn raises the other question, no more answered by the third version of the clinic than the earlier two: "organizing toward what?" The committee structure continues to devote the bulk of the Project's organizing resources to reacting to the problems that workers bring to the workshops—still mostly individually and still mostly after they have been fired—rather than to creating and carrying out a proactive long-term strategy. To ask workers to join an "industry committee" *sounds* like a long-term strategy, but when each committee is composed of ten to twenty workers from six or seven different workplaces in weakly strategically related sectors, it is not one. Organizing around individual post-firing problems may be more consistent with a group's philosophy and may develop leadership better than legal representation, then, but is little more likely to lead to longer-term, strategic collective action.

Although the Workplace Project was free to develop organizing campaigns independent of the clinic, and did so at times, the organization's sense of what was wrong and what needed to be fixed was deeply influenced by the problems workers brought into the clinic. This dynamic was intensified when the database, entirely made up of clinic clients, was used as a way to identify problems and bolster campaigns. Under these influences the group's sights shifted toward strategizing about enforcing minimum rights, away from the broader (and harder to answer) question of how to expand rights or organize beyond existing rights. This was not always a problem. Campaigns that sought enforcement, such as the domestic worker agency campaign and the Unpaid Wages Prohibition Act effort, were important parts of the group's strategy. But the group would have benefited from a complementary approach of generating campaigns that relied on researching the structure of particular labor markets and how their employers and suppliers function, evaluating the power workers had and could build within them, and exploring how various institutions might effectively be pressured to change working conditions, before deciding how to proceed with organizing.

It is possible to imagine a clinic similarly affiliated with and supportive of an organizing effort yet playing a much less prominent role in generating the group's organizing strategy. It seems likely that such a model would avoid some of the problems the Workplace Project faced.

Consider the experience of the United Farm Workers in providing services as a part of its organizing strategy. The UFW is renowned for its service programs. The provision of a wide range of services to union members was philosophically meaningful to its founder, Cesar Chavez, whose Catholicism emphasized service as an act of religious faith. To him, any farm workers' union worthy of the name had to go beyond a traditional economic contract, to help farm workers resolve a range of daily problems.[23] He also believed deeply in the principle of self-help and mutual assistance, and held out the ideal that the union would offer services in ways that emphasized mutual support. Some of the services that the UFW provided, particularly its credit, gas, and food cooperatives, were thus explicitly structured to prefigure and reflect the principles that the UFW was fighting to achieve—that farm workers together could build the power to provide for themselves in ways that none could achieve alone.[24] In this sense, the service component of the UFW was an end in itself, an integral part of building the just world for which the UFW fought.

Although the UFW only briefly incorporated legal help as part of its services, what it did offer members was comparable to the Workplace Project's clinic in many ways. For a short period in the mid-1960s, the union provided legal representation to workers with a wide range of problems as a part of its service programs. This program was canceled when the union realized that it had drained the young attorney in charge, leaving him with no time or energy to figure out how the law might help the union win its battles against the growers. Instead, the union referred most members in need of an attorney for individual matters to the offices of California Rural Legal Assistance, and assembled a staff of lawyers whose primary responsibility was to creatively advance the UFW's external organizing strategy. Nonetheless, the legal department continued to represent a small number of workers with individual claims against growers. And although the service centers the union created had no attorneys, many of the cases its volunteers handled closely resembled those that came through the Workplace Project legal clinic. UFW members could get help with issues such as unpaid wages, unemployment benefits, and workers' compensation claims, as well as assistance with a wide variety of other problems, from access to government benefits to basic tax and immigration matters.[25] In addition, as at the Workplace Project, such services were often provided by "abogadillos" (little lawyers), law students affiliated with the service center or with the UFW legal department. Even when these services were provided by volunteers without legal training, the level and type of interventions were otherwise quite similar.

As the union evolved, service played different roles at different times. In the UFW's early days, the help it offered farm workers was its principal draw. From 1962 to 1965, when the organizing effort was just beginning, organizers held meetings with farm worker families to identify pressing problems, and went to work addressing them. Organizers themselves served members, developing a credit union that gave them much-needed loans, creating a popular death benefit plan, and helping them to obtain drivers' licenses. Many people thus first heard about the union because it had resolved a friend's or relative's problem. In the days when a contract looked like an impossible dream, all of these services became a magnet for the young organization, a way of proving that the promises of "La Causa" were not just castles in the air, and an encouragement to many to sign up and pay dues.

After the union's first grape strike began in 1965, the structure and purpose of UFW services shifted. To take the burden off key organizers, who suddenly had more pressing responsibilities, the union assigned new volunteers to serve members. By 1967, Chavez had established the National Farm Workers Service Center, Inc., a technically separate nonprofit organization with a central office in the union complex in Delano, California, and offshoots in field offices wherever the union's organizing teams were located.[26] Through the Service Center, member benefits were expanded, centralized, and to some degree professionalized. Those services were then used by organizers to encourage farm workers to support the union. Services became a part of the union's story about what it would provide for farm workers, a "downpayment" on that story, a chit that organizers could trade on to call people into organizing, and a source of proof that the union still cared about its members at times or in places where there was little successful organizing.

The UFW sought to make the service experience itself respectful, emphasizing the dignity of the workers and their right to just treatment at the hands of government bureaucracies. But service workers did not ask members to engage in organizing activities focused on the basic problems they brought in the door—they simply fixed them.[27] The separation permitted organizers to concentrate on building the union, and its legal staff to concentrate on the critical question of how law could advance its organizing goals. To be sure, the UFW sometimes encouraged workers to learn how to help themselves and each other. But there was no attempt to make the service experience itself a source of understanding of the need for collective action. Given the context in which the UFW was working, and its own development into a full-fledged social movement, it did not feel it needed service to play this role.

With the grape strike, the union solidified its identity as a movement engaged in a fight for farm workers, not a service organization.[28] Most workers now first heard of the union through news of the strike or of an organizing drive on or near their ranch, not through stories of individuals being helped. Even a worker who came to the union explicitly seeking services would have no doubt about the primary purpose of the organization providing them. The service centers were on union property—often, in field offices, in the same room as the organizers—under the unmistakable protection of the union's red and black eagle flag. In the polarized world of rural California during a UFW drive, in the context of a growing movement, no worker could wander in the door thinking that it was simply a place that facilitated drivers' licenses.[29]

As the UFW began to win contracts, what workers stood to gain by organizing became far greater than any service the union

could offer. Because the UFW's organizing strategy was evident
to all and was already bearing substantial fruit, in the words of
Leroy Chatfield, then the director of the Service Center, it was
clear that service was only organizing's "handmaiden." Service
was important both because of what it symbolized—both proof
and prefiguration of the different kind of life that would emerge
from collective action—and because of the instrumental ways it
interacted with organizing. But it was a minor player compared
to the larger promises of contracts and benefits for which UFW
membership soon came to stand.

Unlike the Workplace Project, which struggled to show workers that organizing was more powerful than individual legal services in the absence of a strategy that provided substantial concrete evidence to bolster the claim, the UFW was able to provide
workers with a roadmap to the changes it sought and, within a
fairly short time, to illustrate its capacity to deliver on its promises through collective action. Its experience indicates that a
clinic may play different roles in organizing at different stages,
working best as a draw in the early days and then receding more
into the background as a member benefit as the collective strategy takes shape. It also suggests that where there is a clear strategy for collective action that has begun to show positive results,
services are likely to be much less of a threat to organizing, and
thus to engender less conflict.[30]

A legal clinic, then, may have a great deal to offer to an organizing strategy under the right conditions. Where many in the
community experience a problem closely related to the issue
around which the group organizes, where the law provides a relatively clear and direct solution to the problem, and where help
enforcing the law is in short supply, a clinic may be a good way
to attract new members, help solve problems that would other-

wise fall by the wayside, and build an information bank, among other supportive roles. But two caveats emerge.

First, a clinic can support a collective strategy, but under most circumstances it should not be the engine for the group's organizing campaigns. Too many factors—the way a clinic filters injustices, selecting only those that have a legal remedy; the way people tend to seek legal services after a problem has happened, which means, in the workplace context, that they are likely to have quit or been fired by the time they arrive at the clinic's doors; and, where the law sets a fairly low standard, the way a clinic will attract only the worst off of any pool of people—weigh against the idea that clinic cases are a good starting point for long-term collective action. Clinics may well find that incorporating collective action in their case resolution makes their work more effective, but to picket in order to win someone's back wages is different from using clinic cases to generate an organizing campaign intended to broadly challenge immigrant working conditions. Organizations are far more likely to arrive at effective, well-targeted, strategic campaigns through independent research and analysis than by relying on a clinic for guidance. And a clinic that is understood as an important but relatively minor component of an organization's overall strategy runs far less of a chance of becoming a tail that wags the dog than a clinic that absorbs most of the group's organizing resources.

Second, however well structured, the combination of legal services and organizing creates tensions that no amount of shifting can eradicate. As difficult as they are, I believe that these conflicts do not obviate, and indeed can be an important part of, what a clinic offers to collective action.

Take the relationship between a "draw" and a "bridge." If a clinic is a first step on the road to organizing, it seems to be only

a very early step—and sometimes a step in the wrong direction.
Simply helping people doesn't get them to organize. It functions
as a draw to an organization but not as a bridge to collective action. As the Workplace Project discovered with the first version
of its clinic, an organization that resolves workers' cases one by
one still has not brought them into a room where they can talk
to each other. And they are unlikely to move spontaneously from
resolving their wage claim to attending meetings, much less
walking a picket line, out of gratitude.

If the organization is set up so that an individual can get legal
services by agreeing to become a member, the quantity of names
on its membership rolls will swell. However, for groups such as
the Workplace Project and many other labor and community efforts, groups that want and need more from their members than
their money and their name on a roster, this is a problem. Offer
people something they want at a bearable price, and they will
join to get it. But then they have joined for the benefit, not the
desire to organize. As Omar Henriquez noted, considering the
clinic in retrospect, "If you said to a worker, 'to have us help you,
you need to go outside and run four times around the block,' he
would do it. But running around the block doesn't make you
understand the need to organize any better."[31]

Unless there is something else that moves people who come to
a clinic toward a belief in the need to organize—something in the
experience of service, or something learned through action and
reflection on its lessons, or a class that changes the angle from
which participants view their experience—they will be members
in name only. And members in name only are not a base from
which a democratic, participatory membership organization can
build power. They are unlikely to be strongly committed to the
group, to be dedicated to developing and carrying out its strat-

egy, or to function well under pressure and over the long term. If a group depends on the participation of its members, then, if it wants to build generative power among people, it will quickly find that it must structure the services it offers so that coming in to be helped is a bridge as well as a draw.[32] The history of the Workplace Project's clinic is in large measure the story of a group trying to balance those two goals while simultaneously seeking to help people resolve the problems they had brought to the clinic.

There are a number of ways to design a legal clinic so that coming in to be helped is the first step on a thoughtful path from service to active membership, but they sort most easily into two basic categories. One is to ask that service recipients do something active for the broader organizing effort in exchange for the services they receive (for example, attend a committee meeting, walk a picket line, take a course on workers' rights or organizing). That approach uses service as leverage to produce participation, without an organic link between the two. But it opens up the possibility that the worker who is required to do one of these things will become committed to organizing in the process, and will choose to continue participating after she has fulfilled her obligation as a result. The other set of approaches seeks to provide the service in a way that reinforces the organization's mission and strategy (for example, by emphasizing self-help and mutual support in the resolution of individual problems, or by responding to individual problems with collective action rather than advocacy). Here the form in which the service is provided is organically related to the organizing effort's overall strategy and enacts or "prefigures" its goals for change.[33]

Despite the Workplace Project's efforts to use both of these sorts of links to resolve the tensions between law and organizing, conflicts persisted. Some of the tensions the Project encountered would probably have eased had the group been able to demonstrate the power of collective action more concretely, through strong organizing strategies generated independently of the clinic, and had it seen the clinic as an important but relatively minor component of its overall strategy rather than as a driving force within it. But other tensions are inherent in the enterprise of bringing service and organizing, two very different approaches to alleviating suffering, into such close proximity.

Lawyering and organizing operate by separate sets of rules, written and unwritten, that guide the choices that lawyers and organizers make about these questions when they do their work. Such rules are helpful because they provide a shortcut through a tangle of balky ethical and tactical issues. But to ease the way, they often discourage consideration of alternate perspectives, preventing people from confronting critically important issues that arise when competing principles clash. And clash they will in a legal clinic that is part of an organizing effort. Individuals approach a clinic with their immediate problems, hoping and believing that the clinic will help resolve them. At that moment, a good outcome from the individual's perspective would be the swift and successful intervention of a lawyer on her behalf, after which she could return to her usual life. The group sponsoring the clinic wants to provide assistance, but ultimately measures its success differently. A good outcome from the group's perspective would see the person move away from an individual focus and a reliance on professionals toward a belief in the collective resolution of systemic problems, and action on that belief.

This is a genuine conflict. And coming face to face with it, I believe, is a good thing. We should not be let off the hook of considering whether we ever think the interests of the individual should be sacrificed to the interests of the group—and if so, when? Is it most important to resolve urgent needs even if that effort absorbs all available resources, or is it most important to uncover and address the root causes of those needs even if it means ignoring immediate suffering? What takes priority, the outcome of a problem-solving effort or the process by which it is conducted? When might these things coincide? What do we fight for, our rights as determined by law already on the books or a just outcome as we independently imagine it? When and how is law helpful to a group trying to build power? Who should decide what priority, what process, and what goals to pursue? These questions, unavoidable in the complicated world where a legal clinic and collective action come together, are pervasive in every effort to make change, unanswerable in the abstract, and worthy of our sustained attention. Only if we can remain attentive to the tensions without being beaten down by their persistence or drawn into the illusion that we can resolve them—only if we can find a way to work in their midst—will we realize the rich rewards of the relationship between law and organizing.

6

NONCITIZEN CITIZENSHIP

The Workplace Project legal clinic was not the only effort in the community charged with enforcing the law about the minimum wage. Several agencies had the same responsibility. Both New York state and the federal government have departments of labor, supposed guarantors of basic legal standards in the workplace. The New York State Department of Labor (DOL) Division of Labor Standards, and the New York minimum wage laws that it administers, were the resources most immigrant workers turned to, largely because federal wage law and the federal DOL did not cover all workers. Federal law excluded those working for small businesses that did not put goods into the "stream of interstate commerce"—such as the mom and pop restaurants, landscaping companies, and small construction firms for which many immigrants worked.[1] Even immigrants who were covered by the federal law often preferred to go to the state agency, because until 1998 the federal DOL had a policy of sharing information with the Immigration and Naturalization Service, so that a report to the feds about unpaid wages could trigger an immigration raid. The state DOL, on the other hand, maintained strict confidentiality.

Over time, the Workplace Project through its clinic learned a great deal about how the state DOL operated (or, more accurately, did not operate) to enforce wage laws. That body of information, and in particular the way it conflicted with the Project's members' beliefs about what sort of enforcement they had a right to, would become the launching pad for one of the organization's most concerted campaigns. The way the campaign was structured, the obstacles it encountered, and its ultimate victory add another layer to our understanding of how rights talk can function within and outside of an organizing effort.

José M. passed his days and much of his nights chopping tomatoes, pitting olives, and tearing lettuce as the salad man at Pizza Novela Restaurant in Oyster Bay, New York. The restaurant was busy and he worked almost around the clock, but he took the job because by the standards of an immigrant restaurant worker in the early 1990s the promised salary of $400 a week was a good wage—if he had been paid. But after the first few weeks of regular cash compensation, his boss began to equivocate. When José would no longer take excuses in lieu of pay, the boss wrote checks for his wages, checks that promptly bounced. Four months after he began work, José quit. All he had to show for the last eleven weeks of his labors were checks returned by the bank, for a total of $4,400.

José brought his claim to the New York State Department of Labor's Long Island office in 1993. A sympathetic Spanish-speaking investigator called Pizza Novela's owner on the spot, and he admitted to owing the wages but said he was unable to pay. The investigator sent José home with the promise that he would be taking his boss to court. When José heard nothing from the

DOL for three months, he returned to the office, only to find that the sympathetic investigator no longer worked there and that his papers had been lost. José knew that Pizza Novela was still in business. Working with another investigator who spoke almost no Spanish, he refiled his claim.

After a full year of silence from the DOL, the restaurant's doors now closed, José was called into the DOL office. The second investigator told him that the office would not be pursuing his case because of "irregularities" in his claim, such as his report that he had been paid partly in cash and partly by check. José protested that he still had the bounced checks in hand, that his employer had admitted to owing the money—and that recovery might still have been possible if the DOL had pursued the case earlier than fifteen months after he filed it. But he walked out with nothing more than eleven useless checks in his pocket.

On a site that soon would be yet another Long Island office building, Leo Cuenca layered bricks and mortar with the tired efficiency of an expert at the end of a long day.[2] Long, but not unusual: 10- or 12-hour shifts, 6 or 7 days a week, had lately become the norm for Cuenca, an immigrant worker in the midst of a Long Island building boom. Working for a well-established construction company, he had come to look forward to a steady paycheck. Steady, however, did not translate to on the up and up. At the end of each 60-hour workweek, in a scenario repeated throughout the industry, Cuenca would open his envelope to find a check for 40 hours of wages at $8 an hour (well below the standard bricklayer rate), neatly typed up with all taxes deducted. Lying under the check was a stack of cash for his remaining 20 hours of work. The cash was also for $8 an hour, instead of the $12 required by overtime laws.

That missing $4 an hour, times 20 hours each week, times 52 weeks a year, began to add up. In August 1994, when the debt amounted to over $5,000 and his efforts to negotiate with his employer proved fruitless, Cuenca brought his case to the Workplace Project, and with the Project's support, to the New York State Department of Labor. There he met with an investigator, who reviewed Cuenca's careful records and shook his head. "Illegal aliens," he said. "Robbing the taxpayer's money." Cuenca opened his mouth to object that he was here legally and, furthermore, that if anyone bore the blame for taking taxpayer money it should be his employer. But he closed it as the investigator began to speak again. "Look," said the man. "Sure, I can go after these wages for you. But then the IRS will be on your back, and you'll owe more in taxes than you get in wages. Want my advice? Forget about it." Patently untrue (after all, Cuenca had already paid taxes on 40 hours of wages per week), the investigator's statement nonetheless hit its mark. Discouraged, Cuenca left the Department of Labor office having decided not to pursue his case.

In 1988, at her cousin's suggestion, Jessica Lopez had gone to seek work at a factory that made bathroom fixtures.[3] The manager had taken her application and called her for work a few days later. When she arrived on the first day, the manager asked her what she would come to think of as *the question:* "What's your other name?" "My other name?" "The one you'll use on your second shift," the manager answered. Remembering her cousin's long workweeks, Lopez realized that the 200 workers in the factory must be working two 40-hour shifts—one under their own name and one under an assumed name. The scheme was the employer's way of avoiding detection for failing to pay overtime wages. Lopez was not happy, but she had no other options. She shook her head, said "Olivia Margas," and walked onto the shop floor.

In 1993, unwilling to be robbed of so much money any longer and exhausted by working 80-hour weeks for years, Lopez was one of three workers who decided that they would turn the factory's owners in. They came to the Workplace Project, and together filed a claim at the New York State Department of Labor. The DOL did not assign an investigator to the case for 20 months. Once the inquiry began, however, it did not take long to confirm the workers' reports. By failing to pay overtime, the factory owner was racking up a debt to his workers of over $1,000,000 each year.

Despite the workers' and the Workplace Project's request to the contrary, and despite the evidence that this system applied to all 200 workers, the DOL refused to broaden its investigation beyond the three claimants. Although the workers explained that they had worked for at least five years under the same regime, the Department of Labor would only look at the employer's records for the two years before the claim was filed, even though the law authorized them to review records going back six years. The total the DOL found those three workers were due for two years was $35,000—not half of what the owner owed them for five years of work; not even 2 percent of what he owed his workforce as a whole just for those two years. And not only did the DOL bring no criminal prosecution against this willful violator of the labor law, but it did not even penalize him with a fine.

By late 1995, Workplace Project members were angry. If the New York State DOL and New York law were all that stood between many immigrants and wageless work, they were a flimsy shield indeed. The law itself was weak—the maximum penalty for an employer who repeatedly or willfully failed to pay legal wages was a mere 25 percent on top of the total the employer owed; the crime of repeated nonpayment of wages was only a misdemeanor. The agency was weaker. The DOL had but one inspector for every 7,000 private businesses on Long Island, and little political will to find and punish violators. Under Governor George Pataki, elected in 1994 as the first Republican to lead New York in over 20 years, the Labor Department had a newly minted mission statement that defined its constituency as "our customers, both workers and employers," a sharp turn away from the previous mission of "protect[ing] the working men, women and children" in the state.[4] Even when it pursued what it called "egregious violators," the agency almost never enforced the minimal penalties at its disposal.[5] The DOL's problems on Long Island were compounded by the fact that it had Spanish-speaking personnel in the office only once every two weeks, for three hours—and no one at other times who could even muster the words to tell an immigrant worker what day to return.

The Workplace Project had been in existence for only three years; it had been a membership organization for only one. But three years was enough to amass a thick file of affidavits and reports about the way that its members and other legal clinic clients had been treated by the state DOL. Beginning in 1993, the Workplace Project kept records of three things: case outcomes, DOL treatment of immigrants seeking assistance at the Long Island office, and DOL handling of cases it accepted. By the end of 1995, the results of this statistic-gathering effort were clear. The Project's computer database contained records of the over 900 Latino workers who had sought help from its legal clinic over the previous three years. It showed that the DOL had rejected many solid cases on capricious and even discriminatory grounds. And it revealed that only two of the 72 Project cases that the DOL did accept over three years, or just 3 percent, resulted in even partial payment to workers. By contrast, over the same period, the Workplace Project, with only one person working half-time on these cases, accepted 234 wage cases for representation and resolved 71 percent of them, winning over $215,000 for 166 workers during that time. The Project's sister organizations in Manhattan, the Latino Worker Center and the Chinese Staff and Workers Association, had similar experiences.

One year was more than enough to build up a sense of outrage.

January 1996. The board at the front of the Workplace Project meeting room is covered with recent statements made by different New York Department of Labor investigators to members who had attempted to file cases with the agency. "I don't like to take claims for domestic workers and restaurant workers." "Claims for housekeepers for overtime . . . are a waste of time." "You have no coworkers so I can't take your case." "We want people coming in here with clean hands." The forty Project members gathered in the room on this cold night tell each other their stories of nonpayment and no redress, and speak of employers who see the level of punishment for violating the wage statute as so slight that the law is irrelevant to their decision about what to pay. The consensus is clear: Wage-enforcement law is ineffective and its keepers are negligent at best, when not overtly hostile to immigrants. Leading the meeting, I ask the group: Why? Who has the power to see that this arrangement is maintained? And, most important, where does the power to change it lie?

February 1996. The list on the board is different tonight. After weeks of *realpolitik* discussion and analysis of the questions raised at the January meeting, Workplace Project members have come together again to develop proposals for change. One man, a Mexican sailor who here works in landscaping, suggests that the Department of Labor impose a much higher penalty for repeat nonpayment—perhaps 200 percent over the amount originally owed. Another proposes a felony charge for willful violators rather than a misdemeanor. Thinking of Jessica Lopez, a third worker suggests requiring the Department of Labor to review employers' files for the full six years permitted by law, rather than just the two years it is looking back now. A domestic worker from Colombia describes her idea of creating a special office to oversee the DOL's work with low-wage workers. Similar processes at the Latino Worker Center and the Chinese Staff and Workers Association are generating other proposals: a prohibition on DOL settlements for less than 100 percent of the amount owed without the workers' permission; a rule that when an employer failed to keep adequate records of wage payment, the burden of proof would shift from the worker (to prove nonpayment) to the employer (to prove that he had paid); a guarantee of translation into Spanish and Chinese.

That the Workplace Project chose to initiate a time-consuming campaign to further the enforcement of minimum wage law might seem to be in tension with its belief that the minimum wage was inadequate. But to the group it felt complementary. Given that so many immigrant workers were paid less than the minimum, giving the law teeth would be an important victory. It was also important to keep fighting for higher wages. The Project and its fellow worker centers saw their campaign as having two prongs: real enforcement and fairer wages. While the legislative effort carried the enforcement prong forward, the

Workplace Project explored the idea of a "living wage" in its membership meetings and continued to experiment with organizing among different sectors of its membership to see what strategies led to wage increases.

In the winter and spring of 1996, the Workplace Project took some tentative steps toward advancing its wage-enforcement proposals. Project members and I gave testimony on the problems with the DOL and our proposed solutions in a legislative hearing sponsored by the Democratic assemblywoman Catherine Nolan, chair of the Assembly Labor Committee. Together with representatives of the Latino Worker Center and the Chinese Staff and Workers Association, the Workplace Project met with the counsel to Assemblywoman Nolan, who drafted a bill in response to our concerns. But none of the three groups did much to support it, and it went nowhere in the 1996 legislative session.

This led to a serious debate within the Workplace Project membership and staff. Compiling a list of dreams was one thing. But for a group of new immigrants, considering leading a battle to make those dreams legislative reality was quite another.

May 1996. A characteristically pessimistic Juan Calderon, a Colombian welder here working as a janitor, stands before his fellow Workplace Project members. How, he argues, can a group like the immigrants gathered in that room lead a campaign to change the law? As he later recalled declaring, "Some of us are afraid even to show our faces. We have no legal status. I don't speak English." No one can deny the truth of his words. Few in the room are bilingual, and almost none can vote: out of the organization's 420 members at the time, approximately 2 percent are citizens, 68 percent are noncitizen legal immigrants, and 30 percent are undocumented immigrants. Rony Martinez, a long-time Project member, echoes Calderon: "If you're not a citizen, how can you make demands? If I can't vote, I'm no one. I'm invisible. How can I protest?"[6]

Gradually, though, the mood shifts. Anger at the Department of Labor and at the weakness of the law, at what employers were allowed to get away with, stirs again in the room. As campaign leader Luz Torres would later reflect, "The thing that made it possible for us to keep going, even when it never seemed like we would win, was knowing how real the problem was, living it daily."[7] A new thought begins to gain currency: "We probably can't win. But we might learn a lot—and what do we stand to lose if we try?" The question is not a rhetorical one. Members are afraid that entering an open political contest will expose not only their ignorance about the political process but their immigration status, rendering them vulnerable to firing and deportation. And yet, as the discussion gathers intensity, the possibility of shaming the Department of Labor, of increasing awareness of the problem, and of learning what it feels like to try to change the law—and the sense that there will be some protection in doing this as a group, under the umbrella of the Workplace Project—begins to hold sway. When the vote is taken about what to do, it is unanimous. The Workplace Project will draft its own bill, the Unpaid Wages Prohibition Act, and with two other worker centers will lead a full-force campaign to pass it in the next legislative session.

If the Project was going to take politics seriously, it had a lot to learn. It was time for more workshops. The focus was Albany and the intricacies of politics as practiced in New York. The prospect was daunting. Even without the complication of the lack of citizenship, to try to pass legislation in New York state was to enter a world of seeming impossibility. The Assembly, dominated by New York City liberals, was and long had been staunchly Democratic, boasting 97 Democrats to 53 Republicans in 1996. The Republicans of the vast upstate farm counties and Long Island controlled the Senate—35 Republicans to 26 Democrats that same year. Not that the date matters much; districts are drawn by the dominant party in each house to ensure that it maintains the same level of control, year after year. In each house of the legislature, one person has absolute say about what reaches the floor: the Assembly Speaker and the Senate majority leader. The power of the controlling political party in each house, and the level of animosity between the houses that has grown up over time, can seem impenetrable. A *New York Times* editorial in 1997 urged voters to approve a constitutional convention because "in New York the chances for reform are so rare, the price of inaction is so great, and the status quo is so wretched."[8]

Looking at this system with an eye toward winning passage of the Unpaid Wages Prohibition Act made one thing was clear. The Assembly would be easy—Labor Committee Chair Nolan would introduce the bill again and gather support. But without strong Republican backing, the Senate would not move. Therefore the bill had to be introduced in the Senate by a Republican, preferably by the chair of the Senate Labor Committee, Nicholas Spano, and it had to have cosponsorship that demonstrated serious Republican support. The Long Island delegation was a natural target.[9] Long Island's delegation to the Senate is made up of nine staunch Republicans. Moderate to conservative, very powerful, tightly adherent to party discipline, it plays a critical role in this political system. With the support of the majority of the Long Island delegation, almost any legislation can pass in the Senate; without it, it can easily wither and die.[10]

But winning Republican support for an immigrant issue in
1996 was no simple matter. The Unpaid Wages Prohibition Act
campaign would be launched in the midst of a tidal wave of anti-
immigrant legislation around the country. Proposition 187 had
recently passed in California, with its attempt to bar undocumented immigrants in that state from using publicly funded
health care, receiving public benefits, or enrolling in the public
schools.[11] At the federal level the immigrant-bashing triumvi-
rate of the Anti-Terrorism Act, the Personal Responsibility Act,
and the Illegal Immigration Reform and Responsibility Act were
voted into law as the campaign intensified in 1996. New York
and Long Island were far from immune to these trends. Suffolk
County was in the midst of a virulent "English-only" battle that
was garnering national attention. Unbeknownst to the Workplace Project, many of the senators whose support the bill would
need to pass had not only voted for but had sponsored some
of the most anti-immigrant and antiworker bills that passed
through the Senate in the mid-1990s. Long Island Republican
Senator Carl Marcellino, who would become the Unpaid Wages
Prohibition Act's primary sponsor, had introduced legislation
that would have denied undocumented children the right to attend public schools, required that schools investigate and report
"suspected illegal aliens," prohibited public hospitals from treating undocumented patients, barred undocumented immigrants
from all public benefits, and mandated cooperation between local police and the INS to enhance immigrant deportations. Every one of the Unpaid Wages Prohibition Act's other eventual
sponsors had voted in favor of each of these provisions every
time they came to the floor, arguing that New York had given
immigrants too easy a ride. As eventual Unpaid Wages Prohibition Act sponsor Senator Marchi had said several years earlier,

"It is street knowledge around the world that we're under a mandate to provide relief . . . We've become a magnet, saying 'Come to New York, and we'll take care of you.'"[12]

On labor issues, things were no better. Bills benefiting workers face a particularly tough road in Albany. Agriculture is still the top industry in New York state, and the Farm Bureau, a private industry organization representing farmers, exerts powerful influence over the Senate. The governor is from an upstate farm family himself. Unions are not a strong force in the legislature.[13] In this context, ostensibly simple legislation can become tangled in debate and rancor for years. For example, a bill guaranteeing clean drinking water to farm workers in the fields had to be reintroduced five times over as many years before finally passing in 1996. Again, although Workplace Project staff and members did not realize this at the time, those whose sponsorship the organization would need for its bill had taken positions against workers on repeated occasions. In 1995, Labor Committee Chair Senator Spano (who would become the "co-prime" sponsor of the Unpaid Wages Prohibition Act) and three others had sponsored a failed bill to repeal the New York corporations law permitting workers owed back wages to collect them from the ten largest shareholders of the company if the company itself did not obey a court judgment. With Senator Spano in charge and four Long Island Senators on the Labor Committee, the Senate had for several years been unwilling to pass legislation bringing New York's minimum wage up from $4.25 an hour to the level of the federal minimum wage, $5.15 an hour.

The Workplace Project membership was sobered by the contrast between the official version of "how a bill becomes law" and the reality of politics in Albany. As José Ramirez says, looking back, "I remember when Omar [Henriquez] showed us how hard it is to pass a law, how many bills get stuck in committees or they are voted against and you have to start all over the next year." But at least the obstacles were clear at the outset. Perhaps because they were so clear, and so daunting, the Workplace Project staff and membership were freed to organize their effort in a way and at a pace that maximized member leadership and made full participation possible. By taking both the process of political participation and the process of passing a bill seriously, the Workplace Project put immigrant workers in a position to learn at first hand about power, politics, and the legislative process, and put Republican senators in a position to learn first hand about the concerns of immigrant workers. The campaign was fed by the desire to learn *what it felt like* to try to change a law—to butt heads against the obstacles of the political process and discover its open doors—rather than by a belief that it could actually succeed.

Full participation meant that the work of figuring out a strategy to win Republican support would be a participatory process. The targets were Republicans, and the goal was to get them to make the bill their own, to actually sponsor rather than just vote for it. But how?

May 1996. A smaller group has gathered tonight, the nascent campaign's strategy committee. As it becomes clearer that the organization cannot win this campaign by viewing Republicans as automatic opponents, I have called the committee of fifteen together with staff to talk about why Republicans are choosing to malign immigrants at this moment, and how to appeal to these unlikely supporters. "The politicians need a scapegoat," says one woman. "They say immigrants take money from the government, that we want welfare, that we don't pay taxes." "Great scapegoat," comments another member sardonically.

"Doesn't bleat back." I ask, *How does what they say compare to your experience?* "I work. And I pay money in taxes." *What about welfare?* "The only time anyone in my family has had to get food stamps was when I wasn't paid for my work." "Anyway, most immigrants can't get welfare." *What do you hear your employers talking about?* "My landscaping boss says if it wasn't for all the other companies underbidding him by hiring 'illegals' and paying cash wages below the minimum, he could pay us more." Others in the room who had worked in landscaping and construction had heard the same thing. They laugh at the idea that the employer won't just pocket the extra money.

But if that is what employers are saying, I ask, *are there ways that the Unpaid Wages Prohibition Act serves the interests that Republicans and business owners claim to have?* Suddenly, ideas come quickly. By putting money into the pockets of workers who had earned it, the bill would avoid the need for families to rely on public benefits—thus the Project could claim that it reduced dependence on welfare. Because the bill would strongly penalize employers who paid illegally low wages, the Project could talk about how it would fight unfair competition and benefit "good" businesspeople. And because it would cost little or nothing to implement, and since the penalties it would generate would go directly to the state's coffers and taxes, the Project could emphasize that the act was a way to increase revenue to the state. The group had found the core of its arguments.

This message was certainly couched in conventional Republican-speak. Indeed, the strategy the group developed was conventional throughout: generate pressure from constituents, from allies, from the press; meet with senators directly to ask for their support and talk to them on their own terms about why this legislation is in their interest. Except, of course, that it was not conventional in the least. Immigrant workers, the constituents most likely to write letters, weren't seen by the senators as constituents at all. Among the allies members would seek were business associations, the groups who at first appeared most likely to oppose the law. And the legislative visits would be carried out by people who could not vote or speak English, asking for the support of senators who were the champions of English-only and immigrants-go-home.

Curious to see what would happen, the Workplace Project staff and members began the work of gathering support. The organization's staff asked for and received endorsements for the act from both the Long Island Association (LIA), Long Island's most respected business group, and the Long Island chapter of the New York State Restaurant Association, on the unfair competition theory that these business groups represented the "good" employers who were being undercut by "bad" employers outside their memberships who failed to pay the minimum wage. The LIA responded to a letter and a brief meeting with a letter of support, convinced by the fairness argument in a boom economy and by its own desire to demonstrate to small business owners that the LIA championed their issues as well as those of larger firms.[14] The New York State Restaurant Association was somewhat harder to convince. This is not surprising, given that restaurants are among the biggest violators of wage and hour laws. The Project argued that the bill was in the best interests of the Restaurant Association's members, presumably the "good" restaurant employers, because they were the ones being directly undercut by the subminimum wage employers in their industry. This put the association in a position where saying no would have been tantamount to admitting that their members were the "bad" employers who routinely violated the law. The association's statewide chapter took no position on the legislation, and was later rumored to be working behind the scenes to stop its passage, but the Long Island chapter did write a letter of support, and subsequently made several positive statements to the press. These unexpected allies would prove immeasurably helpful in the battle that lay ahead.

Their endorsement was eventually complemented those of a more traditional array of supporters, including ACORN, the New York City and State Labor Councils, UNITE! the ACLU, Catholic Charities, nine prominent rabbis, and the Legal Aid Society. Most of these supporters did little other than lend their names to the cause. But several, including Legal Aid and UNITE! provided lobbying support in the final weeks, and UNITE! asked its members to write letters of support in their English classes. Other unions, including the 1199 Health and Hospital Workers Union, United Food and Commercial Workers (UFCW) Local 342-50, and the Long Island Building Trades, also wrote letters of support as the campaign gathered steam.

While staff concentrated on broad institutional endorsements, members approached fellow immigrants, their churches, their unions, and their employers to collect signatures on letters directed toward key senators and the Speaker of the Assembly. About thirty members worked on this throughout the summer of 1996. Their experiences provided a quick check on the initial instinct that this would be a good and easy way for immigrants to promote the campaign.

July 1996. Despite members' best efforts, all has not gone well. Although they have easily communicated to fellow immigrants the unfairness of the situation—"if we steal a candy bar from a store, they put us in jail; if an employer steals a thousand dollars from a worker, he doesn't even get a slap on the wrist"—they have been met with reluctance and even hostility when they asked others to follow up on that sense of injustice by putting their names and addresses on a letter to be sent to a government official. José Ramirez reports, "when I asked people I knew to sign, some wouldn't even hear of it. Some, out of fear, said 'Will it hurt me?' And I would explain, and even then they wouldn't sign. [They thought] how can I give my name? Immigration might show up, or the police, or later someone might call or confront me about my support." Another member stands up to tell the group that she was thrown out of her cousin's home. "'You must be crazy!' my cousin said to me. 'The government is doing everything it can to throw us out and you want me to give them my name and address? Why not a map to our front door!'" Half laughing, shaking her head, she sits back down.

Luz Torres, a domestic worker, is one of the members who asked their employers to sign, a strategy that produced few letters but some interesting reflections. Torres gives her analysis of why she was able to get letters of support from immigrants (the poor, who stood to gain from the legislation) and her wealthiest employers (the very rich, who had little to lose if the bill passed), but not from middle-class people. "The middle class in this country is like a sandwich. There are so many of them, right? . . . I have started to think that middle-class people are brainwashed. Or they don't want to know. They think this country is perfect, clean, that politics or the system here is full of integrity. And it works for the political system, to keep [the middle class] that way. I see it when I try to talk to them. They don't believe the terrible things that happen here. You have to prove it to them, but they refuse to believe it could happen in the United States. That's why I only asked poor people I know, or very rich people I work for, to sign the letters in support of the campaign. They signed, but middle-class people I work for wouldn't. One lady whose house I clean told me, 'You Hispanics are using the Work-place Project to take advantage of the American people.'"

Others report their frustration at attempts to get institutional support. At the beginning of their letter-gathering efforts, members had generated a list of all the local institutions they belonged to—churches, labor unions, and the like. But few held positions of power in those institutions or were connected to powerful people within them. One member reports that a request to her shop steward that the union support the Unpaid Wages Prohibition Act campaign repeatedly got lost before it made its way up through the business agent to anyone with decision-making authority in the local or international union. Another member requested a letter of support from the nun in charge of parish outreach for the Latino community at her Catholic church, who passed the request to the priest who presided over Spanish-language mass, who in turn had to discuss it with the priest in charge of the parish, who then had to take it up the Catholic hierarchy on Long Island. She never received an answer. The only good news on the religious front comes from a member active in a small Latino Protestant congregation run by a charismatic pastor. His pastor, alone among the clergy members approached by members, gave a letter of support in response to his request.

In the end, perhaps not surprisingly, it turned out that the Workplace Project as an institution was much more successful in recruiting institutional support than its individual members. But despite the obstacles they encountered, Project members persevered, collecting over 400 letters, almost all from other immigrants. Each one of those contacts, difficult though it was, served a dual purpose in addition to adding another letter to the pile: it gave members practice in outreach and organizing skills, and it spread the word in the community about the work of the organization.

March 1997. In the cramped Long Island office of yet another Republican senator, Luz Torres concludes her opening presentation about the Unpaid Wages Prohibition Act. The senator leans back in his chair, tie loosened. "Can you tell me that this bill isn't going to flood the state with illegals?" Through the headphones, his question echoes in the ears of his visitors: "Me pueden decir que esta propuesta de ley no causará una inundación de ilegales en el estado?" The senator is looking at the translator, the only white person in the room. The translator, along with ten other people in the room, is looking at José Martinez. Martinez responds: "Esta ley no da a inmigrantes indocumentados ningún derecho que no tenían antes . . ." And as the translator begins to convey his words, the senator, through his headphones, hears the response: "This law doesn't give undocumented immigrants any right they didn't already have. New York already requires that undocumented workers be paid minimum wage, so that employers don't take jobs away from citizens. This bill only raises the penalties to deter repeat violators." Engaged, the senator fires back, "But we have a Department of Labor. And it seems to me they're doing a fine job." Doris Ayarza picks up the thread. "En verdad, el castigo para el patrón que no paga al trabajador no es suficiente para . . . "The truth is, the punishment for an employer who doesn't pay his workers is not sufficient to deter an employer who thinks it's to his advantage to pay less than minimum. For example, . . ." As the afternoon wears away, the meeting continues, back and forth. By the end, the group has interested one more unlikely ally in their cause.

These meetings were the product of intensive work by Workplace Project members and staff. Each team of ten workers chose a leader to make its opening presentation, and then assigned responsibility among its members to address different areas of common senatorial concern. Participants spent long evenings in role-plays, rehearsing their presentations and their responses to the questions it seemed likely senators would ask. Using materials that Project staff had developed on the basis of earlier visits and had constantly revised, participants argued their case against concerns about the bill's impact on business, illegal immigration, and the state coffers, until they were confident of their ability to respond. Much of the material was conventional, the same ground that any lobbying group would cover. In other areas it walked less well-trodden paths: What would they say if the senator asked who in the room could vote? How should they deal with a senator who balked at putting on the translation headphones? What should they do if the senator insisted on speaking with the only white or English-speaking person in the room, the translator, and ignored the workers?

As Workplace Project members visited senator after senator, sometimes accompanied by Latino Worker Center representatives, the Project was making sure that employers who failed to pay the minimum wage were taking a pounding in the press. The public and legislators would have no reason to support this legislation unless they knew about the scores of busboys and dishwashers earning less than $2.50 an hour for 80-hour weeks, the gardeners and landscape workers who often went without pay for weeks on end, and the domestic workers who labored from 6:00 A.M. to 11:00 P.M. for wages of less than $2 an hour. The organization's staff worked with reporters from *Newsday*, the *New York Times*, and local papers throughout the spring of 1997 on stories to build a climate of outrage by emphasizing the still-surprising news that sweatshops had become common on Long Island. The media also conveyed the organization's message that part of the blame for these circumstances lay in weak state laws and inadequate New York State Department of Labor enforcement practices, and reinforced the points that the bill was supported by business organizations and that it would bring revenue to the state in a number of ways.

The press coverage that the group received played a critical role in garnering legislative support for the campaign. When *Newsday* did a Sunday full-cover story on restaurant workers on Long Island being paid less than half the minimum wage (an article on which Project staff and members worked with the newspaper for months), featuring the legislation as an important part of the solution to the problem, it put senators who would have liked to ignore the bill in an awkward position. For example, during the months leading up to the publication of that story, the Project had been in frequent contact with the office of Senate Labor Committee Chair Senator Spano to request that he sponsor the legislation. As Ken Crowe, then *Newsday*'s labor reporter, put the finishing touches on the story, the senator's aide called the Workplace Project to report that he had decided not to become a sponsor. Crowe called him and told him the substance of the story he would be publishing, informed him that the Unpaid Wages Prohibition Act would be featured in the article, and asked if the senator could confirm and explain his refusal to sponsor the legislation. Senator Spano's assistant called back within half an hour to say that the senator would be cosponsoring the bill.

The bill also benefited from editorial support from several key newspapers, the *New York Times* and the politically influential *Schenectady Daily Gazette* among them, and from intensive local press coverage that put constant pressure on legislators in their home districts. This coverage was born of the Project's close attention to relationships with reporters, its persistence, and its ability to back up its claims with numerical data and with the compelling stories of individual workers. With the support of long-time labor journalists such as *Newsday*'s Crowe, the Project succeeded in framing the issue of unpaid wages as a source of shame for Long Island and in presenting the Unpaid Wages Prohibition Act as an important step in remedying that injustice.

June 1997. The Unpaid Wages Prohibition Act is closer to passage than the Workplace Project had ever imagined it would be. The majority of the Long Island delegation have become sponsors, and the bill is finally in position for a vote in the Senate. But before it can get there, two sticking points have arisen, provisions that the Department of Labor is refusing to support: Spanish and Chinese translation, and the creation of an ombudsman's office for low-wage workers. If the DOL pulls its backing, the counsel for the Senate Labor Committee had told me in a call the previous day, the bill is dead. He pushed for an immediate response, but I could not give one. The people with the authority to make a decision like this were the members of the Workplace Project, the Chinese Staff and Workers Association, and the Latino Worker Center, and they took a day to gather. Now that they had, the debate was rough. *They want us to sell out. What good are the higher penalties to immigrants if there's no one at the DOL for them to talk to?* "So, great. We stand on our principles and lose the chance to make it a felony not to pay your workers? To make employers pay *three times* what they owe?" The phone rings: Mónica Santana of the Latino Worker Center. It has decided to support the bill with the cuts. The Chinese Staff and Workers Association has already made a similar decision. At the Workplace Project, members keep debating. *If we give in, it's like saying that it's OK for the DOL not to pay attention to low-wage immigrant workers.* "Right now, we have the Republicans between a rock and a hard place. If we stop, there may not be another moment like this. We may lose everything." At the end of a long evening, consensus moves toward salvage. The members vote to allow those cuts, but to withdraw their support if any more are proposed. The decision is not easy. But it is an important moment of political realism of the kind that only comes with active political participation.

July 1997. With the unexpected sponsorships of key Republicans and the more predictable support of many Democrats, the Unpaid Wages Prohibition Act is in a strong position as it is brought to the floor of the legislature. On July 2, 1997, the Senate and Assembly vote unanimously to pass the act. Ten weeks later, after the Workplace Project leads a prolonged organizing battle against the New York Farm Bureau, the farmers' organization that staunchly opposes the bill, and the *New York Times* publishes a Labor Day weekend editorial urging prompt action, Governor Pataki signs it into law.[15] The campaign for the Unpaid Wages Prohibition Act has ended in victory.

Victory in the legislature did not end the battle. In terms of wage collection, the Unpaid Wages Prohibition Act has had a mixed impact. The campaign briefly succeeded in increasing the speed with which the local New York State Department of Labor office processed claims and in making Spanish-speaking personnel available, and resulted in a new and faster central docketing system for the Department of Labor statewide.[16] But despite Department of Labor officials' recognition that the law provides them with powerful leverage to settle cases under the threat of higher penalties, the department initiated no new push to collect wages in the years following the act's implementation.[17] The first prosecution of an unpaid wages case as a felony did not come until four and a half years after the bill became law.

If it was underused by the Department of Labor, the law proved a potent tool for activists and for activist government officials, particularly New York State Attorney General Eliot Spitzer. The "big stick" of a 200 percent penalty has been wielded by groups as diverse as the American Federation of Musicians and a campaign to organize undocumented Mexican workers of greengroceries in Manhattan.[18] In the case of the greengrocery workers, the law became an element of an organizing strategy. According to Jeff Eichler, the organizing director of UNITE! Local 169, the union responsible for the first several years of the campaign, the greengrocery effort was successful in unionizing Mexican immigrants in 2000 and 2001, in part because of their employers' fear of being charged the 200 percent penalty on the considerable back wages that they owed, a debt resulting from the industry practice of paying subminimum wages. The workers seeking to form a union would offer to forgo pursuit of their claims under the act in exchange for a contract that raised wages and provided other benefits. If the employer refused, the union would work with the attorney general to collect the wages and penalties owed. According to Eichler, the Unpaid Wages Prohibition Act was thus "a very important component" in the effort to draw workers to the union and to pressure their employers.[19] Where employers rejected the union, the campaign went on to collect hundreds of thousands of dollars in wages and penalties on behalf of greengrocery workers under the act, with the support of the attorney general's office.

In a story like this, victory is an unexpected dénouement. Conventionally, power in the legislative system is seen to come from two sources: votes or money. And conventionally, immigrant workers are thought to wield neither. At the time of the campaign, 98 percent of the Project's members were noncitizens, most either undocumented or holding temporary permits not designed to transition to permanent residence. Certainly they were not wealthy. How, then, did this campaign move a Republican Senate and governor to support strong legislation written by and for immigrant workers, at the peak of local and national anti-immigrant sentiment in the Republican Party?

To some extent, we can answer the question of how the act became law quite simply through the traditional lenses of power and interest group politics. Although the campaign for the Unpaid Wages Prohibition Act started in 1996, by mid-1997 what Long Island Republican Senator Carl Marcellino calls "the game of politics" was being played with a new comprehension of a demographic shift long under way. Republicans were late awakening to the realization that Latino voters, reputed to be deeply religious and socially conservative, could be the party's ticket to the next century. Local statistics proved the point. Census data, unquestionably an undercount, put the growth of New York State's Hispanic population at 50 percent between 1980 and 1990, and there would be another 30 percent jump from 1990 to 2000; Long Island saw a leap of 80 percent in its Latino residents between 1980 and 1990, with a further increase of 70 percent to come from 1990 to 2000. As Senator Marcellino observed, "[His-

panics] are a major part of my constituency. . . . Ten or fifteen
years ago you didn't have the same volume of people, there's a
lot more of them here now . . . That's the game of politics, whatever group is there you're going to try to appeal to and try
to bring them under your umbrella to increase your membership."[20] But the Republican Party's vociferous and successful
support of Proposition 187 and federal anti-immigrant legislation in 1996 had proven a deadly move. Even as the numbers of
Latinos were increasing exponentially, they were showing little
attachment to the Republicans, making clear their distaste for a
xenophobic political party.

The Workplace Project and its worker center allies saw this opportunity, and framed their campaign to take advantage of it.
Strategic resourcefulness—the ability to recognize and leverage
new opportunities as they present themselves—is also a source of
power.[21] As a nod toward attracting disgruntled Latinos, an ac-
knowledgment of their potential power in the future, the Unpaid Wages Prohibition Act had appeal. And as the groups presented it, the bill seemed likely to ruffle few other feathers in the
process. It demanded no additional state expenditures; in fact,
through increased collection of penalties and reduced welfare
rolls, it promised to bring additional money into the state's coffers. The severe punishment the bill imposed, a 200 percent civil
fine and a felony with a maximum $20,000 criminal penalty, ap-
plied only to repeat or willful violators of wage payment laws.
The bill applied to all employers and all workers, mentioning immigrants nowhere in its text. The business endorsements of the
legislation and its focus on enforcing existing minimums
against repeat violators rather than on increasing the base wage
seemed likely to avert controversy among employers. Indeed, the
way the bill was constructed meant that any organization or in-

dividual who wanted to oppose it would have had to come out publicly in favor of companies that repeatedly failed to pay their workers. As Senator Marcellino would later reflect, "Nobody heavy came out against it . . . not really anybody. I think frankly once the bill was out there and people understood what it was supposed to do, people were hard pressed to come out opposed to it and not look like some kind of ogre. Even if they were inclined to lean against it, they just kind of walked away from that." Low in financial and political cost, high in presumed appeal to Latino voters: the Unpaid Wages Prohibition Act's attractions are clear.

Part of the reason the act passed, however, is not clear at all. Many businesses that made up a critical part of these senators' constituency and donor base were in industries where wages below the minimum or frequent nonpayment of wages were common practices. The Farm Bureau, representing agricultural employers; small landscaping and construction firms; even the Restaurant Association, despite the endorsement of the bill by its Long Island branch: at least behind the scenes, they were making their interests known. And they had a ready weapon. Helping deserving workers and good businesses was one thing. But that, they claimed, was not the purpose of this bill. *This* bill was, as the *New York Post* said, an "Illegal Worker Protection Act" in disguise. And yet Republican legislators who had previously declared war on "illegals" were willing to champion the Unpaid Wages Prohibition Act. Why did they sponsor the bill despite its obvious benefits to undocumented workers? And, given their vociferously anti-immigrant records, why did these senators treat Workplace Project members who were not citizens, who had no money and no votes to offer, as legitimate political participants?

Faced with a question such as this, it seems reasonable to go directly to the source. A year after the legislation passed, I returned to interview Senators Marcellino and Skelos about their roles.[22] Political expediency—the need for Latino votes and the low political and fiscal cost of this legislation—surfaced frequently in our conversations. But the discussion with each senator kept circling back to his view of immigrants. It is worth considering that some part of what moved the senators had nothing to do with money or votes but instead with a different kind of power, the power of moral suasion that grew from their identification with the immigrant stories that worker participants presented, and thus a willingness to address the suffering they described.

Both senators, like most of their colleagues from the area, were second- or at most third-generation immigrants themselves. Marcellino is the grandson of Italian immigrants, and speaks with pride about his grandfather's work as a laborer and what his family did to make his success possible. "They came the hard way up, that's all. They got their children through school, and their children, my mother and father, worked very hard to get my brother and myself a college education." He is proud of their mastery of English and their assimilation into American society. He emphasizes that life as an immigrant was tough: "Ellis Island—you know, we treat it like it's a shrine right now, but it was an extremely horrible place for the people who came through." Another Republican supporter, Senator Nicholas Spano, is also the grandson of Italian immigrants who made their living in the United States delivering ice and coal. Skelos remembers the labor and suffering of his Greek grandfather: "I mean I came from a background of immigrants, and most of us did in this country, and I saw what my grandfather did. My grandfather was a waiter who was involved in unionizing the restaurant workers, way back. You know, I'm told he was even beat up once because of his labor activities. So, you know, that experience is all there."[23]

Like the country as a whole, these Republican legislators seem to operate on a dual and contradictory mythology of immigration. In their eyes, "good" immigrants built this country. "Good" immigrants, not coincidentally represented in the senators' personal mythologies by their forebears, came legally, quickly learned English, valued education, worked hard, suffered many knocks, and became part of the melting pot. Then there are the "bad" immigrants—the "illegals," non-English-speaking, who come wanting to take from the system, and who have not assimilated. Marcellino emphasized that immigrants should be allowed to "come to the country, but come legally . . . become part of the melting pot . . . People who are illegal are not going to contribute to the society as such. They have to be contributing members, they have to be taxpayers . . . I'd like to see everybody learn English." Skelos, speaking of his grandfather's generation, says "They wanted to work, they wanted to be treated with respect, but they also didn't tolerate people who would abuse the system or take advantage of the system, or want to have government handouts and not work, and had no intention of working."

What is intriguing about the senators' support for the Unpaid Wages Prohibition Act is that work and hard knocks trumped all of the other elements on the list. Workplace Project members may have been undocumented and so uncomfortable with English that the meeting was carried out in Spanish—two of the most reviled characteristics of "bad" immigrants—but they had come to talk about work and hard knocks. And when they, as immigrants, spoke of what they had suffered at the hands of unscrupulous employers while trying to make a better life for their families, they challenged the senators' conception of these new, brown, Spanish-speaking immigrants as takers. They sounded surprisingly like forebears. It was hard for the senators to separate *these* immigrants, sitting before them with dignity and talking about their struggle to be paid for their labor, from their own families and their experiences of building a life in the United States.

From the senators' perspective, their meetings with Workplace Project members represented the first time that most if not all of them had participated in a meeting with immigrants that was run by the immigrants themselves, who spoke to the senator's political interests and made a request that the senators could relate to their own family histories. The unusual structure of the visit made it stand out in a legislator's mind; the image it presented of immigrant workers as hard-working, engaged members of a community made it stay there. As immigrant workers sat before these senators, they told stories that placed them squarely within the worker/forebear tradition, although they were as far from citizens as they could be. In the process they gained a measure of political legitimacy.

Once the senators had identified the immigrant beneficiaries of the legislation as hard-working forebears, they were suddenly concerned about fairness, even as they acknowledged that they were talking about undocumented immigrants. Marcellino said that he felt strongly that immigrants should "come legally. That being said, if you're here, you shouldn't be mistreated or abused. We should be treating everybody fairly." Skelos, in response to a question about whether he saw any inconsistency between his support for legislation that would have denied public schooling and basic health care to undocumented immigrants, and this legislation once it was cast as an "illegal worker protection act," said, "No, because what you have here is people that are trying to be productive and earn a living, and you want to protect people that are looking to be productive and earn a living."

There is no cause to exaggerate the transformation in these legislators, or what immigrants could achieve once accepted by them as political participants. After all, the same senators had kept New York's minimum wage below the federal minimum, tried to undermine even the minimal benefits of the workers' compensation system, and so on, and they gave no sign of reconsidering these positions as a result of their experience with the Unpaid Wages Act. Yet it remains remarkable that conservative senators were able to see noncitizen immigrants as legitimate political actors at all.

Explicitly excluded from citizenship and in many cases forbidden to work, through the Unpaid Wages Prohibition Act campaign immigrants nonetheless came to act like citizens and won recognition for their basic rights as workers. As a Workplace Project member from El Salvador said to a member from Colombia, rushing through the fluorescent-lit underground pathways below the New York State legislative building in Albany during the Unpaid Wages Prohibition Act campaign: "When I crossed a tunnel under the border five years ago, I didn't think the next tunnel I'd find myself in would be this one." The story of the creation and passage of this law by people legally excluded from our political system suggests some further thoughts about the possibilities and the limitations of rights talk.

Conventional citizenship education tends to take a highly

stylized form. The phrase evokes images of immigrants and middle school students memorizing lists of presidents and historic events, with a trip to a state capitol or Washington, D.C., to leaven the class. Most civic education programs focus on the design of our political system, emphasizing a textbook version of democracy: how the people elect the president, how a bill becomes law, how the protections in the Constitution work. They do not explore the problems with our governmental and electoral systems, making no mention of the complex issues of the influence of money on politics, concentrated corporate control of the media, voter ignorance and apathy, or the very real barriers to meaningful participation in politics for most people. Nor do they provide immigrants with opportunities for political action beyond voting and perhaps letter writing.

Such a process not only presents an unrealistic version of how democracy works in the United States, but is based on the erroneous assumption that new immigrants and voters-to-be need nothing more than the title of citizen and some rudimentary classroom education to become effective political participants. This assumption is refuted by a series of recent studies by the political scientist Louis DeSipio. After analyzing significant data on Latino immigrants, DeSipio concludes that "naturalization does not serve as a spur to organizational participation, nor does it promote electoral involvement." In fact, when all other factors (including age, education, source of citizenship, English-language ability, income, employment) were held constant, he found that "the naturalized were *less likely* to register or vote than were the native born" (emphasis added). The only exceptions occurred where there was a powerful system of ethnic leaders and party bosses, as was the case with the New Deal, or strong community pressure to participate, as with the Cubans in

Miami. He concludes that without strong community support and mobilization "new citizens may be more likely to be excluded from U.S. politics than are comparably situated native-born citizens."[24]

In the case of the Unpaid Wages Prohibition Act, for its few citizen members and for many noncitizens as well, the Workplace Project served as the source of community support and mobilization that DeSipio identifies as so important to political participation. Its Workers Course and membership discussions created a dynamic if informal kind of citizenship education, and its organizing campaigns became a channel through which participants could experiment with different forms of political activism.[25] Rights talk and a growing rights consciousness played critical roles in this process.

In its many manifestations at the Workplace Project, rights talk scaffolded these immigrants' belief in themselves as legitimate and effective political actors.[26] Rights talk provided immigrant workers with a structure of support that, over time and with much discussion, changed not only how they saw themselves but what they were capable of doing. Many immigrants initially saw themselves as rights-less in the workplace and excluded from the political sphere. Through the clinic and the Workers Course, they learned about basic workplace laws and began grappling with the meaning of being people with rights on paper that were rarely realized. Indeed, the roots of the Unpaid Wages Prohibition Act lay in the first day of each session of the Workers Course, where immigrants began to talk about their experience with wages and wage enforcement. These conversations were picked up again in the 1995 membership meeting, where members and staff began a detailed exploration of their experience with nonpayment of wages and with their attempts to address the problem through the Department of Labor. The discussions moved on to a close analysis of the law and the failed enforcement system that was supposed to guarantee payment. From there they moved to possible solutions, always on the assumption that participants—the affected people themselves—would be working to close the gap.

As the group made a decision to experiment with leading a real legislative campaign, this exploratory cycle of talk led to more concrete debates about how to carry the campaign forward. The result was very different from a traditional advocacy effort on behalf of poor people. Traditionally, the people who suffer a problem have little to do with crafting a solution. Professional advocates and policy-makers hear of problems at a remove, filtered through the reports of service-providers, the media, or other advocates. The professionals then develop legislative proposals, and design a campaign to carry them forward. If "clients" participate in lobbying at all, they are brought along as victims, to tell the story of how they have suffered, rather than to debate solutions. Policy-makers decide which compromises to make and when to make them.

In the campaign for the Unpaid Wages Prohibition Act, by contrast, the affected people planned and executed the campaign as a part of their work at the organization. The Project's tradition of governance through open debate and ample participation became a model for how to conduct the campaign. Immigrant workers discussed political approaches and ways of communicating their message, explored the interests of those presumed to be their opponents, and prepared themselves to meet them on some combination of the opponents' ground (the "Republican-speak" message, the arguments about the senators' interests) and the immigrants' own (the meetings held in Spanish, the very act of understanding and presenting themselves as political participants to be taken seriously). They made critical decisions about cuts in the bill. Through this process of action and deliberation they built a belief in their ability to act that increased in step with the proof of the effectiveness of their actions.

Growing from the debates and conversations that made up the building blocks of the campaign was a complex process of transformation. As Workplace Project members talked about their rights and about the political system, they made something possible for themselves that they had previously believed impossible. In an unusual sense of the phrase, they *talked themselves into* their own agency. By this I do not mean that they were convincing themselves to have courage where once they were weak, although courage grew hand in hand with agency in the process. Instead, through the process of jointly imagining what they might do, they moved themselves toward the capacity to do it, to make possible what had seemed impossible, to live out what they could not even, before, have conceived of. Through talk—a particular kind of talk, focused on analyzing a situation critically and creating a solution, in a context of institutional support for action—they developed a vision of themselves as legitimate and capable actors in the political system. Along the way, talk became action, and their action and reflection on it strengthened their sense of themselves as effective actors—and built their actual ability to act. The result was a group of people who had begun with talk about rights yet ended up acting in ways not envisioned by the law, indeed in ways beyond the boundaries of the law's definition of who was entitled to do the work of citizenship.

This process touches on all of the critical elements of real citizenship education: an introduction to the ideal model around which politics in the United States is shaped and also to the very different way that it functions in reality, an analysis of how the political process might address concrete problems in participants' lives, the development among participants of a belief in their own capacity and legitimacy as political actors, and the move from talk into action. It also illustrates how important it is that citizenship education take place in the context of an ongoing effort to build organizing institutions in the communities in which immigrants live. An individual campaign will win or it will lose. People join in because it affects them, and leave when it is done. By contrast, a stable organization out of which such campaigns are run can provide training, support, and community to its members before, during, and between campaigns. Through structures to develop internal democracy and member leadership, it can model the democracy it works toward in the outside world. Such community organizations permit the lessons learned in each campaign to feed back into future efforts, the leadership developed to become leadership for the next stage of organizing, the power built to augment the strength of the next campaign, and the creation of an "organizing culture" in a community to lead to consistent opportunities for analysis and change.

It is one thing for a group of immigrants to convince *themselves* that they are legitimate political participants. But what happens when they take that belief outside the walls of the organization? How can a group of noncitizens assert their rights through the political system when most Americans—even those sympathetic to immigration—assume they have no voice there?

Earlier I suggested that immigrants' use of rights talk both within their organizations and in public was analogous to talk about rights by African-Americans in the civil rights movement, and by others in subsequent social movements. But there is, of course, a critical difference. When black people in the 1950s and 1960s talked about their right to "first-class citizenship," they were seeking to realize in fact what was already recognized by law—that they were citizens with the right to vote and to participate politically in other ways as well. So too with others during the second half of the twentieth century: women, gays and lesbians, and disabled people, to name several. Undocumented immigrants and those with short-term documentation can make no such claim. In order to make an argument about their rights, these immigrants first have to fight the public's assumption that they are entitled to none.

A better parallel is to the struggles of African-Americans before the abolition of slavery and the passage of the Fourteenth Amendment, or to women in the suffrage movement, neither yet legally recognized as voters or full citizens. Hendrik Hartog argues that the idea that citizenship can be claimed and enacted by those who do not legally possess it has its origins in the pre–Civil War period. "In the wake of *Dred Scott,*" he contends, "the faith that constitutional rights required legitimation by the Supreme Court declined as a framework of understanding. Concrete constitutional claims, including the rights to vote and other attributes of citizenship, were imagined as inherent in the individual, not as dependent on recognition by public authority." He elaborates: "At the heart of the constitutional aspiration one finds a critique of all restrictive definitions of citizenship, as reproductions of illegitimate hierarchy. Government cannot know in advance who will be capable of exercising rights. And rights holders are those who do what rights holders do. Those who act as autonomous individuals, . . . whether through collective or solitary activities, grow entitled to rights identified with the choices they have made."[27]

Through the campaign for the Unpaid Wages Prohibition Act, then, immigrants whose very presence in the United States was literally illegal, who were not merely symbolically but actually excluded from the political process, made themselves "like citizens," and then they took that sense of themselves, and acted in the way citizens act, and changed the law: They succeeded in the work of citizenship. But they did not do so through a direct challenge to their political exclusion. This was no accident. Like the senators who supported the act, the United States as a whole exhibits a perennial schizophrenia about immigration that oscillates between celebrating the United States's immigrant heritage on the one hand and blaming new immigrants for every ill in the culture, the economy, and the environment on the other. At times, the pendulum swings in immigrants' favor. The mid-1990s was not one of those times.

In an anti-immigrant climate, for noncitizens to make a direct demand that they be allowed to participate politically would have drawn immediate fire from politicians and many others seeking to defend the polity against "illegitimate encroachers." Even independent of the political mood, noncitizens' exclusion from the vote—once an anomaly—is now established beyond dispute, at least at the state and federal levels.[28] Had a legislator questioned their right to act like constituents by visiting him and proposing a law, Workplace Project members would have stated their belief that, as residents of the state who contributed to its well-being through their work, their taxes, and their purchases, they had a right to take part in the political process when they saw a problem going unaddressed. But in the absence of such a challenge, they did not make the right to participate an issue. They just went ahead and did it.

As they acted, they spoke continually in terms of a particular set of rights—the right of laborers to be paid for their work according to the minimum wage laws and the right to protection against abuse on the job. However frequently they were flouted in practice, these rights were uncontroversial as part of the basic package of safeguards that the public and politicians assumed applied to work in this country. As Senator Marcellino pointed out, a politician who opposed them would have looked like an ogre. In this sense, Project members and their worker center allies were safely within the canon when they advanced the Unpaid Wages Prohibition Act proposal. But when they came forward as and on behalf of immigrants not legally entitled to work, arguing that the same rights should apply to all workers, documented or not, they challenged two critical elements of the common understanding. One was that rights on the job applied only to those with a right to be on the job. And the other was that only citizens were entitled to do the work of citizenship, to press for change through the political process. By avoiding a direct confrontation about their right to participate politically, while calling up a rights-based narrative about immigration that resonated with much of the public and many legislators' own family histories of immigrant work, immigrants brokered a sort of truce, described by Senator Marcellino: immigrants should not immigrate without permission—but "if you're here, you shouldn't be mistreated or abused."

Like many truces around rights, this one came at a price. One effect of the way the group carried out the campaign was to reinforce the illusory line between workers and people on public benefits. When legislators were moved by the idea that these immigrants had a right to make a claim on their attention *because they were workers* (in contrast with "immigrant 'takers'" who would be seeking a handout), the Workplace Project's campaign dovetailed with an inaccurate but politically expedient picture of people who work as a particular category of human beings distinguishable from people who rely on government benefits, and reinforced the sense that politicians should be making decisions on a reward-for-work system.[29] The Workplace Project did not believe in these distinctions, and in fact sought to undermine them in its arguments for the bill, which pointed out that workers who do not get paid (or do not get paid enough to survive on their wages) are the same people who must resort to public benefits—that the line between the two is fluid. But its lobbying efforts were read by senators in the opposite way.

The campaign further bore out Hendrik Hartog's observation that "rights talk has shaped what groups demand as their rights, so that what is demanded has often ended close to what those in power wanted to give."[30] Workplace Project members were well aware that the minimum wage they sought to enforce was grossly inadequate. The minimum wage in New York state at the time—$4.25 an hour—left a parent of two children dangling well below the poverty line even when she worked full time. A much higher wage, perhaps $10 or $12 per hour, would have been necessary to meet such a family's basic needs. But arguing for such a wage was not politically feasible in the state legislature. Instead, Workplace Project members sought the enforcement of existing laws. In so doing, they ran the risk of making it look like they endorsed the minimum wage as a fair measure of compensation, a position they assuredly did not endorse.

Yet if what the Unpaid Wages Prohibition Act achieved on paper was no more than a bolstering of existing minimum wage law, what its immigrant proponents accomplished politically was much greater: They brought the problems of immigrant workers into the limelight and reinserted themselves as rightsbearers in a political debate that had sought to eliminate them entirely.

This is the work of citizenship, although it is practiced by those explicitly denied it. Of course, the campaign for the Unpaid Wages Prohibition Act made no one a citizen. In the eyes of the law, its participants were just as much outsiders when it ended as they had been when it began. What it did do, however, was suggest that while the vote and the right to hold public office are aspects of citizenship that can be granted only by the government, the right to seek social change through the political process—a right at the heart of the meaning of citizenship—can be claimed by people who by virtue of their presence and their work are in fact a part of the political community, although they are not yet officially recognized as such.[31]

The campaign for the Unpaid Wages Prohibition Act brought together many of the threads of the Workplace Project's approach to law. It began with members' own experiences of not being paid and of being turned away by the Department of Labor when they sought help. In this sense it had its roots in the legal clinic, in the organization's belief that that the process of resolving individual problems can lead to insight about where the system has gone wrong—here, the recognition of problems with wage-enforcement law and the DOL—and that these insights can be a powerful inducement to join an organization to work on those same issues more systematically. Many members had faced the problem of unpaid wages directly. Their anger and their knowledge of how the system had failed them fueled their desire to carry the campaign forward. To these individual stories was added the impact on the staff of seeing the same employer repeatedly fail to pay workers, season after season, and the experience of repeatedly failing to resolve legal clinic cases through the New York State Department of Labor. In the aggregate, these experiences made clear that the Department of Labor was doing an inadequate job not just in individual cases, but overall, and that wage-enforcement law as a whole was too weak to serve as a real incentive to employers to obey the law. The legal clinic also was the source of concrete evidence that made the campaign much stronger once it was under way. Affidavits sworn out by workers after they returned from an encounter with the DOL, statements typed up by law students who had accompanied workers to the agency, the statistics generated from the legal clinic database, all played critical roles in convincing the press, the public, and legislators that the problem the bill was intended to address was real and substantial. The campaign was also deeply rooted in the Workers Course, in particular the class's grounding in workers' reality, its analysis of the gap between what the law promises and how it actually works, and its push toward imagining a more just and effective solution.

This process put the Workplace Project's members in a strong position to analyze the external world and engage with it effectively. By crafting the legislation as they did, seeking the endorsements they sought, successfully framing the problems immigrant workers faced as basic justice issues resonant with the immigrant tradition, and visiting legislators themselves, members facilitated the conditions under which their campaign could succeed. The result was an unconventional legislative campaign that succeeded in giving New York the toughest wage-enforcement law in the country—and in the process created a group of people disenfranchised by law but more politically active than most citizens.

CONCLUSION

       Despite the evident obstacles, these are exciting times for immigrant worker organizing. A range of unions today are organizing immigrants who work one step up from those in the underground economy, targeting those in more formal jobs that pay a little more than minimum wage, with a slightly higher level of stability and industry identity. And the absence of unions in the worst jobs does not mean an absence of organizing. The growth of worker centers in immigrant communities has ensured that there is action at the very bottom as well.

As grass-roots institutions, worker centers seek to build the collective power of their largely immigrant members and to raise wages and improve working conditions in the bottom-of-the-ladder jobs where they labor. According to the National Study on Immigrant Worker Centers, over 130 such centers have developed around the country today in areas urban, suburban, and rural, in industries from taxi driving to garment manufacturing.[1] The Workplace Project is one of the earlier examples. Among the many others are the Coalition of Immokalee Workers, organizing Haitian, Mexican, and indigenous Guatemalan farm workers in Florida, which has garnered national attention for its sit-down strikes, its efforts to fight farm labor slavery, and its campaign to make Taco Bell accountable for the low wages of the workers who pick the chain's tomatoes; the Korean Immigrant Worker Advocates in Los Angeles, fighting for fair wages for Korean and Latino grocery and restaurant workers; and the Garment Worker Center, in El Monte, California, which brings Asian and Latino garment workers together to talk about their working conditions, pursue wage claims against employers, and carry out political action for legalization and other issues.[2]

Worker centers fight an uphill battle in their efforts to take on the new sweatshops. According to the National Study on Immigrant Worker Centers, most, like the Workplace Project, have been much more successful in enforcing existing workplace laws through legal and political strategies than in bringing direct economic pressure to bear on employers to raise wages.[3] Worker centers remain small, few having membership rolls of more than a thousand, with perhaps 10 percent of those members active on a regular basis in the organization. Not unexpectedly, worker centers are largely foundation dependent, with those that do collect dues from their members suffering from the lack of a union-like automatic deduction mechanism that guarantees their payment.

The challenges worker centers face are unsurprising, the direct result of the structural barriers that led unions to look elsewhere for members in the first place. What is more remarkable, under the circumstances, is what worker centers have been able to achieve nonetheless. They have brought together fragmented, mobile, often desperately poor immigrant workers, the "unorganizable," into vibrant grass-roots organizations. They have confronted a broad spectrum of issues that concern workers, making links between the workplace and the community. And by putting pressure on the government and on resistant employers alike, they have increased compliance with the minimum wage and improved working conditions in the underground economy and the lowest-wage formal work. It is worth reflecting on the insights these aspects of worker centers offer about both labor organizing and lawyering.

The Workplace Project does not offer a "model" for labor organizing. In many ways, the Project's situation was unique. It benefited from the skills and energy of many immigrants who had extensive activist histories in their home countries. It operated in a labor market where large swaths of work were carried out almost exclusively by people who shared a language, an ethnic group, and the experience of recent immigration. It developed in a setting which was off the radar screen of most unions, major foundations, and advocacy groups at the time. This last factor brought obvious disadvantages. But it also gave the organization the space to grow without having to define too early its relationships to other powerful actors in the field, and then, when it began to emerge as a presence, positioned it to gain attention from the media as well as funders in a way that would have been much more difficult in, say, New York City or San Francisco.

The Project developed in ways that reflected its circumstances. It had some success organizing Latino immigrant workers in Long Island by ethnicity and geography. That was not because ethnicity and geography are somehow the answer to the riddle of organizing in the new sweatshops, but because in the Project's particular setting, a number of occupations were filled almost entirely by Latino immigrants who changed jobs frequently but tended to look for work within the bounds of Long Island. Likewise, a legal clinic played an important if contested role within the group. That was not because offering legal services is a universal answer to the question of how to get a new organization off the ground, but because in a context where basic rights exist but are consistently violated, and an organization seeks to organize around the enforcement of those rights, a clinic draws in people with immediate experience of the problem.

The lesson to draw from the Project, then, is not that what it did successfully should be replicated. It is that each context gives rise to a set of obstacles and opportunities, and that organizing in each context requires close attention to them, both at the start and as they change over time. Similar conditions will suggest similar solutions. For all that some of the challenges posed by suburban sweatshops are new, immigrants in Long Island face many of the same difficulties that have confronted other dispersed, mobile, and highly vulnerable workers. As it sought to answer the question of how one set of workers in one particular context could improve their wages and working conditions, the Workplace Project's experiments led it to many of the same forms and tactics that—unbeknownst to its staff and members— have served workers facing similar dilemmas in other eras, as well as in modern times in other contexts. Just as the Project came to organize across occupations in a geographic region, rather than around a relationship with a particular employer, so did a number of the American Federation of Labor (AFL) direct affiliate unions in the late nineteenth and early twentieth centuries, those whose members had a common interest in improving working conditions but labored in a variety of industries. Just as the Project experimented with setting standards through worker-designed "codes of conduct" or worker-determined wage rates rather than by creating contracts through negotiations with individual companies, so too did printers, sailors, and waitresses before World War II, and so do writers, performers, and technicians in the entertainment industry today. All created union structures that linked workers to the union rather than to particular employers and administered their benefits as they move from worksite to worksite. Just as the Project considered creating a worker-run hiring hall for day laborers, so did union-run hiring halls play important roles in many earlier efforts, as they still do today among longshore workers and in the building trades.[4]

Yet some of the success of other unions structured in this way is attributable to factors conspicuously absent in the contexts in which worker centers organize. Unions that represent workers independent of their ties to particular employers accomplish the most where their memberships are concentrated in a particular industry, so that they can make a credible claim to controlling the labor supply, and where the workers they represent are "skilled" and thus in high demand. The majority of worker centers, however, have memberships that cross industrial boundaries; almost all work with immigrants in occupations understood as "low-skilled."[5] Historically, such a structure was also facilitated by a legal regime that permitted unions to require employers to have "closed shops," to hire only union members. Except in the rare cases where unions have exemptions from the current NLRA prohibition on closed shop organizing, as with the building trades, this is not the case today.

In the absence of any of these features, worker centers such as the Workplace Project have shaped organizations around immigrant identity and geographical proximity in order to allow

workers to remain affiliated and to continue organizing on issues related to their work as their jobs change or when they suffer periods of unemployment. In combination with a rights-
based central narrative, organizing by identity has several advantages.[6] It emphasizes the group's pride in who its members are
and where they come from. Workplace Project members brought
very different identities to the organization, but their shared
ethnicity and their common experiences as immigrant workers,
and the vision for change that they developed through the organization, proved to be a powerful glue. Furthermore, worker centers that are organized around ethnicity put down deep roots in
the communities where they are located, both drawing strength
from and building leadership for other local institutions such as
ethnic churches and home country associations. Deep roots can
also be the impetus for organizing around nonlabor issues of
broad concern to the community, from campaigns for immigration reform to fights for fair housing.

A workers' association not based on industry raises two questions, however. One is how far mono-ethnic identity can go in a
world of multiethnic workplaces. Organizing as Latinos worked
for Workplace Project members because so many very low-wage
jobs in Long Island were held almost exclusively by Latino immigrants. But where African-Americans, whites, or other immigrant groups worked alongside them, an ethnic association of
workers showed the potential to divide rather than unite the
workforce. A possible response is suggested by the recent alliance
between four Los Angeles worker centers, several multiethnic
themselves, to form the Multi-Ethnic Immigrant Workers Organizing Network, or MIWON: the Korean Immigrant Worker
Advocates, with its Korean and Latino members; the Garment
Worker Center, organizing Latino, Chinese, and Thai workers;

the Pilipino Worker Center; and the predominately Latino day laborers and domestic workers projects of the Coalition for Humane Immigrant Rights of Los Angeles. Through MIWON, low-wage immigrant workers in Los Angeles come together across ethnicity to learn about their rights and develop joint campaigns to improve their living conditions. Although MIWON's work to date has been focused on winning legalization for undocumented immigrants—an interest shared by all group members—it also provides an image of how individual worker centers might combine to organize workers of different races and ethnic groups in a particular workplace or industry.

The other question is about power and strategy. An associational structure solves the problem of keeping workers affiliated as they change jobs, but how can a membership so diffused among industries exert the power it takes to raise wages and improve working conditions? In other words, what happens *after* the worker center structure has, in the words of Workplace Project member Juan Carlos Molina, "brought two domestic workers, two factory workers fired when they got pregnant, and two car-wash guys" into a room together? One result has been worker centers' emphasis on change through the political process, where industry identity matters little and the goal is to achieve improvements for workers in general. But to do *only* this would be to ignore opportunities for worker centers to pursue more focused economic pressure where their memberships concentrate in one or more occupations in which they might be able to exercise some leverage. To this end, there are several options they might consider.[7]

One would be to experiment with organizing toward a contract for some part of their membership, as a few centers have already done on a small scale. Worker centers such as the Workplace Project, located in areas without a dominant industry and where workers rarely identify strongly with one of the twenty or more common immigrant job categories, could choose to target a particular locally rooted industry—say, car washes, or landscaping; recruit members heavily among immigrants currently employed in those jobs; and develop an organizing campaign that targets all (or all key) employers in the industry simultaneously in order to keep nontargeted employers from undercutting those who raise wages.[8] Such a campaign would need to be based on the sort of intensive research about the labor market, employers, and consumers that the best union research departments routinely do as a part of organizing campaigns and that worker centers historically have not done. Tactically, it could combine worker pressure with boycotts, media exposure, government inspections, and other corporate campaign elements as appropriate. A successful campaign of this nature holds out the hope of making jobs in the targeted industry more stable and better paying, and thus increasing the number of workers who remain in them.[9] Meanwhile, the organization would not have to sacrifice the flexibility and other advantages of its broad associational form. Indeed, in such an effort, solidarity from among the center's general membership base offers the additional advantage of reducing the numbers of workers from other industries who might cross picket lines in the targeted industry.

Collaborative work that encompasses and goes beyond cross-ethnic and cross-racial alliances is also crucial in this regard. The workers with the least power have long relied on, and benefited greatly from, the solidarity of other workers sympathetic with their cause. Garment workers organizing in Chicago in the early 1900s had the active support of the bakers and teachers unions, the Women's Trade Union League, and of reformers such as

Jane Addams, whose Hull House shared many features with the worker centers of today. Longshore workers in San Francisco did not win the central union hiring hall they so ardently sought until workers across the city went out on a general strike in their support in 1934. Waitresses in the pre–World War II era got help from truck drivers who refused to deliver milk to restaurants that hired nonunion servers and from chefs with clout who would not cook in nonunion kitchens. Sympathy strikes, once widespread, are now largely illegal. But the question remains how organized workers can help the unorganized.[10]

This raises the issue of strategic alliances between worker centers and unions. From the outside, unions and worker centers seem like an ideal match, and yet their collaborations have often been fraught with tension.[11] When worker centers and unions work together on a particular campaign, worker centers often complain that the union expects the center to pour all its resources into an effort that may help only a fraction of the center's membership. If the campaign is successful, the workers begin to pay dues to the union and often shift their primary affiliation as well. If it fails, the union pulls out and leaves the center to pick up the pieces among frustrated and demoralized workers. For their part, unions often interpret worker centers' reluctance to collaborate as willful blindness to the best interests of their members, whose only chance of a contract will come if the union wins. They dismiss worker centers as service organizations or utopian experiments in democracy with little promise of having an economic impact on workers' lives.

Lately, several new worker centers have been born of community-union partnerships. These include worker centers initiated by the Interfaith Worker Justice Center in Madison, Wisconsin, Morganton, North Carolina, and Chicago. Thoughtful about the strengths of each half of the partnership and mindful of the pitfalls, these new collaborations may model a way of working together that other unions and worker centers can emulate. Context remains critically important; there is no blueprint for the relationship. In some settings, where the interests of both institutions overlap, there will be meaningful opportunities for unions and worker centers to work together on concrete campaigns. In others, the support is more likely to be symbolic—a union's token donation to a worker center, a worker center's token presence on a union picket line. And in still other circumstances, a more conflictive relationship may be appropriate, for example when a worker center has consistently tried to help its members who belong to a union address issues of nonrepresentation and has been met with hostility.

No matter what the nature of their relationship, worker centers and unions that seek to take on the new sweatshops will need to remain open to a wide range of answers to the question of how best to set and maintain wages and working standards, depending on the context or contexts in which they operate. At its root, a "union" is not defined by one kind of structure or strategy. It is defined by a group of workers seeking to resolve the problems they face on the job, to do so collectively, and to do so in ways that reflect the best hope for shifting power in the context in which they work. If the new sweatshops are to be organized it will not be by creating a one-size-fits-all model in a diverse world of work, but by a process that works outward from intimate familiarity with a local context, using that knowledge to craft strategies and organizational forms that fit the best with the structure of a particular labor market. And the more these experiments are regarded as a part of, rather than standing outside, the labor movement, the more the movement stands to flourish through their presence.

The Workplace Project's experience also emphasizes the importance of democracy in organizing. The Project's internal process was designed to maximize participation by staff, members, and volunteers, to several ends. One was to create a highly participatory organization, on the belief that a group thus structured would be legitimate, vibrant, and sustainable in the long term. Another was to address difficult challenges creatively, by bringing many minds together to generate solutions that made organic sense in relation to the problems they sought to address, and then bringing them together again to reflect on how those efforts played out once put in place and to revise them accordingly.

The skeleton of the Workplace Project's internal process was its democratic structure, but its lifeblood was a democratic culture—intensive deliberation and debate at every level. It is useful to distinguish between the two. Democratic *structure* is made up of guarantees: that there will be levels of leadership elected from among the members, that those leaders will have the power to govern the organization, that there will be regular opportunities for input, and so on. The Workplace Project's active membership, its all-immigrant-worker board of directors, its organizing committees, and its frequent staff meetings all reflect this commitment. But structure is only the first step, dry and meaningless without creating a genuine *culture* of democracy. By democratic culture I mean not just voting and *Robert's Rules of Order* and the other trappings we associate with democratic decision-making, but a commitment to sharing information widely and to creating a series of opportunities, informal as well as formal, for the issues facing the group to be understood and discussed by members and staff alike. I mean the practice of democracy as a jazz quartet practices: the daily exercise of the skills, the interaction and the improvisations that make participation meaningful, rich, and effective. To have a truly *democratic institution,* structure and culture need to coincide to make bottom-up participation and control real as the way the organization functions. The Workplace Project reached for this goal, even if it did not always attain it.

I think it is fair to say that although this focus on broad participation is an important strain in the community and labor organizing traditions in the United States, it is far less common than a top-down model. In the labor context, some unions do actively seek to put members in the center of analyzing issues, discussing priorities, and setting strategy. But many others make a sharp distinction between the few moments at which organizing is called for—the union election or a contentious moment in contract negotiations—and the vast rest of the time, when the union's role is to collect dues and "service" its existing members according to the contract. Other more activist unions use innovative organizing tactics, ask workers to take risks as a part of organizing campaigns, and justly pride themselves on being militant and movement oriented. Yet many of these unions remain very top down in approach, equating organizing simply with mobilizing. Members are not called on to understand or critique the context in which they work, to consider strategic options, or to make decisions about which course of action to pursue. The leadership of the union does all of that. Once the decisions are made, union staff mobilize workers to carry them out. In this model too, mobilizing is confined to critical moments.

There is certainly no consensus within the labor movement that this is the moment to emphasize democracy. Many would agree with SEIU Building Trades director Steven Lerner, who argues that unions should worry about building power through increased numbers now and defer concerns about how unions are run internally until after that is achieved.[12] He and others view a participatory approach to organizing as a drag on union efficiency and a diversion in the midst of a pitched battle. A counter-current within the labor movement, represented most effectively by Teamsters for a Democratic Union, maintains by contrast that "democracy *is* power,"[13] that unresponsive and unaccountable unions lose the commitment of their members, while those that seek to engage the membership in the governance of their union and in the union's strategic decision-making gain strength through that process. Where union democracy efforts have prevailed, as well as in other union locals with a similar focus on bottom-up organizing, the commitment to member engagement has played important roles in winning union victories and sustaining members' involvement over time.[14]

The Workplace Project experience lends support to the position that democracy can bolster organizing capacity. As immigrant workers participated in the organization, they developed a new understanding of where their experience fit in the local and global economic and political structure and a new capacity to imagine and debate alternative responses. When workers and staff came together repeatedly to debate and make strategic decisions and to reflect on the results of the course of action they had chosen, they were able to arrive at, implement, and then evaluate approaches that were not part of the standard labor organizing repertoire. Other gains were evident as well. Workers were more willing to take action because they had been a part of the process of determining which action to take, and to stick with an organizing effort whose payoff was only visible in the long term because they understood and agreed with its analysis and approach. And the substantial involvement and commitment of immigrant workers was, in turn, an important component of what made the organization's campaigns credible and compelling to the public. Far from undermining its capacity to act, the emphasis on worker participation increased the Project's innovativeness, its strength, and its effectiveness.

The labor movement today faces challenges that bottom-up organizing alone cannot resolve. Both the need for a consistent strategy against corporations in far-flung locations and the demand for massive union restructuring in response to changes in the economy require centralized decision-making. But there is plenty of room to focus also on building democracy within the governance of union locals, and to approach both times of peak organizing activity as well as the more routine moments of running the union as opportunities to develop workers' organizing acumen and their leadership. The strength that grows from a bottom-up approach in the context of established union structures will be essential to the revitalization of the labor movement.[15]

For at least the last quarter of the twentieth century, activist lawyers and legal scholarship have been plagued by questions about whether lawyers inevitably dominate and derail collective action, and whether law has much if anything to offer to social change.[16] I have a sense that the tide has turned. As a quiet but persistent chorus of voices maintained all along, we seem to be reaching a consensus that there is little use in asking questions about law and organizing in grand or abstract terms.[17] The real issue is, what kind of lawyers, in what kind of relationships with community groups or movements, using what sorts of strategies, make sense in which contexts?

I offer the Workplace Project's uses of law in this spirit, as one effort to address these questions in a particular setting. Some of what the Workplace Project did with the law was quite straightforward. It used court cases and legislative strategies as part of substantive efforts to remedy the abuses workers suffered and to raise their wages. It taught immigrants about their rights, lobbied for changes in the law, and wrangled with administrative agencies about enforcement. It asked lawyers for help on transactional questions: incorporating the organization and its cooperatives and drafting their by-laws. Law also played a role in defending the Project's right to protest, for example when lawyers negotiated with the police to maximize the group's ability to picket. Other worker centers have needed legal defense against lawsuits filed in retaliation for their organizing. These are fairly conventional uses of a lawyer's skills, in the sense that each seeks to deploy the law for the purpose for which it was written, or to obtain a legal victory, as at least one of its goals. If law is a screwdriver, all of these strategies are screws.

But in the hands of the creative, a screwdriver has other uses—it can pry lids off cans, prop open doors, make a hole in a wall. So too with law as a way to advance the goals of organizing. At times, a legal strategy will have an organizing goal that is as or more important than legal victory. The Workplace Project's legal strategies often combined the two: a legal clinic that sought to tackle the problem of unpaid wages *and* to attract new members; legal rights education that strove to teach people what their rights were and at the same time to encourage them to critique those rights as a way to begin a broader conversation about justice and collective action; a legislative campaign fought to win, to build skills and leadership among the membership, and to illustrate an alternative concept of citizenship. There are other ways to use law in this vein as well. A group may bring large numbers of individual claims not only to win the cases but to jam up a system, bringing it to a crisis point that illustrates the need for comprehensive change. It may decide to pursue a lawsuit, but to make key decisions about strategy on the basis of what advances the larger organizing vision, rather than on the basis of what approach is most likely to win in court. This might lead to a decision to involve members in the preparation of a lawsuit to a far greater degree than a conventional lawyer would; to use a legal hearing as an occasion for protest, to inform the public of their struggle and to build alliances, to build their members' sense of their own voice and power, or to challenge the working of the legal system as unfair; to bring a lawsuit on a collateral matter in order to pressure an opponent; to sue in order to distract attention from a losing campaign; or even to reject a high settlement offer and risk a likely loss in court in the belief that the injustice of defeat will galvanize further organizing. None of these examples is meant to suggest that legal strategies could, much less should, substitute for organizing. Instead they illustrate how law might be one way to jump-start and bolster collective action.[18]

One field in which this can play out is, of course, labor. Most lawyers representing unions in the second half of the twentieth century, whether at labor-side law firms or within union legal departments, have had practices shaped largely by the limitations of the NLRA. They argue the union's case in the NLRA-related disputes that arise over the course of an organizing campaign, facilitate the processing of grievances, and litigate where the union has been sued or where there are opportunities to expand its capacity to organize. All of these are highly important functions. But the ways that the Workplace Project and a number of other worker centers have developed law as an organizing tool suggests that there are other powerful roles that law can play in workplace struggles and in organizing efforts more broadly. This approach harkens back to a proud but largely forgotten tradition in labor movement history.

Although their work is no longer well known, waves of lawyers in the labor movement over the past eighty years have used law to build collective power in much this way. This approach seems to have been strongest at moments when an upsurge in worker organizing coincided with the lack of a settled legal framework to channel the collective energy. Thus, in the 1930s and 1940s, lawyers such as Lee Pressman, the general counsel to the Steel Workers Organizing Committee beginning in 1936 and to the Congress of Industrial Organizations (CIO) from 1937 until 1948, and Maurice Sugar, a lifelong labor lawyer and the United Auto Workers' general counsel from 1939 to 1947, sought at different times to teach workers their rights in ways that would facilitate organizing, to use legal cases as an occasion to strengthen worker solidarity or to argue the workers' case to the public, to craft union constitutions that would facilitate rank-and-file participation, to forge labor-community alliances, to develop new legal theories to support controversial organizing tactics such as the sit-down strike, to fight for judicial rulings, new laws, and indeed new government institutions that would create a legal framework to facilitate industrial unionism, and—in Sugar's case—to initiate the founding of the National Lawyers' Guild, which would become a haven for generations of lawyers who worked in support of organizing.[19]

From the 1950s onward, the standard labor lawyer became much more of a technician, helping unions to navigate the law rather than to shape it or to craft organizing strategy. In industries where the NLRA did not apply, though, or in places where its rules were a poor fit with workers' organizing needs, lawyers again developed more aggressive and creative strategies in support of organizing. The legal department of the United Farm Workers in the 1960s and 1970s, to which I have referred repeatedly here, is a case in point. Operating on an unregulated playing field, UFW lawyers deployed "legal karate and the law of the jungle," using the courtroom as a stage on which to tell the union's story to the public, bringing lawsuits to pressure growers to agree to unionization, and lobbying and litigating in an effort to reshape the rules of organizing so that they would support rather than hinder farm workers' efforts. When the UFW succeeded in passing California's Agricultural Labor Relations Act, imposing a legal framework on the organizing process, most UFW lawyers similarly turned to more technical roles within the movement, pressing for the union's interests within the newly established rules of the game.[20]

Written to govern a world of work now on the decline, interpreted against the interests of workers by generations of conservative courts, and administered by a backlogged, hamstrung, and sorely underfunded administrative agency, the National Labor Relations Act is now more of an impediment to organizing than the manifesto for the right of workers to bargain collectively envisioned by its pro-labor drafters and early supporters. As the NLRA fades into irrelevance for whole categories of workers, or, worse still, shackles the development of innovative responses to the poor working conditions they face, lawyers have begun to think again about law as a way to help workers generate power. The National Employment Law Project, for example, acts as both a law and policy think tank and a central source of legal support for unions and other groups organizing workers on the fringes of the labor movement, including subcontracted workers, day laborers, undocumented workers, unemployed workers, and people on workfare.[21] Other smaller organizations seek to play similar roles in particular regions: the DC Employment Justice Center in Washington, D.C., the Mississippi Center for Workers Human Rights in Greenwood, Mississippi, and the nascent Northwest Workers Justice Project in Portland, Oregon, to name a few. Lawyers at innovative unions like SEIU and at individual worker centers do similar work, as do law professors and law students who provide support for efforts from law school clinics such as the NYU Immigrants Rights Clinic at New York University Law School. In each of these efforts, law is sometimes a technical tool and sometimes a way to leverage power, and sometimes it is both and other things as well.

This wealth of experience, and the Workplace Project's practice in particular, suggest several ways that law might support the organizing of the lowest-wage workers beyond the important straightforward approaches of litigating to enforce rights, lobbying to claim new ones, and defending organizing efforts on the ground. One is the link between individual representation and organizing. A few unions do provide legal representation for their members on matters not directly related to union business. UNITE!'s former Immigration Project, which for twenty years assisted UNITE! members with their immigration claims, was a case in point. But these services, as well as others such as health clinics and education programs, are usually offered only as benefits to existing members, and are not explicitly linked to organizing in any way. By contrast, unions that seek to organize new immigrants in low-wage industries—take the building trades for an example—might consider creating wage claim clinics structured to introduce potential members to unions in their area. Of course such clinics will confront the same tensions that the Workplace Project clinic faced. Unions cannot assume that the transition from "client" to "active member" under such a system will be automatic; they, too, will have to struggle with how a relationship begun through individual representation can be the first step on the road to collective action. But here as with the Workplace Project clinic, such tensions can be generative, shedding light on the gaps between what the workers outside the union want and need and what the union wants from them, and focusing the union's attention on how to build a bridge between the two.

Another idea is to draw on the approach to rights education that leads to citizenship education, and on the resulting political participation, as ways to reinvigorate the labor movement with new immigrant members and new vitality.[22] As the Unpaid Wages Prohibition Act campaign illustrated, conversations that start with immigrants' urgent interest in learning basic rights, move on to focus a critical lens on the gap between the conditions under which participants live and work and the way they feel they should be treated (both according to the law and according to their developing vision of the human rights to which they as human beings are entitled), and lead to concrete action toward change, can be a launching pad for immigrant worker activism. The sense of "citizenship" and the political experience that results would be an invaluable source of union power.

The labor movement itself provides the beginning of an example, through its participation in the current campaign for immigrant legalization. The AFL-CIO's pro-amnesty vote in early

2000 was a first step. Unions truly woke up to amnesty's galvanizing potential, however, when over 20,000 workers crammed the Sports Arena stadium in Los Angeles for a pro-legalization rally called by the Los Angeles County Federation of Labor that fall. Derailed for more than a year after the events of September 11, 2001, the movement toward a new immigrant amnesty has begun again to gather steam. In the fall of 2003 HERE led an effort to organize an Immigrant Worker Freedom Ride, bringing buses of immigrants from all over the country to culminating rallies in Washington, D.C., and New York City. The buses made stops at immigrant and labor strongholds, building support for workers' rights and for the idea that years of hard labor in the United States should entitle a worker to gain legal status—and jumpstarting immigrant political participation in the process. If taken to the next level, so that groups all over the country use immigrants' interest in legalization as a starting point for study of the history of immigration and immigrants' rights, analysis of the political system, and local alliance-building and organizing that feed into the national plan, the result could be the sort of surge in strategic capacity and confidence and leadership that would redound to the benefit of any union involved in organizing those same workers on the job. It would also support the process of creating real citizenship among new immigrants, whose active and informed political participation will be essential to shaping how this country responds to the challenges of local and global change for generations to come.

Many of these reflections on the role of law are equally applicable beyond the context of the battle against sweatshops. Critical approaches to rights education, efforts to integrate litigation and lobbying strategies with organizing, and visions of lawyering that move beyond these court and legislative arenas, are all available to groups seeking to make change in other arenas. In environmental justice work, in struggles to fight unfair welfare policies, in community economic development efforts, in civil rights battles, and many other areas as well, groups have experimented with multiple ways that law can be a tool that builds organizational power, community power, and the power of the broader movements of which each are a part.[23] Seeing law as this sort of a component of a social change effort represents no small shift from a more traditional perspective on lawyering. But it is worth the effort. In situations where change will not happen until the balance of power shifts, a vision of law as a part of a larger strategy to move power is the best vision we have.

Immigrant workers are not deluded about the scale of the challenges they face. As Workplace Project member and organizer Carlos Canales said in late 2001, "I feel like right now we are on the tip of an iceberg. The Workplace Project is a tiny ant, with a tiny ant's needle, trying to break that iceberg down." In the context of a globalized economy, he remarks wryly, even a substantial local victory "is as if we've just taken a toenail off of one of the feet of an octopus." And yet at the same time, Canales suggests one response to the resulting feeling of impotence. It may be, he concedes, that the struggle of the ant against the iceberg is unlikely to break it down. But when a few chips fall to the ground, "it reaffirms this idea that *we can,* that workers can." With such small victories, the omnipresent and overwhelming sense of powerlessness and irrelevance that immigrant workers feel in the face of forces that they cannot control may begin—just begin—to dissolve. Canales argues that in the global economy

immigrant workers "are the accomplices of capital. We are partners, like it or not. Because we have been exploited but we are
not robots, we are human beings. In that sense organizations
[like the Workplace Project] that democratize are important, to
keep hope alive, to keep giving the idea that we can get there . . .
They are sending the message to the rest of the workers that although global conditions may not have changed, battle after
battle after battle we will be winning terrain, winning terrain."[24]

Some of what will determine the future ability of worker centers and the very low-wage immigrants whom they represent to
win terrain is beyond our ability to predict. Their work takes
place in a shifting context. For those who are poised to notice,
the future may bring fractures in what once looked fixed, and
with them unexpected opportunities to build power and make
change. Over time, new opportunities will arise for alliances, for
working with or against employers, for lobbying legislators. A social movement may emerge. Under pressure from outside and
within, the labor movement itself may move toward broader acceptance of the need to be flexible with regard to strategy, funda-
mentally committed to worker participation, active in seeking
out alliances both locally and globally, and stanch in its support
of the wide range of workers' interests in the workplace and the
community. Any of these shifts would fertilize the ground in
which the scattered seeds and fragile shoots of worker centers
now grow.

To date, the Workplace Project and other groups like it may
not have been able to overcome the structural problems of immigrant work in a globalized world. But what they *have* done is
critically important. In an area where no one has figured out a
broad and viable strategy for change, the Workplace Project has
built a stable, democratic organization of immigrant workers as

a base from which to carry out some noteworthy experiments in challenging the conditions of work in the underground economy. Through those experiments, it has begun to learn about where the realm of the possible lies in terrain that once looked impossible. It has changed lives in ways that are more than individual, developing leadership among immigrants who are at once deeply committed to *this* organization and well positioned to lead future organizing efforts there or elsewhere. In the process, it has shown that, try as we might to assess power with a clear, cold eye, to pin it down on the page according to the characteristics of a community or a labor market, there is often room for surprising change.

NOTES
ACKNOWLEDGMENTS
INDEX

NOTES

INTRODUCTION

1. Jeffrey S. Passel, Randy Capps, and Michael Fix, *Undocumented Immigrants: Facts and Figures,* Urban Institute, Washington, D.C., Jan. 12, 2004.

2. Thomas Maier, "Surge in Immigrant Worker Deaths," *Newsday,* Oct. 29, 2001, p. A14.

3. Howard Wial, "Minimum-Wage Enforcement and the Low-Wage Labor Market," MIT Task Force on Reconstructing America's Labor Market Institutions Working Paper 11, Aug. 1, 1999, p. 22. The .6 percent figure represents union density for the bottom tenth of wage distribution in the United States and is based on Wial's analysis of 1997 Current Population Survey data.

4. I paraphrase Evelina Dagnino, who calls this the "right to have rights" in "On Becoming a Citizen: The Story of Dona Marlene," in Rina Benmayor and A. Skotnes, ed., *Migration and Identity: International Yearbook of Oral History and Life Stories III* (New York: Oxford University Press, 1994), p. 74.

1. THE NEW SWEATSHOPS

1. A "sweatshop" is defined by the U.S. General Accounting Office as a workplace in violation of two or more basic laws governing working conditions, such as those about wages, safety, and child labor: "'Sweatshops' in the U.S.: Opinions on Their Extent and Possible

Enforcement Options," *GAO/HRD-88–130BR* (Briefing Report to the Honorable Charles E. Schumer, House of Representatives, 1988), p. 16.

2. Much of the credit for this hiatus goes to strong garment work unions operating in a largely domestic context with the support of New Deal labor legislation. Edna Bonacich, "Organizing Immigrant Workers in the Los Angeles Apparel Industry," 4 (1) *Journal of World-Systems Research* 10-19 (Winter 1998); Max Zimny and Brent Garren, "Protecting the Contingent Workforce: Lessons from the Women's Garment Industry," paper reprinted as a part of the Subcontracted Worker Initiative Strategy Forum of the National Employment Law Project (NELP), 1994, available at *http://www.nelp.org/docUploads/zimny%2Epdf.*

3. Marc Cooper, "The Heartland's Raw Deal: How Meatpacking Is Creating a New Immigrant Underclass," *The Nation,* Feb. 3, 1997, pp. 11-17. See also Eric Schlosser, *Fast Food Nation* (New York: Houghton Mifflin, 2001).

4. Patrick J. McDonnell, "Thai Sweatshop Workers Savor Freedom's Joys," *Los Angeles Times,* Aug. 13, 1995, p. B1; Julie Su and Chanchanit Martorell, "Exploitation and Abuse in the Garment Industry: The Case of Thai Slave-Labor Compound in El Monte," in Marta Lopez-Garza and David R. Diaz, ed., *Asian and Latino Immigrants in a Restructuring Economy: The Metamorphosis of Southern California* (Stanford: Stanford University Press, 2001), pp. 21-45; Ian Fisher, "U.S. Indictment Describes Abuses of Deaf Mexican Trinket Sellers," *New York Times,* Aug. 21, 1997, p. A1; Joseph P. Fried, "Deaf Peddlers Were Tortured with Stun Guns, Enforcer Says," *New York Times,* Oct. 24, 1997, p. B5; John Bowe, "Nobodies: Does Slavery Exist in America?" *The New Yorker,* April 21, 2003, pp. 106-133; Mireya Navarro, "In the Land of the Free: A Modern Slave," *New York Times,* Dec. 12, 1996, p. A22; Stephanie Armour, "Part 1: Some Foreign Household Workers Face Enslavement," *USA Today,* Nov. 19, 2001, p. 1A; Jimmy Breslin, *The Short Sweet Dream of Eduardo Gutierrez* (New York: Crown, 2001).

5. On some of the other depoliticizing and dehumanizing effects of emphasizing sweatshop horror stories, see Leti Volpp, "Migrating Identities: On Labor, Culture, and Law," 27 *North Carolina Journal of International Law and Commercial Regulation* 507 (2002).

6. The physical effects of these injuries are compounded by their economic impact on the workers. See Thomas Maier, "Paying Injury's Price: Immigrants Rarely Compensated for Workplace Harm," *Newsday*, July 24, 2001, p. A4.

7. Nurith C. Aizenman, "Harsh Reward for Hard Labor: For Many Hispanic Immigrants, Work Injuries End Dreams of a New Life," *Washington Post*, Dec. 29, 2002, p. C1.

8. Interview with Zoila Rodriguez, Dec. 6, 2001. Unless otherwise indicated, all further quotes from Rodriguez are from this interview.

9. Thomas Frank, Olivia Winslow, and Victor Ramos, "Island's Changing Face: Census Says 23.6% of Long Island's 2.75M People Are Minorities," *Newsday*, March 16, 2001, p. A2.

10. Somini Sengupta, "Our Evolving Suburbia: New 'Locals' Are Immigrants," *Newsday*, Nov. 5, 1995, p. A4.

11. Bart Jones, "A Salvadoran Boom: Census: Group's LI Population Gaining on Puerto Ricans," *Newsday*, June 27, 2001, p. A5. The Salvadoran General Consulate in Brentwood, Long Island, estimates there are 150,000 to 200,000 Salvadorans on Long Island (consul's communication with Jason Yan on behalf of the author, July 2003); for a list of cities in El Salvador ranked by population, see *http://www.world-gazeteer.com/t/t_sv.htm*. From a population of more than 6 million, it is estimated that more than 1 million Salvadoran refugees have fled to the United States since the 1980s. Jon Ward, "Salvadoran MS-13 Gang Rated among the Most Violent," *Washington Times*, Aug. 24, 2002, p. A10; *http://www.populationworld.com/ElSalvador.php*; Mae M. Cheng, "Research: Census Off on Hispanics," *Newsday*, July 6, 2001, p. A4. Frank, Winslow, and Ramos, "Island's Changing Face," p. A2.

12. Suffolk County Legislature 1994 resolution, "America First Welfare Reduction Program."

13. "Philosophy and Mission Statement of the Sachem Quality of Life Organization" (copy on file with the author); Victor Chen, "Farmingville Faces Off over Immigrant Workers," *Newsday*, Aug. 24, 1999, p. A30, quoting Steve Merschoff, a resident who attended the SQL antiworker demonstration. The Workplace Project captured the events of the 1999 hearing on videotape; it was also reported by Paul Vitello, "Melting Pot at Boiling Point," *Newsday*, Oct. 24, 1999, p. A4.

14. The Farmingville attackers were convicted and jailed; see Andrew Smith, "Guilty of All Counts in Worker Beatings," *Newsday*, Aug. 17, 2001, p. A5; Elissa Gootman, "2nd Man Gets 25-Year Term for Beating Mexican Laborers," *News York Times*, Jan. 10, 2002, p. B5. In the years after my departure from the Workplace Project, an important aspect of the Project's work came to be organizing day laborers to fight anti-immigrant sentiment and its effects.

15. Audrey Singer, "America's Diversity at the Beginning of the 21st Century: Reflections from Census 2000" (Washington, D.C.: The Brookings Institution, 2002), p. 11, citation omitted; U.S. Department of Housing and Urban Development, "The State of the Cities 1998," available at *http://www.huduser.org/publications/polleg/tsoc98/contents.html*.

16. Janice Fine, "Community Unions in Baltimore and Long Island: Beyond the Politics of Particularism" (Ph.D. diss., Massachusetts Institute of Technology, 2003), pp. 88–89. Fine notes that Long Island lost a total of 53,000 defense-related jobs between 1986 and 2000. James Bernstein, "The LI Brain Drain: Study: Little Aid to Laid-Off Defense Workers," *Newsday*, Dec. 21, 1994, p. A7; my calculations are based on Bureau of Labor employment statistics (Jan. 1970–June 2003), available at *www.bls.gov*.

17. H. J. Cummins, "LI Jobs Forecast: Slow Growth; Planners: Most New Posts to Be in Services," *Newsday*, June 18, 1993, p. 4; Judy Temes, "Next Generation Long Island's Technology Firms Build on Defense Work Brainpower," *Crain's New York Business*, June 27, 1994, p. 21; Pearl M. Kamer, *The LIPA Annual Business Fact Book: A Comprehensive Guide to Business Activity on Long Island* (Uniondale, NY: Long Island Power Authority, 2001), cited in Fine, "Community Unions," p. 91, n. 21; Fine, "Community Unions," p. 91.

18. Fine, "Community Unions," pp. 95–99.

19. The vast majority of courts have concluded that undocumented immigrants are covered by the Fair Labor Standards Act and by state wage and hour laws, by the health and safety protections of the Occupational Safety and Health Act, and by the antidiscrimination provisions of Title VII. The 4th Circuit is the exception here; see *Egbuna v. Time Life Libraries, Inc.*, 153 F.3d 184 (4th Cir. 1998), *cert. de-*

nied, 119 S.Ct. 1034 (1999). Workers compensation for on-the-job injuries is available to undocumented immigrants in most states, but it is limited in some and contested in others. For a recent case upholding the right, see the Minnesota Supreme Court's decision in *Correa v. Waymouth Farms, Inc.,* 664 N.W.2d 324 (2003). For a recent case limiting some elements of the right, see the Pennsylvania Supreme Court's holding in *Reinforced Earth Company v. Workers' Compensation Appeal Board,* 810 A. 2d 99 (PA, 2002). One workplace benefit universally denied to undocumented workers is unemployment insurance, because of the requirement that recipients be "ready, willing and able" to accept another job; 26 USC § 3304(a)(14)(A). Because of their lack of working papers, undocumented immigrants are not considered "able" to work. See *Zapata v. Levine,* 375 N.Y.S.2d 424 (3d Dep't 1975). In its 2002 *Hoffman Plastic* decision, the Supreme Court affirmed that undocumented immigrants were "employees" protected by the National Labor Relations Act, but held that they were not entitled to the usual penalties of back pay or reinstatement when fired in retaliation for organizing. Although limited in its holding to the NLRA, *Hoffman Plastic* created a great deal of concern among immigrants and their advocates about its possible extension to other areas.

20. Alan Finder, "Despite Tough Laws, Sweatshops Flourish," *New York Times,* Feb. 6, 1995, p. A1; Howard Wial, "Minimum-Wage Enforcement and the Low-Wage Labor Market," MIT Task Force on Reconstructing America's Labor Market Institutions Working Paper 11, Aug. 30, 1999, pp. 10-11. According to its most recent statistics, OSHA has 1,123 inspectors for 111 million workers. On the U.S. Department of Labor "Hot Goods" efforts in the garment industry, see Bonacich, "Organizing Immigrant Workers," p. 16; Wial, "Minimum-Wage Enforcement," p. 13. On legal loopholes, see Wial, pp. 25-26.

21. New York Committee for Occupational Safety and Health, "Tip of the Iceberg: Top OSHA Violators in New York City, Long Island, and Lower New York State, Special Report" (1993), p. 3. A decade later in 2003, national statistics were even lower: one inspector per 6,233 private businesses nationwide. See *www.osha.gov/as/opa/oshafacts.html;* David Barstow, "U.S. Rarely Seeks Charges for Deaths in Workplace,"

New York Times, Dec. 22, 2003, p. A1; Michael Yates, *Power on the Job: The Legal Rights of Working People* (Boston: South End Press, 1994), pp. 248–249.

22. New York State Assembly Committee on Labor, "Testimony of Jennifer Gordon," Feb. 16, 1996.

23. Compare U.S. Department of Labor, "Memorandum of Understanding," *DLR No. 113* (June 11, 1992), p. D-5, with *DLR No. 227* (Nov. 25, 1998), p. E-1.

24. 45 CFR §§ 1626.3–4 (1997); 45 CFR § 1610.3 (1997).

25. Robert L. Bach, "Building Community among Diversity: Legal Services for Impoverished Immigrants," 27 *University of Michigan Journal of Law Reform* 639, 657 (1994).

26. Paul Buhle, *Taking Care of Business: Samuel Gompers, George Meany, Lane Kirkland, and the Tragedy of American Labor* (New York: Monthly Review Press, 1999), p. 44.

27. Gonzalo F. Santos, "Modern Human Migration, the History of 'Immigration Problems' in California, and the Options for the XXI Century," in Charles F. Hohm, ed., *California Social Problems* (New York: Addison Wesley-Longman, 1997), pp. 178–179, n. 30.

28. See, for example, Robert H. Zeiger, *The CIO, 1935–1955* (Chapel Hill: University of North Carolina Press, 1997); Ruth Needleman, *Black Freedom Fighters in Steel: The Struggle for Democratic Unionism* (Ithaca: Cornell University Press, 2003).

29. Linda C. Majka and Theo J. Majka, *Farm Workers, Agribusiness, and the State* (Philadelphia: Temple University Press, 1982), pp. 186, 261; interview with Jerry Cohen, July 22, 1999. Unless otherwise indicated, all further quotes from Cohen are from this interview. Interviews with former UFW attorneys Barbara Rhine, March 27, 2000, and Peter Haberfeld, March 28, 2000; on Chavez's "private border patrol," see Jeff Coplon, "Cesar Chavez's Fall from Grace, Part II," *The Village Voice,* Aug. 21, 1984, p. 20; Susan Ferriss and Ricardo Sandoval, *The Fight in the Fields: Cesar Chavez and the Farmworkers Movement* (New York: Harcourt Brace, 1997) p. 244.

30. Fine, "Community Unions," pp. 95–99.

31. Conversation with Nadia Marín-Molina, 2002. That this union might have seen the day labor sites as an opportunity rather than an opponent is illustrated by the example of the ironworkers union in

Washington D.C., which has actively sought to build alliances with organized day laborers in Maryland's Prince Georges County. Greg Simmons, "Unions Court Day Laborers," *Silver Spring Gazette,* Jan. 30, 2002, p. A1.

32. All cites are from Janice Fine interviews of Workplace Project members in 1996 and 1997, "Community Unions," pp. 102-103.

33. Interview with Juan Carlos Molina, Dec. 19, 2001. Unless otherwise indicated, all further quotes from Molina are from this interview.

34. Interview with Maria Aparicio, Dec. 17, 2001. Unless otherwise indicated, all further quotes from Aparicio are from this interview.

35. Interview with Carmen Lelys Maldonado, Feb. 21, 2002. Unless otherwise indicated, all further quotes from Maldonado are from this interview.

36. Interview with Carlos Canales, Dec. 17, 2001. Unless otherwise indicated, all further quotes from Canales are from this interview.

37. Sarah Mahler, *American Dreaming,* (Princeton: Princeton University Press, 1995), chap. 4, pp. 84-104.

38. Fair market rent for a two-bedroom apartment on Long Island in 2002 was $1,230 a month, or $14,760 a year. Bruce Lambert, "Housing Pinch on L.I. Causes New Group to Push for More Rentals," *New York Times,* April 25, 2002, p. B1.

39. Interview with Samuel Chavez, Dec. 6, 2001. Unless otherwise indicated, all further quotes from Chavez are from this interview.

40. Roger Waldinger and Claudia Der-Martirosian, "Immigrant Workers and American Labor: Challenge . . . or Disaster?" in Ruth Milkman, ed., *Organizing Immigrants: The Challenge for Unions in Contemporary California* (Ithaca: ILR Press, 2000), p. 74.

41. Popular understanding has it that the sojourner attitude stands in stark contrast to that of earlier generations of immigrants. Marc Wyman demonstrates, to the contrary, that between 1880 and 1930, from a quarter to a third of European immigrants returned home permanently. For some groups, such as the Italians, the rates were as high as 50 percent. *Round-Trip America: The Immigrants Return to Europe, 1880-1930* (Ithaca: Cornell University Press, 1993), p. 6-10. For a discussion of the predictably negative impact of this attitude on labor organizing at the time, see ibid., pp. 66-70.

42. "Samuel Chavez et. al., vs. American Tissue Company, Shahram

Roozrokh and Gulan Farooq," Complaint and Jury Trial Demand, June 26, 1998.

43. Roger Waldinger et al., "Helots No More: A Study of the Justice for Janitors Campaign in Los Angeles," in Kate Bronfenbrenner et al., ed., *Organizing to Win: New Research on Union Strategies* (Ithaca: ILR Press, 1998), p. 117.

44. Interview with Rodolfo Sorto, Dec. 17, 2001. Unless otherwise indicated, all further quotes from Sorto are from this interview.

45. Peter Dicken, *Global Shift: Reshaping the Global Economic Map in the 21st Century,* 4th ed.(New York: Guilford Press, 2003), p. 53.

46. Mark Landler, "Hi, I'm in Bangalore (But I Can't Say So)," *New York Times,* March 21, 2001, p. A1; Crayton Harrison, "A Different Accent on Service: New Challenges Arise as U.S. Firms Move Call Centers Overseas," *Dallas Morning News,* Sept. 15, 2002, p. 1H. Increasingly, high-paying white-collar jobs are following the lower-paying jobs overseas; see Steven Greenhouse, "I.B.M. Explores Shift of White-Collar Jobs Overseas," *New York Times,* July 22, 2003, p. C1.

47. Bonacich lays out some of these factors in "Organizing Immigrant Workers," p. 14. For another argument that profitability even in industries like the garment industry is not as much about labor costs as one might assume, see Frederick H. Abernathy, John T. Dunlop, Janice H. Hummond, and David Weil, *A Stitch in Time: Lean Retailing and the Transformation of Manufacturing* (New York: Oxford University Press, 1999), pp. 11, 15–16.

48. *Textile Workers Union of America v. Darlington Manufacturing Co.,* 380 U.S. 263 (1965); Terry Collingsworth, "Resurrecting the National Labor Relations Act: Plant Closings and Runaway Shops in a Global Economy," 14 *Berkeley Journal of Employment and Labor Law* 72, 85–104 (1993); on predictions versus threats, see *NLRB v. Gissel Packing Co.,* 395 U.S. 575, 618 (1969), citing *Darlington,* n. 20; *Darlington,* at 274–276; Collingsworth, "Resurrecting the National Labor Relations Act," pp. 99–104.

49. Before their merger into UNITE! for example, the ILGWU and the Amalgamated Clothing and Textile Workers Union (ACTWU) supported workers organizing with a Dominican union at the Bibong Apparel Corporation, an export-processing plant in the Dominican

Republic. UNITE! has continued to support union struggles in Latin America and the Caribbean. Jonathan Werberg, "Internationalism and Trans-Nationalism in American Labor: Cross-Border Organizing, 1199, and LCLAA" (B.S. thesis, Massachusetts Institution of Technology, 2003), p. 34, citing Laura McClure, "Garment Unions UNITE," 17 (6) *Multinational Monitor* 14–16 (June 1995). Other unions have developed or joined transnational solidarity campaigns that seek to improve global working conditions more broadly. See Thalia G. Kidder, "Networks in Transnational Labor Organizing," in Sanjeev Khagram, James V. Riker, and Kathryn Sikkink, ed., *Restructuring World Politics: Transnational Social Movements, Networks, and Norms* (Minneapolis: University of Minnesota Press, 2002), pp. 269–293. Much less common, but particularly interesting, are the stories of unions in different countries that have begun to coordinate their efforts across national borders as they organize workers in the same transnational companies. See Andrew Banks and John Russo, "The Development of International Campaign-Based Network Structures: A Case Study of the IBT and ITF World Council of UPS Unions," 20 *Comparative Labor Law and Policy Journal* 543 (1999).

Although the term "cross-border solidarity" is most often used to describe efforts where the problems are in other countries and the support comes from the United States, this is not always the case. For a reverse example, see Terry Davis, "Cross-Border Solidarity Comes Home," 23 *Labor Research Review* 23–29 (1995). .

50. When work is globally interconnected, a U.S.-based union may not even be able to ask unions in other countries for support. The court in *Dowd v. International Longshoremen's Ass'n.*, 975 F.2d 779 (1992), for example, held that a U.S. union's request for Japanese unions to refuse to unload fruit loaded by nonunion stevedores in Florida would have resulted in illegal secondary pressure on U.S. shipping companies to use union stevedores. The waters were muddied a few years later by the decision in *International Longshoremen's Ass'n v. NLRB*, 318 U.S. App. D.C. 80 (1995), in which a different circuit court, considering similar facts, reached the opposite conclusion. For a discussion of these issues generally, see James Atleson, "The Voyage of the Neptune Jade: Transnational Labour Solidarity and the Obstacles of Do-

mestic Law," in Joanne Conaghan, Richard Michael Fischl, and Karl Klare, ed., *Labour Law in an Era of Globalization: Transformative Practices and Possibilities* (Oxford: Oxford University Press, 2002), pp. 379–399.

51. Tim Shorrock, "Labor's Cold War," *The Nation,* May 19, 2003, p. 15; Buhle, *Taking Care of Business,* pp. 136–158.

52. Martin Khor articulates this position in "The World Trade Organisation, Labour Standards, and Trade Protectionism," 45 *Third World Resurgence,* 30–34 (1994). Lance Compa outlines the controversy in ". . . And the Twain Shall Meet? A North-South Controversy over Labor Rights and Trade," *Labor Research Review,* 23 (1995): 50–65. And William Grieder discusses differing perspectives among unions in different countries in chap. 4 of his book, *One World, Ready or Not: The Manic Logic of Global Capitalism* (New York: Touchstone Press, 1997).

53. *Plyler v. Doe,* 457 U.S. 202, 72 L. Ed. 2d 786 (1982). The majority of states deny undocumented immigrants resident tuition rates at publicly funded colleges and universities, thus making attendance financially prohibitive for many. Recently, however, several states—California and Texas among them—have passed laws that grant in-state tuition to undocumented immigrants who graduate from a high school in the state, can show proof of past in-state residence, and sign a pledge to apply for permanent residence at the earliest opportunity.

54. Other immigration categories include "diversity immigration," which offers visas on a lottery basis to would-be immigrants from countries with historically low numbers of immigrants to the United States, and high-end business visas for those who can afford to invest large sums of money (at least $1 million) to open a new firm in the United States.

55. Manuel Castells and Alejandro Portes, "World Underneath: The Origins, Dynamics, and Effects of the Informal Economy," in Castells Portes and Lauren A. Benton, ed., *The Informal Economy: Studies in Advanced and Less Developed Countries* (Baltimore: Johns Hopkins University Press, 1989), p. 12.

56. Saskia Sassen-Koob, "New York City's Informal Economy," in Portes and Benton, ed., *The Informal Economy,* p. 71. For a description of the

internal immigrant informal economy in Long Island, see Mahler, *American Dreaming.*

57. Friedrich Schneider with Dominik Enste, "Hiding in the Shadows: The Growth of the Underground Economy," *Economic Issues,* No. 30 (Washington, D.C.: International Monetary Fund, March 2002). Globally, the informal sector makes up a much higher percentage of the total economy: for example, 62 percent of employment in Mexico and 93 percent of employment in India takes place in the informal sector. Martha Alter Chen, Renana Jhabvala, and Frances Lund, "Supporting Workers in the Informal Economy: A Policy Framework," (Geneva: ILO, 2002), p. 7.

58. Beth Barrett, "Cash Economy Threatens Wages, Tax Base," *Los Angeles Daily News,* May 6, 2002, p. N1.

59. Castells and Portes, "World Underneath," p. 12; for a rare detailed, data-based analysis of the work lives of undocumented immigrants in one city, see Chirag Mehta, Nik Theodore, Iliana Mora, and Jennifer Wade, "Chicago's Undocumented Immigrants: An Analysis of Wages, Working Conditions, and Economic Contributions" (University of Chicago Center For Urban Economic Development, February 2002), available at *http://www.uic.edu/cuppa/uicued/Publications/ RECENT/undocimmigrants.htm;* Lin Lean Lim, "Women and Men in the Informal Economy: A Statistical Picture," (Geneva: ILO, 2002) p. 10; Chen, "Supporting Workers in the Informal Economy," pp. 7–8; Steven Greenhouse, "Wal-Mart Raids by U.S. Aimed at Illegal Aliens," *New York Times,* Oct. 24, 2003, p. A1; Steven Greenhouse, "Illegally in the U.S., and Never a Day Off at Wal-Mart," *New York Times,* Nov. 5, 2003, p. A1.

60. Barrett, "Cash Economy Threatens Wages," p. N1, quoting Julie Butcher, who is identified as "general manager" of SEIU Local 347 in Los Angeles.

61. 99th Congress, 2nd sess., 1986, H.R. Rept. 682(I), p. 58. But see the Supreme Court's subsequent decision in *Hoffman Plastics v. NLRB,* 535 U.S. 137 (2002).

62. In 1990, just as immigrant janitors at Shine Building Maintenance in Silicon Valley began organizing a drive to join the SEIU, their employer demanded that they produce new documentation of their

right to work. This demand decimated the union leadership, end-ing the organizing effort. David Bacon, "Immigration Law: Bringing Back Sweatshop Conditions," *Labor Center Reporter,* #306 (Institute of Industrial Relations, UC Berkeley, 1999), p. 1, 4–6. Letters that the So-cial Security Administration sends to employers who submit Social Security payments on behalf of employees with invalid numbers can play out in a similar way. National Immigration Law Center, "Social Security Administration 'No-Match' Letters," March 2003, p. C-17.

63. AFL-CIO lobbyist Jane O'Grady, quoted in Julia Malone, "A Hesitant House Takes Up Immigration Bill," *The Christian Science Monitor,* June 11, 1984, p. 1.

64. David Bacon, "Unions Take on Immigration-Related Firings," *Z Magazine,* July/August 2000, p. 28.

65. *Sure-Tan, Inc. v. NLRB,* 467 U.S. 833 (1984).

66. *Hoffman Plastics v. NLRB* is in fact but one of many legal obstacles to organizing immigrants under the NLRA. In the most extreme cases, some immigrant-heavy industries are completely excluded from the NLRA, domestic work and farm labor among them. Other immi-grant workers, such as day laborers, are vulnerable to the challenge that they are they are not employees but independent contractors, prohibited from organizing under the NLRA. Employers have histor-ically phoned in tips to the INS as soon as an organizing drive be-gins. Hard work by advocates resulted in the INS Operations In-struction (OI) 287.3a, forbidding the INS to carry out a raid at a workplace without lengthy internal consultation where the agency has been notified of an ongoing labor dispute. For the first decision terminating deportation proceedings after a raid that violated the OI, see *In the Matter of Herrera-Priego,* Decision of the Immigration Judge, July 7, 2003. In the wake of *Hoffman,* both the U.S. Depart-ment of Labor and the Equal Opportunity Employment Commis-sion (EEOC) have confirmed that they intend to continue enforcing wage and hour, OSHA, and antidiscrimination provisions of federal law on behalf of undocumented immigrants. U.S. Department of La-bor, "Fact Sheet #48: Application of U.S. Labor Laws to Immigrant Workers: Effect of *Hoffman Plastics* decision on laws enforced by the Wage and Hour Division," available at *http://www.dol.gov/esa/regs/*

compliance/whd/whdfs48.htm; U.S. Department of Labor, *"Hoffman Plastic Compounds, Inc, v. NLRB,* Questions and Answers"; "EEOC Reaffirms Commitment to Protecting Undocumented Workers from Discrimination," EEOC Press Release, June 28, 2002.

Nonetheless, since *Hoffman* employers have been more aggressive in arguing that their undocumented employees are not entitled to the protection of these and other workplace laws. National Employment Law Project, "Used and Abused: The Treatment of Undocumented Victims of Labor Law Violations since Hoffman Plastic Compounds v. NLRB" (Sept. 2003), available at *http://www.nelp.org/docUploads/Used%20and%20Abused%20101003%2Epdf.*

67. Bureau of Labor Statistics (BLS), 2002 statistics, available at *ftp://146.142.4.23/pub/news.release/union2.txt;* Carol Zabin with Katie Quan and Linda Delp, "Union Organizing in California: Challenges and Opportunities," *The State of California Labor, 2001 Report,* p. 13. As of 2002, manufacturing accounts for only 16 percent of U.S. employment (BLS), and for a more or less equivalent percentage of all unionized workers. The public sector accounts for 15.9 percent of all work in the United States (BLS), but 46 percent of all union membership. AFL-CIO website, available at *http://www.aflcio.org/aboutunions/joinunions/whyjoin/uniondifference/uniondiff10.cfm.*

68. Bob Ortega, *In Sam We Trust: The Untold Story of Sam Walton and How Wal-Mart Is Devouring America* (New York: Times Books, 1998); Karen Olsson, "Up against Wal-Mart," *Mother Jones,* March/April 2003, pp. 54-59.

69. Rachael Cobb, "Unionizing the Home Care Workers of Los Angeles County," unpublished paper, Massachusetts Institute of Technology, 1999 (on file with the author); Linda Delp and Katie Quan, "Homecare Worker Organizing in California: An Analysis of a Successful Strategy," 27 (1) *Labor Studies Journal* 1-23 (2002).

70. Although the skilled/unskilled dichotomy accurately reflects one aspect of reality—that workers with recognized skills have a far greater capacity to control the flow of labor, and thus greater bargaining power, than those without—the terms ignore the way that workers develop and apply distinctive experiences and abilities in all jobs. This was recognized by no less a craft union man than AFL president

Samuel Gompers at the turn of the last century. Dorothy Sue Cobble, "Reviving the Federation's Historic Role in Organizing," Institute for the Study of Labor Organizations, Working Papers, March
10, 1996, pp. 1–43, pp. 23–24.

71. Howard Wial, "The Emerging Organizational Structure of Unionism
in Low-Wage Services," 45 *Rutgers Law Review* 671 (1993).

72. A few courts have decided cases in these workers' favor. See *Vizcaino
v. Microsoft Corp.*, 173 F.3d 713 (9th Cir. 1999).

73. Catherine Ruckleshaus and Bruce Goldstein, "The Legal Landscape
for Contingent Workers in the United States," available at *http://
www.nelp.org/docUploads/pub42%2Epdf*, a part of the National Employment Law Project's Subcontracted Worker Initiative Strategy Forum.

74. Before its legislative overruling via the Taft-Hartley Act in 1947, the
ruling case had been *NLRB v. Hearst Publications, Inc.*, 322 U.S. 111
(1944), which stated a much broader standard for coverage. The
problems of rules written for another era have been compounded by
the arthritic slowness of the National Labor Relation Board's process for deciding if a violation of the NLRA, an "unfair labor practice," has occurred, and by the weakness of its remedies. For a discussion of the ineffectiveness of the NLRB in addressing the common
unfair labor practice of firing workers suspected of being union supporters, see Paul Weiler, *Governing the Workplace: The Future of Labor
and Employment Law* (Cambridge: Harvard University Press, 1990),
pp. 234–240.

75. NLRA § 8(b)(4)(B). The garment industry, which is similarly structured, was long ago granted a specific exception to the prohibition
on secondary action, allowing garment workers and their unions to
exert economic pressure against jobbers, contractors, and manufacturers. Zimny and Garren, "Protecting the Contingent Workforce,"
pp. 7–8. Outside the garment industry, advocates have recently had
some success in arguing that the ultimate employer bears a responsibility for the wages and working conditions of its contractors' employees. In 2003, for example, the National Employment Law Project
negotiated settlements with Duane Reade and Gristede's for millions of dollars in back wages owed to delivery workers who were
contracted through middlemen to work for those stores. Steven

Greenhouse, "Gristede's Deliverymen to Share in $3.2 Million Wage Settlement," *New York Times,* Dec. 18, 2003, p. B2.

76. *Malbaff Landscape,* 172 N.L.R.B. 128 (1968); *Burns International Security Services, Inc.,* 406 U.S. 272 (1972). The construction industry was granted a specific exception to this rule in NLRA § 8(f), which permits prehire agreements obligating employers to hire only union labor for a particular construction job.

77. Dorothy Sue Cobble and Leah F. Vosko, "Historical Perspectives on Representing Nonstandard Workers," in Francoise Carre, Marianne A. Ferber, Lonnie Golden, and Stephen A. Herzenberg, ed., *Nonstandard Work: The Nature and Challenges of Changing Employment Arrangements* (Champaign: Industrial Relations Research Association, 2000), pp. 291-312.

78. Fine, "Community Unions," chaps. 2-3; Dorothy Sue Cobble, "Lost Ways of Organizing: Reviving the AFL's Direct Affiliate Strategy," 36 (3) *Industrial Relations* 278-301 (1997); Cobble, "Lost Ways of Unionism: Historical Perspectives on Reinventing the Labor Movement," in Lowell Turner, Harry C. Katz, and Richard W. Hurd, ed., *Rekindling the Movement: Labor's Quest for Relevance in the Twenty-First Century* (Ithaca: Cornell University Press, 2001) pp. 82-96.

79. Cobble, "Lost Ways of Organizing."

80. Cobble, "Organizing the Postindustrial Work Force: Lessons from the History of Waitress Unionism," 44 (3) *Industrial and Labor Relations Review,* 419-436 (1991); Cobble, *Dishing It Out: Waitresses and Their Unions in the Twentieth Century* (Chicago: University of Illinois Press, 1991).

81. On unionism in the entertainment industry, see Lois Gray and Ronald Seeber, ed., *Under the Stars: Essays on Labor Relations in Arts and Entertainment* (Ithaca: Cornell University Press, 1996). On longshore workers, see David Wellman, *The Union Makes Us Strong: Radical Unionism on the San Francisco Waterfront* (Cambridge: Cambridge University Press, 1995); Charles P. Larrowe, *Shape-Up and Hiring Hall: A Comparison of Hiring Methods and Labor Relations on the New York and Seattle Waterfronts* (Berkeley: University of California Press, 1955); Bruce Nelson, *Workers on the Waterfront* (Chicago: University of Illinois Press, 1988).

82. Cobble, "Organizing the Postindustrial Work Force," p. 431. Some

unions—such as construction unions—have carved out exceptions to the law that permit "prehire agreements," an analog to closed-shop agreements. NLRA § 8(f) permits construction unions to sign agreements with employers that the employers will hire only union workers.

83. Waldinger, "Helots No More"; Wial, "The Emerging Organizational Structure of Unionism"; Catherine L. Fisk, Daniel J. B. Mitchell, and Christopher L. Erickson, "Union Representation of Immigrant Janitors in Southern California: Economic and Legal Challenges," in Milkman, ed., *Organizing Immigrants,* pp. 199–224.

84. Nonetheless, SEIU's strategies do come close to the legal line at times, and the union has been brought before the NLRB on allegations of secondary activity. Fisk, "Union Representation of Immigrant Janitors in Southern California," pp. 214–221; interview with Orrin Baird, Associate General Counsel of SEIU, Oct. 16, 2003.

85. Cobb, "Unionizing the Homecare Workers of Los Angeles County"; Delp and Quan, "Homecare Worker Organizing in California."

86. Miriam Wells, "Immigration and Unionization in the San Francisco Hotel Industry," in Milkman, ed., *Organizing Immigrants,* pp. 109–129.

87. Karen Olsson, "The Shame of Meatpacking," *The Nation,* Sept. 16, 2002, pp. 11–16; Cooper, "The Heartland's Raw Deal"; David Bacon, "The Kill-Floor Rebellion," *The American Prospect,* July 1, 2002, pp. 20–23.

88. David Johnson, "Model Organizing Campaign Doubles Union Membership in Nine Months," *Labor Notes,* May 2002, p. 16.

89. Janice Fine, *Immigrant Worker Centers: Building a New American Community at the Edge of the Dream* (Washington, D.C.: Economic Policy Institute, 2004).

2. THE WORKPLACE PROJECT STORY

1. Workplace Project Mission Statement, on file with the author.

2. Joel Handler, *Social Movements and the Legal System: A Theory of Law Reform and Social Change* (New York: Academic Press, 1978), pp. 18–25.

3. I knew this from consulting work I had done with Central American organizations during law school. It is confirmed by the Mumford

Center's analysis of 2000 Census data, available at *http://mumford1 .dyndns.org/cen2000/HispanicPop/HspSort/salSort.htm.* See also the Mumford Center's Report, *The New Latinos: Who They Are, Where They Are*, Albany, NY, Sept. 10, 2001.

4. All last names have been deleted to protect privacy.

5. Under New York state law, there was a penalty for "repeat or will-ful non-payment of wages" equivalent to 25 percent of the amount owed. NY CLS Labor §218 (1996 version). Under the federal Fair La-bor Standards Act, the penalty was an amount equal to the amount owed. Employers rarely if ever paid the penalty, because the govern-ment agencies in charge of enforcement did not pursue it, because courts did not often impose it, or because, if imposed, the penalty was too hard to collect. State of New York, Office of the State Comp-troller, 1994 Report 94-S-56; Howard Wial, "Minimum-Wage Enforce-ment and the Low-Wage Labor Market," MIT Task Force on Recon-structing America's Labor Market Institutions Working Paper 11, Aug. 1, 1999.

6. Janice Fine, "Community Unions in Baltimore and Long Island: Be-yond the Politics of Particularism" (Ph.D. diss., Massachusetts Insti-tute of Technology, 2003), p. 114.

7. Not all low-wage job categories were dominated by Latinos. Factory owners, for example, tended to hire a diverse range of workers, in part to play workers of different races and ethnic groups off against each other. See Saru Jayaraman, "Letting the Canary Lead: Power and Participation among Latina/o Immigrant Workers," 27 *New York Uni-versity Review of Law and Social Change* 103–109, 106 (2001–2002), Fine, "Community Unions," pp. 103–104.

8. The Workplace Project was fortunate that none of its protests re-sulted in SLAPP (Strategic Litigation against Public Participation) lawsuits. Worker centers protesting unpaid wages have at times been the target of SLAPP suits, including the Korean Immigrant Workers Advocates in Los Angeles, which was sued by a restaurant owner af-ter protesting the restaurant's failure to pay overtime wages, and the Chinese Staff and Workers Association and the National Mobiliza-tion against Sweatshops, which were sued by the New York garment

manufacturer Street Beat after protesting the company's illegally low wages. Both lawsuits were eventually defeated under anti-SLAPP laws in the respective states.

9. *So Goes a Nation: Lawyers and Communities* (Sight Effects, 1997). The documentary, which explores three organizations' approaches to community lawyering, was also released on CD-Rom as an attachment to 25 *Fordham Urban Law Journal* (1998). It was prepared by New York Lawyers for the Public Interest in conjunction with the Stein Center at Fordham Law School.

10. See Fine, "Community Unions," p. 136.

11. This is not a function of an independent union's worker center sponsorship, but of its resource-intensive nature. Administrative costs are high. With so few members, it is nearly impossible to establish effective benefit structures and strike funds. See, e.g., Mae M. Ngai's review of Peter Kwong, "Forbidden Workers" in *New Labor Forum,* Fall/Winter 1998, pp. 151-157.

12. See, e.g., Ruth Milkman and Kent Wong, "Organizing the Wicked City: The 1992 Southern California Drywall Strike," in Ruth Milkman, ed., *Organizing Immigrants: The Challenge for Unions in Contemporary California* (Ithaca: Cornell University Press, 2000), pp. 169-198; Immanuel Ness, "Community Labor Alliances: A New Paradigm in the Campaign to Organize Greengrocery Workers in New York City," in Benjamin Shepard and Ronald Hayduk, ed., *From ACT UP to the WTO: Urban Protest and Community Building in the Era of Globalization* (New York: Verso, 2002), pp. 57-73; Leon Fink, *The Maya of Morganton: Work and Community in the Nuevo New South* (Chapel Hill: University of North Carolina Press, 2003).

13. Nadia Marin interview, Oct. 10, 1999 (before the Workplace Projects's new industry committees were launched).

14. There was one more major day labor site in northern Nassau County, in the city of Glen Cove. Because of the distance and the configuration of highways in Long Island, Glen Cove was not a likely source of competition for workers in Inwood. In addition, the Glen Cove site was managed by a social service agency, Fuerza Unida of Glen Cove.

15. Personal observation; John Leonardo and James O'Shea, "A Quantitative Analysis of 'Shape-Ups' on Long Island: A Report Prepared for

the Workplace Project," Hofstra University, Jan. 1997 (paper on file with the author); Abel Valenzuela and Edwin Melendez, "Day Labor in New York: Findings from the NYDL Survey," April 11, 2003, available at *http://www.newschool.edu/milano/cdrc/pubs/daylabor.pdf*.

16. Notes from a meeting with Pastreich, Feb. 28, 1997. Janice Fine made similar observations as she guided the group through its analysis of the options for its day labor program in the spring of 1997.

17. Fine, "Community Unions," p. 128.

18. Many observers have remarked on this aspect of the relationship. See, e.g., Mary Romero, *Maid in the U.S.A* (New York: Routledge, 1992), pp. 123–126.

19. The FLSA did not include private household workers until 1974, following intensive advocacy by the National Committee on Household Employment. Pierrette Hondagneu-Sotelo, *Doméstica: Immigrant Workers Cleaning and Caring in the Shadows of Affluence* (Berkeley: University of California Press, 2001), p. 212. Even now its coverage is limited to those who devote at least 20 percent of their time to housekeeping (excluding many babysitters and personal care attendants). Live-in employees are not covered by the FLSA's overtime protections. 29 U.S.C. § 213(b)(21) (2003). Some state wage and hour laws have more expansive coverage of domestic workers while others exclude them entirely. The National Organization for Women (NOW) Legal Defense and Education Fund, *Out of the Shadows: Strategies for Expanding State Labor and Civil Rights Protections for Domestic Workers* (1997), pp. 3–5. See also Tera W. Hunter, *To Joy My Freedom: Southern Black Women's Lives and Labors after the Civil War* (Cambridge: Harvard University Press, 1997), in particular chap. 4; Peggie R. Smith, "Organizing the Unorganizable: Private Paid Household Workers and Approaches to Employee Representation," *79 North Carolina Law Review* 45, 52–71 (2000).

20. Hondagneu-Sotelo, *Doméstica,* p. 16.

21. Its success served as a model for other efforts, including a much broader campaign by domestic worker organizations in New York City in 2001 and 2002 that succeeded in passing a city ordinance imposing a code of conduct on domestic work placement agencies. Chisun Lee, "Domestic Disturbance: The Help Set Out to Help

Themselves," *The Village Voice*, March 19, 2002, p. 31; Steven Greenhouse, "New Protections for Nannies are Approved by Council," *New York Times*, May 15, 2003, p. B3.

22. For interviews with many of the women who founded and work in the UNITY cooperative, see Drucilla Cornell, *Between Women and Generations: Legacies of Dignity* (New York: Palgrave MacMillan, 2002).

23. Juan Calderon interview, June 17, 1998. Unless otherwise indicated, all further quotes from Calderon are from this interview.

24. In 1997 the Workplace Project created an associate member category that would have permitted a worker to join at a lower level in order to receive membership benefits. Approved as an attempt to build the organization's membership rolls, the plan was not promoted by the group, and the Workers Course—both in its traditional form and a shorter, two-day *cursillo*—remained the primary point of entry to membership.

25. In 2001, the Association of Community Organizations for Reform Now (ACORN) and the Working Families Party succeeded in passing a living wage ordinance in Suffolk County. It covered only workers laboring under county service contracts worth $10,000 or more and those whose employers received subsidies or incentives from the county. Elissa Gootman, "Suffolk County Votes to Mandate a Living Wage," *New York Times*, July 28, 2001, p. B1. These provisions affected few of the small and underground businesses for which the majority of immigrants worked, with the notable exception of the home health care industry. Since that time, however, several cities around the country have passed much broader living wage ordinances that cover all workers within the city. San Francisco's Proposition L, raising the minimum wage in that city to $8.50, is a model for such laws. It passed on Nov. 4, 2003. Steve Rubenstein and Alan Gathright, "Measures: Panhandling Limits, Minimum-Wage Hike Passed by S.F. Voters," *San Francisco Chronicle*, Nov. 5, 2003, p. A20.

3. PATHS TO PARTICIPATION

1. Less than a third of worker centers have memberships larger than 500. Janice Fine and Jon Werberg, "National Study on Immigrant Worker Centers—Draft Worker Center Survey, Preliminary Analysis," unpublished ms., Nov. 6, 2003.

2. Mancur Olson, *The Logic of Collective Action: Public Goods and the Theory of Groups* (Cambridge: Harvard University Press, 1965).

3. Between a quarter and a third of the active membership in 1997 had first come to the organization through the legal clinic. Author's calculation; Janice Fine, "Community Unions in Baltimore and Long Island: Beyond the Politics of Particularism" (Ph.D. diss., Massachusetts Institute of Technology, 2003), p. 118.

4. For an account of a similar dynamic in another setting, see Leon Fink's description of how Guatemalan Mayan immigrants to Morganton, North Carolina, were taken aback when they found that the labor courts that had for some years existed in their country were nowhere to be found in the United States. Fink, *The Maya of Morganton: Work and Community in the Nuevo New South* (Chapel Hill: University of North Carolina Press, 2003), pp. 65–67.

5. See also Fine, "Community Unions," p. 120.

6. Interview with Janice Fine, 1977, no date.

7. Ibid.; Fine, "Community Unions," p. 117.

8. Fine interview; Fine, "Community Unions," p. 121. Words in brackets are mine.

9. Interview with Raul Lopez, June 17, 1998. Unless otherwise indicated, all further quotes from Lopez are from this interview.

10. For a resounding "no," see Steve Jenkins, "Organizing, Advocacy, and Member Power: A Critical Reflection," 6 (2) *Working USA* 56–89 (2002). I draw on—and, in part, take issue with—his arguments here.

11. See, e.g., Rachel L. Swarns, "Immigrants Feel the Pinch of Post-9/11 Laws," *New York Times,* June 25, 2003, p. A1.

12. Lani Guinier and Gerald Torres offer the image of a group engaged in trying to build a beautiful sandcastle together as a metaphor for the value of collaborative work independent of its impact on the outside world, in *The Miner's Canary: Enlisting Race, Resisting Power, Transforming Democracy* (Cambridge: Harvard University Press, 2002), p. 141. Feminists in particular have advanced the idea that a group of people working together to create something are building power through that act. This concept has variously been labeled "generative power," "power-with," and "power-to," in contrast with the more traditional concept of power as "power-over," or the power to compel someone else to do something. Bernard M. Loomer, "Two Kinds of

Power," 15 (1) *Criterion* 11-29 (1976); Jean Baker Miller, "Women and Power," in Judith V. Jordan, Alexandra G. Kaplan, Jean Baker Miller, Irene P. Stiver, and Janet L. Surrey, ed., *Women's Growth in Connection: Writings from the Stone Center* (New York: The Guilford Press, 1991), pp. 197-205; Nancy C. M. Hartsock, "Political Change: Two Perspectives on Power," in *The Feminist Standpoint Revisited and Other Essays* (Boulder: Westview Press, 1998), pp. 15-27.

13. There is a long tradition of participatory organizing in the United States, which Francesca Polletta traces in her book, *Freedom Is an Endless Meeting: Democracy in American Social Movements* (Chicago: University of Chicago Press, 2002). For the argument that sites where participatory organizing happens have played critical roles in fomenting and supporting social movements in the United States, see Sara M. Evans and Harry C. Boyte, *Free Spaces: The Sources of Democratic Change in America* (Chicago: University of Chicago Press, 1986).

14. This example is taken from SEIU's home health campaign. Rachael Cobb, "Unionizing the Home Care Workers of Los Angeles County," unpublished paper, Massachusetts Institute of Technology, 1999 (on file with the author); Linda Delp and Katie Quan, "Homecare Worker Organizing in California: An Analysis of a Successful Strategy," 27 (1) *Labor Studies Journal* 1-23 (2002).

15. Several scholars have documented this effect in union organizing campaigns that are run in strongly participatory ways. See Katherine Sciacchitano, "Unions, Organizing, and Democracy: Living in One's Time, Building for the Future," *Dissent* 47 (2) 75-81 (2000). On a similar process and outcome in a very different context, that of the Harvard Union of Clerical and Technical Workers' long and ultimately successful effort to organize the staff of Harvard University, see John Hoerr, *We Can't Eat Prestige: The Women Who Organized Harvard* (Philadelphia: Temple University Press, 1997).

16. In her history of participatory democracy in social movements in the United States, Polletta points out a number of times and places where participatory democracy was a source not just of internal but of external strength for organizing efforts, *Freedom Is an Endless Meeting*, pp. 2-3.

17. See Bill Fletcher and Richard W. Hurd, "Is Organizing Enough?

Race, Gender, and Union Culture," *New Labor Forum,* Spring/Summer 2000, pp. 59–70. There are a variety of perspectives on how to achieve this. For one slice of the debate, contrast the view of the positive role identity caucuses play in this regard in Ruben J. Garcia, "New Voices at Work: Race and Gender Identity Caucuses in the U.S. Labor Movement," 54 *Hastings Law Journal* 79 (2002), with the opposition to such caucuses expressed in Michael Selmi and Molly S. McUsic, "Difference and Solidarity: Unions in a Postmodern Age," in Joanne Conaghan, Richard Michael Fischl, and Karl Klare, ed., *Labour Law in an Era of Globalization: Transformative Practices and Possibilities* (Oxford: Oxford University Press, 2002), pp. 430–446.

18. Marshall Ganz, "Resources and Resourcefulness: Strategic Capacity in the Unionization of Californian Agriculture," 105(4) *American Journal of Sociology* 1003–1062 (2000).

19. Jenkins, "Organizing, Advocacy, and Member Power," p. 84.

4. RIGHTS TALK AND COLLECTIVE ACTION

1. This was one of the central concerns of left legal scholars from the 1960s through the early 1980s. Stuart Scheingold's influential book, *The Politics of Rights: Lawyers, Public Policy, and Political Change* (New Haven: Yale University Press, 1974), argued that to believe that law, and litigation in particular, would create social change was to succumb to the "myth of rights." Critical Legal Studies proponents such as Mark Tushnet, Duncan Kennedy, and Peter Gabel carried that argument forward, positing that talk about rights and even rights-based strategies are incompatible with successful social movements. See, e.g., Mark Tushnet, "An Essay on Rights," 62 *Texas Law Review* 1363, 1371–1382 (1984); Peter Gabel, "The Phenomenology of Rights-Consciousness and the Pact of the Withdrawn Selves," 62 *Texas Law Review* 1563, 1586–1597 (1984).

2. On teaching about rights as a starting point for social change, see Margaret Schuler and Sakuntala Kadirgamar-Rajasingham, ed., *Legal Literacy: A Tool for Women's Empowerment* (New York: Women, Law, Development International / OEF UNIFEM, 1992); Margaret Schuler, ed., *Empowerment and the Law: Strategies of Third World Women* (New York: Women, Law, Development International / OEF UNIFEM,

1986); George Andreopoulos and Richard Pierre Claude, ed., *Human Rights Education for the Twenty-First Century* (Philadelphia: University of Pennsylvania Press, 1997); Ingrid Eagly, "Community Education: Creating A New Vision of Legal Services Practice," 4 *Clinical Law Review* 433 (1998).

3. The line is far from absolute. For one, substantive laws all have procedural parts that explain how the rights in that law will be enforced. More important, procedural laws have substantive consequences: The way the NLRA sets up the "game" of labor organizing often predetermines who will win and who will lose, and thus what workers can ask for or even whether they dare to think seriously about asking in the first place.

4. The continuum does not always run from reality to law to justice. In a variety of situations, as Fran Ansley has pointed out to me, it is flipped: law to reality to justice. That is certainly the case described in *Whigs and Hunters: The Origin of the Black Act* (London: Allen Lane, 1975), E. P. Thompson's book about the draconian—but rarely enforced—English Poor Laws.

5. For an exploration of the way that divisions present in home-country communities can play out in labor organizing struggles in the United States, see Leon Fink, *The Maya of Morganton: Work and Community in the Nuevo New South* (Chapel Hill: University of North Carolina Press, 2003).

6. Sarah Mahler, *American Dreaming: Immigrant Life on the Margins* (Princeton: Princeton University Press, 1995).

7. Mahler made similar observations during her study of the Salvadoran and Peruvian communities on Long Island in the early 1990s—the same communities from which the Workplace Project drew its membership. *American Dreaming*, p. 4.

8. See Janice Fine, "Community Unions in Baltimore and Long Island: Beyond the Politics of Particularism" (Ph.D. diss., Massachusetts Institute of Technology, 2003), p. 119.

9. See, e.g., Michael Walzer, *Exodus and Revolution* (New York: Basic Books, 1986). For a comparison of the use of religious narratives in movements on the left and right see Rhys H. Williams, "From the 'Beloved Community' to 'Family Values': Religious Language, Sym-

bolic Repertoires, and Democratic Culture," in David S. Meyer, Nancy Whittier, and Belinda Robnett, ed., *Social Movements: Identity, Culture, and the State* (New York: Oxford University Press, 2002), pp. 247-265.

10. For the sake of clarity, I make a sharp distinction between "internal" and "external" organizing. But in truth, the line is never so easy to draw. As Nancy Whittier has observed, "movements' internal dynamics interact with their external contexts." This is true on the level of structure, as groups take forms that respond to outside opportunities and ideologies. It is also true on the level of meaning: "movements, institutions, and the state incorporate and reformulate each others' meanings even as they challenge them." Whittier, "Meaning and Structure in Social Movements," in Meyer, Whittier, and Robnett, ed., *Social Movements,* pp. 293-294.

11. In his class on organizing at Harvard's Kennedy School of Government, the sociologist (and former UFW Executive Committee member) Marshall Ganz connects the "emotional" process of building a group's values and its understanding of its identity (heart), the "analytical" process of developing its strategy (head), and the development of skills necessary to realize that strategy (hands). Ganz, "Organizing Notes" (Harvard Kennedy School of Government, 2000).

12. Ellen Carol DuBois, "Outgrowing the Compact of the Fathers: Equal Rights, Woman Suffrage, and the United States Constitution, 1820-1878," in David Thelen, ed., *The Constitution and American Life* (Ithaca: Cornell University Press, 1988), pp. 176, 181. See also Martha Minow, "We, the Family: Constitutional Rights and American Families," in Thelen, ed., *American Life.* On rights talk in the antislavery movement, see Eric Foner, "Rights and the Constitution in Black Life during the Civil War and Reconstruction," in Thelen, ed., *American Life,* pp. 203, 212.

13. This is different from the work rules enshrined in a contract, the predominant form of labor organizing after the New Deal. See William Forbath, *Law and the Shaping of the American Labor Movement* (Cambridge: Harvard University Press 1991) p. 84; David Montgomery, *Workers Control in America* (New York: Cambridge University Press, 1980), p. 16.

14. Forbath, *Shaping of the American Labor Movement,* esp. pp. 128-166; James Pope, "Labor's Constitution of Freedom," 106 *Yale Law Journal* 941 (1997).

15. Pope argues that much of the blame for the failure of this vision to be integrated into law should be laid at the feet of labor attorneys of the era. "Labor's Constitution," p. 1027; Pope, "The Thirteenth Amendment versus the Commerce Clause: Labor and the Shaping of American Constitutional Law, 1921-1957" 102 *Columbia Law Review* 1 (2002).

16. Forbath, *Shaping of the American Labor Movement,* pp. 136-139, 145.

17. Foner, "Black Life," p. 216: "Black religion reinforced black republicanism"; Francesca Polletta, "The Structural Context of Novel Rights Claims: Southern Civil Rights Organizing, 1961-1966," 34 *Law and Society Review* 367, 391 (2000).

18. Studies of the relationship of rights to social movements include Susan Olson, *Clients and Lawyers: Securing the Rights of Disabled Persons* (Westport, CN: Greenwood Press, 1984); Martha F. Davis, *Brutal Need: Lawyers and the Welfare Rights Movement, 1960-1973* (New Haven: Yale University Press, 1993); Michael McCann, *Rights at Work: Pay Equity Reform and the Politics of Legal Mobilization* (Chicago: University of Chicago Press, 1994); David Engel and Frank Munger, *Rights of Inclusion: Law and Identity in the Life Stories of Americans with Disabilities* (Chicago: University of Chicago Press, 2003); Elizabeth M. Schneider, "The Dialectic of Rights and Politics: Perspectives from the Women's Movement," 61 *New York University Law Review* 589 (1986); Neal Milner, "The Dilemmas of Legal Mobilization: Ideologies and Strategies of Mental Patient Liberation Groups," *Law and Policy,* Jan. 1986, pp. 105-129; Polletta, "The Structural Context," pp. 367-406.

19. Engel and Munger, *Rights of Inclusion,* p. 83. Talk about rights at work may have special resonance. As Judith Shklar has noted, work is a particularly important component of how people in the United States have come to understand the way standing as a citizen is earned. Shklar, *American Citizenship: The Quest for Inclusion* (Cambridge: Harvard University Press, 1991).

20. Patricia Williams, "Alchemical Notes: Reconstructed Ideals from Deconstructed Rights," 22 *Harvard Civil Rights–Civil Liberties Law Review*

401, 414 (1987). See also Martha Minow, "Interpreting Rights: An Essay for Robert Cover," 96 *Yale Law Journal* 1860, 1887, n. 108 (1987).

21. Formal rights are not the only source of a change in identity and action. Perhaps the best example is in the area of gay and lesbian rights in the United States, where formal law has lagged behind a sense of pride among gay and lesbian people and even behind their broadening social acceptance. See Thomas B. Stoddard, "Bleeding Heart: Reflections on Using the Law to Make Social Change," 72 *New York University Law Review* 967, 968–71 (1997).

22. See, e.g., Engel and Munger, *Rights of Inclusion;* Patricia Ewick and Susan Silbey, *The Common Place of Law* (Chicago: University of Chicago Press, 1998); Ewick and Silbey, "Making Resistance Thinkable: Desired Disturbances of Everyday Legal Transactions," paper given at New York Law School, Dec. 2001; Lucie White, "Subordination, Rhetorical Survival Skills, and Sunday Shoes: Notes on the Hearing of Mrs. G.," 38 *Buffalo Law Review* 1 (1990). See also Sally Engle Merry, *Getting Justice and Getting Even: Legal Consciousness among Working Class Americans* (Chicago: University of Chicago Press, 1990), pp. 146–149, discussing individual emotions as resistance in court settings.

   For critiques of this individual focus, see Joel Handler, "A Reply," 26 *Law and Society Review* 819–824 (1992); Michael McCann and Tracey March, "Law and Everyday Forms of Resistance: A Socio-Political Assessment," 15 *Studies in Law, Politics, and Society* 207–236 (1995); Francesca Polletta, "The Laws of Passion" (reviewing Susan Bandes, ed., *The Passion of Laws*), 35 *Law and Society Review* 467–493 (2001); William H. Simon, "The Dark Secret of Progressive Lawyering: A Comment on Poverty Law Scholarship in the Post-Modern, Post-Reagan Era," 48 *University of Miami Law Review* 1099 (1994); Gary Blasi, "What's a Theory For? Notes on Reconstructing Poverty Law Scholarship," 48 *University of Miami Law Review* 1063 (1994).

23. Critical race theorists such as Kimberlé Crenshaw, Patricia Williams, and Richard Delgado have pointed out the related ways that rights have long been an important source of legitimization and an important framework for claims-making for people of color: Williams, "Alchemical Notes;" pp. 408–415; Crenshaw, "Race, Reform, and Re-

trenchment: Transformation and Legitimation in Antidiscrimination Law," 101 *Harvard Law Review* 1331 (1988); Delgado, "The Ethereal Scholar: Does Critical Legal Studies Have What Minorities Want?" 22 *Harvard Civil Rights–Civil Liberties Law Review* 301 (1987).

24. Anthony Amsterdam and Jerome Bruner, *Minding the Law* (Cambridge: Harvard University Press, 2000), pp. 231–232 (italics deleted).

25. Williams, "Alchemical Notes." Engel and Munger also suggest that "rights become active in situations where potential rights holders perceive a disparity between the treatment they expect and the treatment they actually receive." *Rights of Inclusion,* p. 165. The process I describe is to some extent about using rights to change the treatment immigrant workers expect.

26. Staughton Lynd has suggested that some kinds of rights are more likely than others to encourage and support collective action for the benefit of community, in "Communal Rights," 62 *Texas Law Review* 1417, 1421 (1984). He posits a set of what he terms "communal rights," even as he acknowledges that "rights do not come neatly divided into inherently individual and inherently communal" packages.

27. This was well expressed by M. D. Mistry, the founder of a union for migrant construction workers and other "non-standard" workers in Gujarat, India, whom I met on a research trip there in 1999: "A law can't bring about social change. Of course movements will put pressure on the government to change the laws. But the problem is then that people begin obsessing on the law itself, forgetting how it was achieved. They abandon the movement and fixate on the law. That makes no sense. You have to recognize that it's a constant process: pressure so that a law is enacted, pressure so that it is enforced." Interview with Mistry, Nov. 15, 1999.

28. So much talk about enforcement could also elide the ways that the gap between reality and law is the manifestation of the workings of power, an intentional distance between political promises and the will to execute them. The Indian advocate and legal scholar Rajeev Dhavan points out this danger in his analysis of "gap theory," which he critiques for its assumption that the distance between reality and legal promises is an accidental side effect of policy-making rather than a deliberate one. Dhavan, "Introduction," Marc Galanter, *Law and Society in Modern India* (New York: Oxford University Press, 1989), pp.

xxiii–xxiv. On the failure of legal and social science scholarship to effectively understand the gap problem, see Richard Abel, "Law Books and Books about Law," 26 *Stanford Law Review* 175, 184–189 (1973).

29. As Martha Minow has argued, "'Rights' can give rise to 'rights consciousness' so that individuals and groups can imagine and act in light of rights that have not been formally recognized or enforced." "Interpreting Rights," p. 1867.

30. Ibid., p. 1874. Footnotes omitted.

31. Polletta, "The Structural Context," p. 378. Poletta goes on to posit the circumstances under which novel rights claims are more likely to arise and succeed.

32. Amsterdam and Bruner, *Minding the Law,* pp. 236–237. To capture the characteristic of simultaneous restraint and freedom, Martha Minow uses the image of rights as a language, "Interpreting Rights," p. 1892. Similarly, see William Forbath on the language of law, *Shaping of the American Labor Movement,* p. 171.

33. Minow, "Interpreting Rights," p. 1877; see also Hendrik Hartog, "The Constitution of Aspiration and 'The Rights That Belong to Us All,'" in Thelen, *American Life,* pp. 353, 368.

34. Forbath, *Shaping of the American Labor Movement.*

35. Schneider, "The Dialectic of Rights."

36. For a discussion of how this dynamic played out in a labor struggle in London nearly two centuries ago, see Marc W. Steinberg, "Toward a More Dialogic Analysis of Social Movement Culture," in Meyer, ed., *Social Movements,* pp. 208–225.

5. A Legal Clinic and Organizing

1. Many of the 550 sought help with issues other than unpaid wages or benefits. Where the claims were for wages or benefits due, on average the Project won 70 percent of its cases.

2. In some circumstances, though, immigrants from El Salvador and other countries with strong popular movements can be especially active participants in organizing efforts in the United States.

3. Ann Withorn, "To Serve the People: An Inquiry into the Success of Service-Delivery as a Social Movement Strategy." (Ph.D. diss., Brandeis University, 1978), p. 49.

4. With regard to foundations, counter-intuitively, it was easier to fund

the Workplace Project's organizing work than its legal services programs. Very few foundations will fund a small legal clinic that is tightly linked to organizing. The small progressive foundations that the Project relies on have been much more interested in funding the group's organizing and education work.

5. The database was also a unique source for the news media of statistics about Long Island's immigrant workers and their problems on the job. This indirectly supported the Project's organizing efforts by leading to many relationships with reporters that later generated publicity for campaigns.

6. Model Code of Professional Responsibility EC 5-1 (1981); Model Rules of Professional Conduct R. 1.7(b) (1983).

7. *NAACP v. Button,* 371 U.S. 415 (1963), *BRT v. Virginia,* 377 U.S. 1 (1964). See also George E. Bodle, "Group Legal Services: The Case for BRT," 12 *UCLA Law Review* 306 (1965). For a brief discussion of this question in the legal-clinic-as-organizing-tool context, see William Simon, "The Dark Secret of Progressive Lawyering: A Comment on Poverty Law Scholarship in the Post-Modern, Post-Reagan Era," 48 *University of Miami Law Review* 1099, 1109 (1994).

8. A few legal services offices select cases differently, through an approach that puts strategy at the forefront. Gary Bellow and Jeanne Charn advocate a version of this approach that they call "focused case pressure." Gary Bellow and Jeanne Charn, "Paths Not Yet Taken: Some Comments on Feldman's Critique of Legal Services Practice," 83 *Georgetown Law Journal* 1633, 1645–1650 (1995); Gary Bellow, "Steady Work: A Practitioner's Reflections on Political Lawyering," 31 *Harvard Civil Rights–Civil Liberties Law Review* 297, 299 (1996).

9. When the legal case and organizing work are intermingled, nonlawyers such as organizers, social workers, and member-volunteers may not be covered by lawyer-client confidentiality protections. As a result, information that a client provided in confidence may become public either through the nonlawyer's communication with others or through "discovery" carried out by the opposing side during a lawsuit. Ingrid Eagly and Scott Cummings express concern about this in "A Critical Reflection on Law and Organizing," 48 *UCLA Law Review* 443, 506–509 (2001). Only lawyers or others under their direct supervision can practice law. Yet a legal clinic involves so-called lay-

people in the presentation of rights and the resolution of cases, which can leave an organization vulnerable to charges of unauthorized practice of law. Ibid., pp. 513-516. A clear policy that only the lawyers in the organization can give legal advice, and careful separation of legal and organizing work in the handling of cases, can reduce the level of both of these ethics concerns. But building a firewall between law and organizing runs counter to the integrated relationship between the two that a legal clinic like the Workplace Project's seeks to achieve.

10. Interview with Jerry Cohen, UFW general counsel, July 22, 1999.

11. Ibid.

12. See Simon, "The Dark Secret of Progressive Lawyering," p. 1107.

13. Interview with Nadia Marín-Molina, May 23, 2003.

14. Saru Jayaraman, "Letting the Canary Lead: Power and Participation among Latina/o Immigrant Workers," 27 *New York University Review of Law and Social Change* 104 (2001-2002).

15. Interview with Saru Jayaraman, May 3, 2001.

16. For a description of another legal clinic that gained considerable benefit from workers speaking to each other about their problems in a group format, see Lucie White, "To Learn and to Teach: Lessons on Lawyering and Power from Dreifontein," 1988 *Wisconsin Law Review* 699, 730-732 (1988). Note, however, that the people attending the South African legal clinic White describes did receive the assistance of a lawyer after they strategized possible solutions with each other.

17. Jayaraman interview; Marín-Molina interview. See also Julien Martin Ross, "A Fair Day's Pay: The Problem of Unpaid Workers in Central Texas" (MPA thesis, University of Texas, 2003), p. 101 (based on interviews with Marín-Molina and Carlos Canales).

18. Jayaraman, "Letting the Canary Lead," p. 105; Jayaraman interview.

19. Marin-Molina interview. See also Jayaraman, "Letting the Canary Lead."

20. Rinku Sen, *Stir It Up: Lessons in Community Organizing and Advocacy* (San Francisco: Jossey-Bass, 2003), p. 46.

21. Steve Jenkins, "Organizing, Advocacy, and Member Power: A Critical Reflection," 6 (2) *Working USA* 67 (Fall 2002). See also Ross, "A Fair Day's Pay."

22. Because workers were so mobile, this would have mattered less if the

Workplace Project had been able to organize a high percentage of low-wage Latino workers on Long Island. Their continued affiliation with the Project would have allowed them to organize wherever they ended up, and with a mass base they would have found fellow members at their new workplace.

23. Interview with Eliseo Medina, June 22, 2000. The UFW Service Center's first director, LeRoy Chatfield, emphasizes that "Cesar was very determined not to let the union become just a union . . . There was more to life, more needs, than the union could fill." Interview with Leroy Chatfield, Feb. 27, 2000.

24. Chatfield interview.

25. Ronald B. Taylor, *Chavez and the Farm Workers* (Boston: Beacon Press, 1976), pp. 215–216; Withorn, "To Serve the People," p. 272; interview with Jessica Govea, Oct. 13, 1999; Medina interview.

26. The Service Center's "Inc."—its status as a separate nonprofit 501(c)(3) entity—allowed it to receive foundation money, which the union could not do. Thus as well as the source of core services, the Service Center became a source of funding for a variety of work, including organizer training and some legal services. Chatfield interview.

27. Interview with Gilbert Padilla, Feb. 28, 2000; Chatfield interview; Govea interview.

28. Interview with Marshall Ganz, May 25, 2000; Medina interview.

29. Chatfield interview; Ganz interview; Govea interview. See also Withorn, "To Serve the People."

30. Contemporary examples support this hypothesis. In the midst of a union democracy campaign among immigrant meatpackers in Pasco, Washington, Teamsters for a Democratic Union (TDU) helped the workers file a lawsuit for wage and hour violations against the meatpackers' employer, IBP. In a 2003 decision, the Ninth Circuit Court of Appeals proposed a formula for calculating the money owed to the workers that would result in a judgment of over $7 million dollars. *Alvarez v. IBP, Inc.,* 339 F.3d 894 (2003). IBP has filed an appeal of the decision with the U.S. Supreme Court. During the ongoing organizing effort, the lawsuit has provided evidence of TDU's commitment to the immigrant meatpackers' interests, served as a vehicle to attract new activists, and become a point of contact

between members. The case has not been without conflicts. In particular, as the suit dragged on after its filing in 1999, with a long series of "victories" followed by appeals, workers became cynical about the likelihood that the legal strategy would actually result in money in their pockets. Nonetheless, coming as it did in the midst of a vibrant organizing effort with the clear goal of reforming the union, the lawsuit never threatened to become the focus of TDU's relationship with the workers. Interview with David Levin, TDU organizer, Nov. 11, 2003.

31. Interview with Omar Henriquez, Jan. 14, 2000.
32. On the characteristics of a successful movement service, see Withorn, "To Serve the People," p. 127.
33. One example of a prefigurative approach is the self-help health services developed by the women's movement in the 1970s, which were designed to make the service a transformative experience. See Sandra Morgen, *Into Our Own Hands: The Women's Health Movement in the United States, 1969–1990* (Piscataway: Rutgers University Press, 2002), pp. 359-414. See also Withorn, "To Serve the People."

6. NONCITIZEN CITIZENSHIP

1. 29 U.S.C. §§ 203, 207, 208.
2. The name and some identifying details have been changed to protect confidentiality.
3. The name and some identifying details have been changed to protect confidentiality.
4. Transcript of New York State Assembly Committee on Labor Hearing, Feb. 16, 1996, pp. 22-23.
5. State of New York, Office of the State Comptroller, 1994 Report 94-S-56. The DOL imposed penalties in only 2 percent of the cases it settled over three years, thus sacrificing as much as $6.7 million in revenues.
6. Interviews with Juan Calderon, June 17, 1998, and Rony Martinez, June 17, 1998. Unless otherwise indicated, all further quotes from each are from their respective interviews.
7. Interview with Luz Torres, June 17, 1998. Unless otherwise indicated, all further quotes from Torres are from this interview.
8. This chronic dysfunction resulted in New York state receiving the

lowest credit rating of any state except Louisiana. Clyde Haberman, "Albany Sets Bad Example for California," *New York Times,* July 25, 1997, p. B1. Richard Perez-Peña, "Scorn for Albany Unites Forces Urging a New Constitution," *New York Times,* Oct. 26, 1997, p. A31; "Call a Constitutional Convention," *New York Times,* Oct. 28, 1997, p. A22.

9. The Workplace Project might not have recognized this—or a number of other strategic opportunities—without the guidance of insiders who supported the legislation. Geri Reilly, associate counsel on labor for the Assembly, was a critical source of this kind of insight.

10. The Long Island delegation is important to the New York state Republican Party. It is very large, and Long Island is a high-income area that brings in more money for the Republican Party than any other region. State Republicans wanted to keep the Long Island delegation and their constituents happy, and thus were very responsive to the agenda of the state senators from Long Island. Telephone interview with Geri Reilly, Oct. 2, 1998.

11. Proposition 187 never went into effect. Some of its provisions were barred by court injunction soon after passage. Eventually, negotiations between opponents and a by-then more pro-immigrant state administration in 1999 largely invalidated the measure.

12. Nicholas Goldberg, "Move in State to Cut Aid to Poor," *Newsday,* March 11, 1993, p. 19.

13. Governor Pataki's 1998 State of the State address is at *http://www.nysl .nysed.gov/edocs/governor/stateofstate/1998/sos98.html;* Senator Charles Schumer's website at *http://www.senate.gov/~schumer.* Andy Logan, "Family Businesses," *New York Times,* July 12, 1998, p. 24. Although New York City is more heavily unionized than the country as a whole, the rest of the state has a much lower unionization rate. Unions had grown used to doing business in Albany during the long reign of Democratic governors, but have had a difficult time developing an effective strategy to promote their legislative agenda under a Republican governor. Reilly interview.

14. Interview with Mitch Pally, June 8, 1998.

15. Steven Greenhouse, "Bill Seeks to Make Sure Immigrants Get Paid," *New York Times,* June 30, 1997, p. B4.

16. Author's notes from her meeting with Rhina Ramos and Michael Hoffman, then Workplace Project executive director, and Richard Polsinello, Joaquin Bermudez, and Manuel Fruchter, Department of Labor, July 2, 1998 (hereafter cited as July 2 DOL meeting).

17. Richard Polsinello, director of the Labor Standards Division of the New York State Department of Labor, states that the Unpaid Wages Prohibition Act has been a "strong enforcement tool that has given us real leverage against employers." July 2 DOL meeting. Yet in 1998 the DOL collected just $5,209,415 for 8,548 workers; in 1996 it had collected $5,370,851 for 12,643 workers and in 1995 it had collected $5,728,902 for 13,376 workers. Richard Polsinello, "Worker Protection Data, Division of Labor Standards" (facsimile sent to the author, Oct. 12, 1999). On the failure of the DOL to take advantage of the tools offered it by the new law in the six years after passage, see Jordan Rau, "A Fight for Fair Pay," *Newsday*, April 11, 2004, p. A6.

18. A business representative of the musician's union gave public testimony in 1998 that the mere mention of the law's provisions was often enough to provoke the payment of substantial wages owed musicians. In one case, the business agent merely "read the employer the Unpaid Wages Prohibition Act and sent him a copy. Because of a fear of being pursued under this new law, a check was sent out immediately to the employee." Peter Voccola, senior business representative, American Federation of Musicians Local 802 (presentation to the Standing Committee on Labor of the New York State Assembly, May 19, 1998).

19. Interview with Jeff Eichler, March 21, 2002. For a description of this campaign, see Victoria Malkin, "The New York Greenpeace Campaign: Immigrant Organizing in Ethnic Niches," in Aristede R. Zoloberg and Alison Joy Clarking, ed., *Sharing Integration Experiences: Innovative Community Practices on Two Continents* (New York: New School University, 2003), pp. 43–53.

20. Interview with Senator Carl Marcellino, June 24, 1998. All other quotes from Senator Marcellino are from this interview.

21. See, e.g., Marshall Ganz, "Resources and Resourcefulness: Strategic Capacity in the Unionization of Californian Agriculture," 105 (4) *American Journal of Sociology,* 1003–1062 (2000).

22. I also called Governor Pataki's office to try to arrange an interview. No one in the office returned my calls.

23. Joseph Berger, "When County Politics Is a Family Business: Westchester Feels the Spanos' Presence," *New York Times,* April 26, 1996, p. B1; interview with Senator Dean Skelos, July 23, 1998. Parts of this chapter are based on an earlier piece of mine, *The Campaign for the Unpaid Wages Prohibition Act: Latino Immigrants Change New York Wage Law,* International Migration Policy Program Working Paper no. 4 (Washington, D.C.: Carnegie Endowment for International Peace, Sept. 1999), available at *www.ceip.org.*

24. Louis Desipio, "'Making Citizens or Good Citizens?' Naturalization as a Predictor of Organizational and Electoral Behavior among Latino Immigrants," 18 (2) *Hispanic Journal of Behavioral Sciences,* 210, 207, 211 (1996); Louis Desipio and Jennifer Jerit, "Voluntary Citizens and Democratic Participation: Political Behaviors among Naturalized U.S. Citizens" (unpublished paper on file with the author, 1998); see also the preliminary results of an ongoing study by Audrey Singer and Greta Gilbertson, *Naturalization in the Wake of Anti-Immigrant Legislation: Dominicans in New York City,* Working Paper no. 10, International Migration Program (Washington, D.C.: Carnegie Endowment for International Peace, 1998).

25. Although the context is obviously quite different, this approach to citizenship education has interesting parallels to the early civil rights movement's Citizenship Schools, begun by the Highlander Center in 1957. For a history of these schools, see Aldon D. Morris, *The Origins of the Civil Rights Movement: Black Communities Organizing for Change* (New York: Free Press, 1984), pp. 149-155, pp. 236-239; Carl Tjerandsen, *Education for Citizenship: A Foundation's Experience* (Santa Cruz, CA: Emil Schwarzhaupt Foundation, 1980), pp. 139-231; Myles Horton with Judith Kohl and Herbert Kohl, *The Long Haul: An Autobiography* (New York: Teacher's College Press, 1998), pp. 96-112.

26. The term "scaffold" is Jerome Bruner's, but it describes a phenomenon first noted by the Russian psychologist Lev Vygotsky. Jerome Bruner, "Vygotsky: A Historical and Conceptual Perspective," in James V. Wertsch, ed., *Culture, Communication, and Cognition: Vygotskian Perspectives* (Cambridge: Cambridge University Press, 1985), pp. 21-34.

27. Hendrik Hartog, "The Constitution of Aspiration and 'The Rights That Belong to Us All'," in David Thelen, ed., *The Constitution and American Life* (Ithaca: Cornell University Press, 1988), pp. 372, 359.
28. Many states in this country once permitted noncitizens to vote. See Gerald L. Neuman, "'We Are the People': Alien Suffrage in German and American Perspective," 13 *Michigan Journal of International Law* 259 (1992); Jamin B. Raskin, "Legal Aliens, Local Citizens: The Historical, Constitutional and Theoretical Meanings of Alien Suffrage," 141 *University of Pennsylvania Law Review* 1391 (1993). Noncitizen voting represented an attempt by underpopulated states to increase their voting numbers and thus their national political clout. Today no states and only a handful of local governments permit noncitizen voting, although the issue has recently resurfaced in several major cities.
29. For a fuller exploration and critique of this political fault line see Lucy A. Williams, "Beyond Labour Law's Parochialism: A Reenvisioning of the Discourse of Distribution," in Joanne Conaghan, Richard Michael Fischl, and Karl Klare, ed., *Labour Law in an Era of Globalization: Transformative Practices and Possibilities* (Oxford: Oxford University Press, 2002), pp. 93-114.
30. Hartog, "The Constitution of Aspiration," pp. 353, 368.
31. For other examples of and reflections on noncitizen-citizenship, see Paul Johnston, "Transnational Citizenries: Reflections from the Field in California," 7 (2) *Journal of Citizenship Studies* (July 2003), 199; "Citizens of the Future: The Emergence of Transnational Citizenship among Mexican Immigrants in California," in T. Aleinikoff and D. Klusmeyer, ed., *Citizenship Today: Global Perspectives and Practices* (Washington, D.C.: Carnegie Endowment for International Peace, 2001); William V. Flores and Rina Benmayor, ed., *Latino Cultural Citizenship: Claiming Identity, Space, and Rights* (Boston: Beacon Press, 1997).

CONCLUSION

1. Janice Fine and Jon Werberg, "Draft Worker Center Survey, Preliminary Analysis: November 6, 2003," unpublished ms., National Study on Immigrant Worker Centers. The national study is a project of the Economic Policy Institute.

2. On worker centers, see Janice Fine, *Immigrant Worker Centers: Building a New American Community at the Edge of the Dream* (Washington, D.C.: Economic Policy Institute, 2004); Miriam Ching Yoon Louie, *Sweatshop Warriors: Immigrant Women Workers Take on the Global Factory* (Boston: South End Press, 2001); Rinku Sen, *Stir It Up: Lessons in Community Organizing and Advocacy* (San Francisco: Jossey-Bass, 2003); Anaga Dalal, "Cleaning Up Exploitation," *Ms. Magazine,* March–April 1998, p. 12 (on the New York worker center Workers' Awaaz); Elizabeth Kolbert, "The Unfashionable Mr. Lam," *Mother Jones,* September–October 2001, pp. 60–65; Peter Kwong, "Chinese Staff and Workers Association: A Model for Organizing in the Changing Economy?" 25 (2) *Social Policy* 30–39 (Winter 1994).

3. Fine, *Immigrant Worker Centers.*

4. See Joshua Freeman, *Working Class New York* (New York: The New Press, 2000), p. 42.

5. Fine and Werberg, "Draft Worker Center Survey."

6. For an argument that identity-based organizing should be an important part of labor's response to globalization, see Maria L. Ontiveros, "A New Course for Labour Unions: Identity-Based Organizing as a Response to Globalization," in Joanne Conaghan, Richard Michael Fischl, and Karl Klare, ed., *Labour Law in an Era of Globalization: Transformative Practices and Possibilities* (Oxford: Oxford University Press, 2002), pp. 417–428.

7. For more detailed development of a similar theme, see Edna Bonacich and Fernando Gaspasin, "Organizing the Unorganizable," *The State of California Labor: 2001 Report* (Los Angeles: University of California Institute for Labor and Employment, 2001), available at *http://www.ucop.edu/ile/scl/2001/ch15.pdf,* in the section titled "Worker-Centered versus Workplace Centered Organizing."

8. Howard Wial, "The Emerging Organizational Structure of Unionism in Low-Wage Services," 45 *Rutgers Law Review* 671 (1993).

9. One example of such a campaign is the effort to organize deli or greengrocer workers in New York City. Immanuel Ness, "Community Labor Alliances: A New Paradigm in the Campaign to Organize Greengrocery Workers in New York City," in Benjamin Shepard and Ronald Hayduk, ed., *From ACT UP to the WTO: Urban Protest and Com-*

munity Building in the Era of Globalization (New York: Verso, 2002), pp. 57-73. A campaign to organize laundry workers on a similar model was launched in the wake of the greengrocer campaign. Denny Lee, "Labor Groups Set Their Sights on a Surprising Foe: The Corner Laundry," *New York Times,* June 8, 2003, sect. 14, p. 6.

10. Steven Fraser, *Labor Will Rule: Sidney Hillman and the Rise of American Labor* (New York: The Free Press, 1991), pp. 58-65; Bruce Nelson, *Workers on the Waterfront: Seamen, Longshoremen, and Unionism in the 1930s* (Urbana: University of Illinois Press, 1988), chaps. 5 and 6; Dorothy Sue Cobble, "Organizing the Postindustrial Work Force: Lessons from the History of Waitress Unionism," 44 (3) *Industrial and Labor Relations Review* 419-436 (1991); Cobble, *Dishing It Out: Waitresses and Their Unions in the Twentieth Century* (Chicago: University of Illinois Press, 1991). On the history of sympathy strikes, see David Montgomery, *Workers' Control in America* (Cambridge: Cambridge University Press, 1979), pp. 18-27.

11. Perhaps as a result, 82 percent of worker centers surveyed by the National Study on Immigrant Worker Centers in 2003 reported just "occasional" collaborations with unions, while only 15 percent were in an ongoing partnership or were union sponsored. Fine and Werberg, "Draft Worker Center Survey."

12. Steven Lerner, "Three Steps to Reorganizing and Rebuilding the Labor Movement," *Labor Notes,* December 2002. The full version of this article is available only on the *Labor Notes* website at *http://www.labornotes.org/archives/2002/12/e.html.*

13. See Mike Parker and Martha Gruelle, *Democracy Is Power* (Detroit: Labor Notes, 1999) (emphasis mine). See also Katherine Sciacchitano, "Unions, Organizing, and Democracy: Living in One's Time, Building for the Future," 47 (2) *Dissent* 75-81 (Spring 2000).

14. Examples include the Harvard Union of Clerical and Technical Workers and the SEIU nursing home campaign that Katherine Sciacchitano describes, both noted in Chapter 3. See also Dan Clausen, *The Next Upsurge: Labor and the New Social Movements* (Ithaca: Cornell University Press, 2003), pp. 197-199.

15. Clausen, *The Next Upsurge.*

16. Critical Legal Studies scholars were some of the voices expressing

concern about the relationship of rights-based strategies to social change. Other pieces, more focused on the specific arena of litigation, included Marc Galanter, "Why the Haves Come Out Ahead: Speculations on the Limits of Legal Change" 9 *Law and Society Review* 95 (1974); Gerald N. Rosenberg, *The Hollow Hope: Can Courts Bring about Social Change?* (Chicago: University of Chicago Press, 1991). A final group of articles looked at the individual lawyer-client relationship and explored the ways that even well-intentioned lawyers dominated their poor clients. See, for example, Anthony Alfieri, "Speaking Out of Turn: The Story of Josephine V.," 4 *Georgetown Journal of Legal Ethics* 619 (1991); Alfieri, "Reconstructive Poverty Law Practice: Learning Lessons of Client Narratives," 100 *Yale Law Journal* 2107 (1991); Lucie White, "Subordination, Rhetorical Survival Skills, and Sunday Shoes: Notes on the Hearing of Mrs. G.", 38 *Buffalo Law Review* 1 (1990).

17. The quiet chorus was largely led by sociologists rather than lawyers or legal scholars. Some of the more critical work also contains suggestions for how lawyers might better approach law and support communities seeking social change. See, for example, Stuart Scheingold, *The Politics of Rights: Lawyers, Public Policy, and Political Change* (New Haven: Yale University Press, 1974). Others who write critically about what lawyers too often do to undermine poor people and community organizing see hope in changing the ways lawyers interact with their clients. See, for example, Gerald López, *Rebellious Lawyering: One Chicano's Vision of Progressive Law Practice* (Boulder: Westview Press, 1992); William P. Quigley, "Reflections of Community Organizers: Lawyering for Empowerment of Community Organizations," 21 *Ohio Northern University Law Review* 455 (1994).

18. There is a small but growing literature on law and organizing. It includes Stephen Wexler, "Practicing Law for Poor People," 79 *Yale Law Journal* 1049 (1970); Steve Bachmann, "Lawyers, Law, and Social Change," 13 New York University *Review of Law and Social Change* 1 (1984–1985); Lucie White, "To Learn and Teach: Lessons from Dreifontein on Lawyering and Power," 1988 *Wisconsin Law Review* 699 (1988); Richard Klawiter, "La Tierra es Nuestra! The Campesino Struggle in El Salvador and a Vision of Community-Based Lawyer-

ing," 42 *Stanford Law Review* 1625 (1990); López, *Rebellious Lawyering;* Quigley, "Reflections of Community Organizers;" Jennifer Gordon, "We Make the Road by Walking: Immigrant Workers, the Workplace Project, and the Struggle for Social Change," 30 *Harvard Civil Rights–Civil Liberties Law Review* 407 (1995); and Ingrid Eagly and Scott Cummings, "A Critical Reflection on Law and Organizing," 48 *UCLA Law Review* 443, 506-509 (2001). For a useful bibliography on the topic, see Melinda Davis and Loretta Price, "Seeds of Change: A Bibliographic Introduction to Law and Organizing," 26 *New York University Review of Law and Social Change* 615 (2000-2001).

19. I thank Alan Hyde for drawing my attention to this tradition in labor lawyering. See Gilbert Gall, *Pursuing Justice: Lee Pressman, the New Deal, and the CIO* (Albany: State University of New York Press, 1999); Christopher Johnson, *Maurice Sugar: Law, Labor, and the Left in Detroit* (Detroit: Wayne State University Press, 1988). Lawyers' interpretations of rights did not always coincide with those advanced by workers, however. James Gray Pope, "Labor's Constitution of Freedom," 106 *Yale Law Journal* 941 (1997); Pope, "The Thirteenth Amendment versus the Commerce Clause: Labor and the Shaping of American Constitutional Law, 1921-1957," 102 *Columbia Law Review* 1 (2002).

20. Jerry Cohen interview, July 22, 1999; Marshall Ganz interview, May 25, 2000; Miriam J. Wells and Don Villarejo, "State Structures and Social Movement Strategies: The Shaping of Farm Labor Protections in California," *Politics and Society,* forthcoming; Philip Martin, *Promise Unfulfilled: Unions, Immigration, and Agricultural Workers* (Cornell: ILR Press, 2003).

21. See the organization's website, *www.nelp.org.* Lawyers at other public interest litigation centers with missions that extend beyond workers' rights can and do play similar roles. See, for example, the reflections of Julie Su, the lawyer at the Asian Pacific American Legal Center in Los Angeles who led the representation of Thai and Latino workers in the garment worker slavery case I referred to in Chap. 1. Julie A. Su, "Making the Invisible Visible: The Garment Industry's Dirty Laundry" 1 *Journal of Gender, Race, and Justice* 405 (1998).

22. For a related argument, *see* Paul Johnston, "Citizenship Movement Unionism," in Bruce Nissen, ed., *Unions in a Globalized Environment:*

Changing Borders, Organizational Boundaries, and Social Roles (Armonk: M. E. Sharpe, 2002), pp. 236–263.

23. On environmental justice, see Sheila Foster and Luke Cole, *From the Ground Up: Environmental Racism and the Rise of the Environmental Justice Movement* (New York: New York University Press, 2000), as well as a number of other articles by Cole. On community economic development, see William Simon, *The Community Economic Development Movement: Law, Business, and the New Social Policy* (Durham: Duke University Press, 2002); Scott Cummings, "Community Economic Development as Progressive Politics: Toward a Grassroots Movement for Economic Justice," 54 *Stanford Law Review* 399 (2001). On racial justice work, see Penda Hair, *Louder Than Words: Lawyers, Communities, and the Struggle for Justice* (New York: The Rockefeller Foundation, 2001).

24. Carlos Canales interview, Dec. 17, 2001.

ACKNOWLEDGMENTS

To say simply that many people have helped me in the process of writing this book would be to reduce a banquet to a brown-bag lunch.

At the Workplace Project I had the extraordinary privilege of working with hundreds of immigrants, many of them undocumented. Their tenacious, creative fight against some of the worst that work in this country has to offer is the inspiration for this book. As with all organizing efforts, the Project has been and continues to be the product of a massive collaborative effort involving hundreds of people. In choosing to emphasize the organization's programs and the systemic challenges it faced in this book, rather than providing a narrative that focused on the contributions of individuals, I have given many who were instrumental in the Project short shrift. My greatest respect and my deepest gratitude go to all those who worked for the Workplace Project while I was there, including Eduardo Bolaños, Samuel Chávez, Carmen Fernández, Romelinda Grullón, Omar Henriquez, Randy Jackson, Rob MacKay, Nadia Marín-Molina, Rúriko Mata-Banegas, Rhina Ramos, Zoila Rodriguez, Laura Saborío, Alan Siege, and Esly Umanzor, and to all those who have joined the staff since; to the organization's many volunteers and interns over the years, essential to its success, and in particular to those who have volunteered their support for a decade or more, including Juan Calderon, Jeanette Katz, Nelson Sol-Castillo, and Rodolfo Sorto; and to its board and members, who are at its very core. Many thanks also to the Echoing Green Foundation, which gave me the seed money to begin the Workplace Project, and to the Central American Refugee Center (CARECEN) in Hempstead, New York, which hosted the Project in its first two years.

As I write this, I have been gone from the Workplace Project as long as I was there. To write a book about an organization that I founded, but that continued to live a life of its own after I left, proved a challenging task. I particularly appreciate the openness of members and staff who shared their thoughts with me about various aspects of the organization's work after I left, in a series of interviews I conducted between 1998 and 2002. They include Lilliam Araujo, María Aparicio, Juan Calderón, Carlos Canales, Samuel Chavez, Omar Henriquez, Saru Jayaraman, Raúl López, Carmen Leys Maldonado, Rony Martinez, Juan Carlos Molina, Nadia Marín-Molina, Eduardo Platero, Rhina Ramos, Zoila Rodriguez, José Ramirez, Angela Sarmiento, Rodolfo Sorto, and Luz Torres. These formal interviews were enriched by countless informal conversations with a wide range of members, volunteers, and current and former staff. For her skilful leadership, her willingness to engage in discussions with me as this book evolved, and, most difficult, her generous support of my writing what I thought even when it did not necessarily agree with her perspective, I will be forever indebted to my successor, Nadia Marín-Molina.

At its inception this book had a much broader scope, including a focus on the United Farm Workers and how that union used legal strategies to advance its organizing goals. Some of that material remains embedded here, although I will provide a fuller accounting elsewhere. Interviews with Gary Bellow, LeRoy Chatfield, Jerry Cohen, Marshall Ganz, Jessica Govea, James Lorenz, Eliseo Medina, Peter Haberfeld, Gilbert Padilla, and Barbara Rhine during 1999 and 2000 provided me with invaluable insight into this topic.

I have worked on this book in many places. I so appreciate the generosity of my former neighbors Gigi and the late Sylan Schendler, who gave me the keys to their Brooklyn apartment during two summers so that I would have a peaceful place to write. The Blue Mountain Center in Blue Mountain Lake, New York, proved a beautiful and supportive retreat for me at several critical moments, as it has been for many artists, writers, and activists over the years. Elaine Greenstein rented me a room in her home to use as an office when my second child's arrival put a decisive end to my illusion that my family's apartment could be a productive workplace. And the warm welcome that my colleagues at Fordham Law School gave me during my first year on the faculty created an ideal atmosphere in which to bring this project to its conclusion.

Much of this book was written during a time when I had no full-time institutional affiliation, and I want to recognize a number of people who went out of their way to help me overcome that obstacle and gain access to books and research materials. Dean Tony Kronman was generous enough to grant me faculty library privileges at Yale Law School for the three university-library-bereft years after I stopped teaching there. "Invaluable" is an overused accolade, but Gene Coakley at the Yale Law Library provided me with truly invaluable assistance in searching down even the most obscure references swiftly and with a sense of humor. Once I reached Fordham, Juan Fernandez and others at the law library made sure I had the materials I needed. I have benefited greatly from research assistance from law students as well, for which I would like to thank Julie Chinitz, Saru Jayaraman, Kristi Graunke, Jason Yan, and Hal Blanchard. My thanks also to Kim Holder and Kristin Connelly for their able help with the final preparation of the manuscript.

I have received financial support from several sources during the years I worked on this book. The Open Society Institute provided me with an Individual Project Fellowship that enabled me to devote myself to research and writing for a year and a half immediately after I left the Workplace Project. The Ford Foundation also provided funding at that stage. I would have had to relegate this work to the back burner, however, had it not been for the tremendous good fortune of receiving a MacArthur Fellowship in 1999. For that grant and the freedom it gave me I will always be grateful.

Many people read part or all of the manuscript at various stages of its development. For their patience, their insights, and their wide-ranging perspectives, I thank Rick Abel, Fran Ansley, Sameer Ashar, Lenore Azaroff, Jerome Bruner, Matthew Capece, Dorothy Sue Cobble, John Feffer, Janice Fine, Pam Galpern, Marshall Ganz, Lani Guinier, Omar Henriquez, Randy Jackson, Steve Jenkins, David Levin, Sarah Ludwig, Nadia Marín-Molina, Martha Minow, Leslie Newman, Matt Noyes, Steven Pitts, Francesca Polletta, Bill Quigley, Rhina Ramos, Zoila Rodriguez, Florence Roisman, Linda Steinman, Kathy Sreedhar, Susan Sturm, Carlos Vanegas, Michael Wald, Lucie White, and Michael Wishnie. My thanks also go to Cynthia Peters, whose editing acumen was very helpful at an earlier stage of the draft, and to my editors at Harvard University Press, Kathleen McDermott and Nancy Clemente, whose persistence and precision have made this a much better book.

Several people in particular provided me with critical support as the idea for this book took shape and as I struggled to put my experiences and ideas into a coherent form. All my thanks to Fran Ansley for showing me how a commitment to law teaching and a commitment to activism can walk hand in hand; to Lucie White for pushing me always to recognize the contradictions in the categories I set up and for her friendship, which I hold dear; to Danny Greenberg for teaching me by his example what it means to be a world-class mentor; to the late Gary Bellow for his consummate illustration of engaged and reflective practice; to Leslie Newman for her perceptive readings at particularly difficult moments in the writing process; to Rick Abel for his consistent encouragement and his invariably useful suggestions; to Francesca Polletta for her fine work on participatory democracy and for introducing me to sociologists' thinking about many of the same issues that engaged me from a different perspective; to Susan Sturm and Martha Minow for their guidance and their warm welcome as I made the transition from practice to writing and teaching; to Dorothy Sue Cobble for challenging me to tell a more complicated and truer version of labor history; and to Pam Galpern and David Levin, who in supporting me as I wrote the book met their customary gold standard both for true friendship and for political commitment. Indeed, all of my friends deserve credit here. Their faith in me was a fuel I burned liberally when my own reserves ran low.

Of all my readers, two reviewed every draft from beginning to end, and for that among other reasons deserve special mention. Janice Fine, who came into my life when she arrived at the Workplace Project in 1996 to study it for her dissertation, has been an unwavering source of support ever since. In between carrying out interviews and observing meetings, she also helped the Project examine and reshape its organizing strategies with domestic workers and day laborers, a critical contribution. Her steady friendship, her incisive mind, and her determination to do organizing justice on the page and in action shaped not only this book but how I see my work and how I live my life. My partner Linda Steinman also read draft after draft, deftly walking the line between loving spouse and gimlet-eyed critic. She was with me, supportive if faintly dubious, at the stove on the summer morning in 1991 when I began to talk about founding the Workplace Project as I stripped the skins off fresh tomatoes. She is with me still, one organization, one book, two children, and countless batches of tomato sauce later. I could not be more blessed.

Our family is immensely fortunate to be surrounded by a densely woven web of friends and relatives. All my respect and thanks to Joan Baptiste, without whose care our children, Sophie and James, would not be the marvels that they are and without whose work this book could never have been written. I am proud to be an honorary member of the Steinman family. Most especially, I want to recognize Michael and Roberta Gordon; Andra, Randy, and Diego Gordon-Gatica; Ann Gordon, Mollie Rosenberg, and the rest of my extended family. Their support, sense of humor, and love is a constant source of joy in my life.

Index

Sarmiento, Angela, 33, 135–136, 158–159
Schneider, Elizabeth, 182
Seal-It factory, 89–90
SEIU. *See* Service Employees International Union (SEIU)
September 11, 2001, attacks, 19, 51
Service Employees International Union (SEIU), 32, 61–63, 73, 90, 293
Shop stewards, 32, 69, 89, 90, 255. *See also* Unions
Skelos, Dean, 105–106, 265, 267–268
Slavery, 101, 166, 274
Social Security, 45, 50, 57
So Goes A Nation (documentary film), 87
Sorto, Rodolfo, 38, 123–124, 130, 134–135
Spano, Nicholas, 247, 249, 265–266
Spitzer, Eliot, 261
Strikes, 60, 62, 181
Subcontracting, 22, 52, 53, 56–57, 58–59, 62
Suffolk County, 19, 248
Sugar, Maurice, 297

Taco Bell, 282
Taft-Hartley amendments, 61
Teamsters for a Democratic Union, 63
Teamsters Union, 32, 33
Temporary work, 56–57
Title VII, 57
Torres, Luz, 106, 246, 254, 256

Umanzor, Esly, 99, 124
UNICCO, 54
Unions: and amnesty, 300–301; and benefits, 62, 63; and closed-shop

agreements, 61, 285; competition with, 220; control of labor supply, 61; craft, 52; culture of, 292–293, 294; direct affiliation of, 59–60, 284; and direct vs. indirect employment, 58; dues support for, 55–56; and employers, 61; and globalization, 41–44; hiring halls of, 61, 285; history of, 59; in home countries, 38; and immigrants, 27–28, 31–33, 36–39, 53, 54, 59, 63–64, 299–300; and Immigration and Naturalization Service, 32; and landscape work, 56; and language, 32; lawyers for, 296–298; Long Island, 30–33, 58; and New York politics, 249; occupational, 60–61; organizing by, 27–39, 300–301; participatory approach in, 293; and rights talk, 166; and service work, 53–56; and sojourner attitude, 36–37; and specific industries, 52–53, 54, 55, 58, 59, 91; and underground economy, 48–49; and undocumented workers, 50; and Unpaid Wages Prohibition Act, 253, 255; and wage competition, 30, 53; and worker centers, 289–290; and workers, 285; and the Workplace Project, 31, 32, 69, 85, 89–91, 109–110, 283
United Farm Workers, 29–30, 63–64, 163, 209–210, 227–231, 298
United Food and Commercial Workers, 31–32, 63, 89
United Mine Workers, 29
UNITE HERE! 73, 253, 261
UNITY household cooperative, 69, 104
Unpaid Wages Prohibition Act, 110, 139, 237–280 passim; benefits of,